On the
Genealogy of
Morality

Appended to the recently published *Beyond Good and Evil* as a supplement and clarification.

FRIEDRICH NIETZSCHE

On the Genealogy of Morality

A Polemic

Translated, with Notes, by
Maudemarie Clark and Alan J. Swensen

Introduction by Maudemarie Clark

Hackett Publishing Company, Inc.
Indianapolis/Cambridge

Friedrich Nietzsche: 1844–1900

Copyright © 1998 by Hackett Publishing Company, Inc.

Cover design by Brian Rak and John Pershing
Text design by Meera Dash

Printed in the United States of America

05 04   3 4 5 6 7 8 9

For further information, please address

Hackett Publishing Company, Inc.
P. O. Box 44937
Indianapolis, Indiana 46244–0937

Library of Congress Cataloging-in-Publication Data

Nietzsche, Friedrich Wilhelm, 1844–1900.
    [Zur Genealogie der Moral. English]
    On the genealogy of morality/Friedrich Nietzsche; translation
and notes by Maudemarie Clark and Alan Swensen; introduction by
Maudemarie Clark.
        p. cm.
    Includes bibliographical references and index.
    ISBN 0-87220-284-4 (cloth : alk. paper).
    ISBN 0-87220-283-6 (pbk. : alk. paper).
    1. Ethics.   I. Clark, Maudemarie.   II. Swensen, Alan J.
III. Title.
B3313.Z73E5 1998
170—dc21   98-37868
                                                        CIP

Contents

Introduction

1. Nietzsche's Path to the End of the Twentieth Century

When Nietzsche's *Genealogy* was published in 1887, there was little reason to think it would become an important book, much less a recognized masterpiece. Indeed, its prospects for success could hardly have looked much worse. Great things had certainly been expected of its author. Born in 1844 on the birthday of King Friedrich Wilhelm IV of Prussia, after whom he was named, Nietzsche survived major trauma in his early childhood: the death of his beloved father when he was not yet five, followed by the death of his younger brother the next year. A precocious student, he was awarded admission to the famed Pforta, from which he graduated in 1864 with a thesis in Latin on the Greek poet Theognis. He began university studies at Bonn, where he registered as a theology student, in accord with family expectations that he would follow in his father's footsteps (which were also those of both grandfathers) and enter the ministry. Instead, he transferred to Leipzig, where he studied philology, becoming the protégé of the well-known classical philologist, Friedrich Ritschl. With Ritschl's strong endorsement, Nietzsche was appointed to the chair of classical philology at the University of Basel in 1869 at the unprecedented age of twenty-four and was made a full professor the following year. The scholarly world eagerly awaited his first book, expecting it to secure his reputation as a brilliant young scholar.

When his first book, *The Birth of Tragedy Out of the Spirit of Music*, eventually appeared in 1872, it did win him considerable attention in scholarly circles, but not the sort young scholars seek.[1] Torn between philosophy and classical scholarship since his discovery of Schopenhauer in 1865, Nietzsche attempted to combine the two disciplines in this book by using Schopenhauer's ideas about knowledge and reality to interpret the origins of Greek tragedy and to urge the possibility of its spirit's reemergence in the modern world—in the music of his great friend and father-figure, Richard Wagner. Nietzsche hoped that the book would establish his credentials as a philosopher, for he now contemplated leaving his posi-

---

1. The attention was due to the polemic against it immediately published by Ulrich Wilamowitz-Möllendorff, which was answered that same year by Nietzsche's friend Erwin Rohde. Wilamowitz responded to that the next year.

tion in classics and being appointed in philosophy at Basel. Given its often rhapsodic tone and the absence of footnotes and other traditional scholarly trappings, the book certainly did not look much like a work of classical scholarship. But it did not look much like a work of philosophy either. In the end, it managed only to damage his reputation as a classical scholar. Few philology students registered for his courses during the first years following its publication, and the chair in philosophy went to some-one else. As he makes clear in his preface to the new edition of 1886, Nietzsche himself eventually recognized *The Birth of Tragedy* as an "almost inaccessible book"—"badly-written, ponderous, embarrassing, image-mad, image-confused"—in short, an altogether "impossible book" (BT:P 3).[2]

Serious health problems, undoubtedly exacerbated by his increasing feeling of being unsuited to the life of academic scholarship, forced him to resign his chair in 1879, allowing him to escape and begin life anew as a writer of philosophy. The first five books he published in this new role, however—*Human, All Too Human*; *Daybreak*; *The Gay Science*; *Thus Spoke Zarathustra*; and *Beyond Good and Evil*—sold so few copies that no publisher would touch his *Genealogy*. It was printed by what we would now call a "vanity press"; Nietzsche himself had to pay the complete cost of its publication. In the hope of finding readers, he also spent a consid-erable amount of his own money publishing new editions of his earlier works, which was not easy for him since his retirement had left him with only a modest pension.[3] Money worries were among the central prob-lems that afflicted and occupied him during these years—exceeded only by his continuing health problems and the absence of readers and of suit-able companions, which left him feeling very much alone. His relations with most of his family and friends (above all, with Wagner) had broken down or were on thin ice—due, at least in part, to his philosophical views and their development—and his relationship with his homeland was even worse. A few readers had appeared elsewhere, but there seemed to him to be none among Germans, as his many critical comments about

2. The acronyms used to cite Nietzsche's books are listed in the Selected Bibliog-raphy, as are the books cited in the footnotes.

3. Nietzsche had also paid for the publication of *Thus Spoke Zarathustra* and *Beyond Good and Evil*, and the "new editions" were actually old editions, which he bought back from his former publishers and repackaged with new prefaces. For detailed information about Nietzsche's publication and connected financial woes, see William H. Schaberg (1995).

the Germans make clear. He was increasingly appalled by the political atmosphere (especially the nationalism and anti-Semitism) he saw developing in Germany following the Franco-Prussian War and the establishment of the second *Reich* (1871), with Bismarck, who had engineered both, in almost complete control. Although he made visits there, Nietzsche did not choose to live in Germany after he left Basel, but spent the greater part of the life left to him in voluntary exile, traveling and living alone in pensions in various other European countries, always in search of conditions that would improve his deteriorating health and facilitate his work.

But Nietzsche's prospects were actually much worse than they would have seemed to a contemporary observer. When his *Genealogy* appeared in November of 1887, he was little more than a year away from a complete mental and physical breakdown, which would overtake him in Turin, on January 3, 1889, bringing his productive life to an end. Before his collapse, he was able—incredibly enough—to write five new books: *The Case of Wagner, Twilight of the Idols, The Anti-Christ(ian), Ecce Homo,* and *Nietzsche Contra Wagner.* But his breakdown would eventually leave both his body and his spirit, as it was now embodied in his literary estate, under the control of his unphilosophical and unscrupulous sister, Elisabeth Förster-Nietzsche. It is almost universally agreed that she had no aptitude for philosophy, no understanding of her brother's philosophy, and a set of values quite antithetical to Nietzsche's own. He was an atheist who was disgusted by anti-Semitism; she was a devout Christian who married a leading anti-Semite, Bernhard Förster (whom Nietzsche detested), who was hard at work founding a colony in Paraguay for Aryans, *Nueva Germania.* Elisabeth joined her husband in Paraguay for a time and, when he committed suicide (a few months after Nietzsche's breakdown), she took over the affairs of the colony. But she soon returned to Germany, where she fought for and won complete control of Nietzsche's unpublished work, including the letters he had sent to others. She began preparing a biography of Nietzsche, helped found the Nietzsche Archive to edit and publish his literary estate and to promote his philosophy, and was ready to assume physical custody of him when their mother, with whom Nietzsche had been living, died in 1897. Elisabeth moved Nietzsche to Weimar, the symbol of Germany's highest cultural achievements and the city to which she had already moved the Nietzsche Archive. He died in Weimar on August 25, 1900.

Elisabeth did have a positive short-term effect on Nietzsche's reputation, helping to defend his name from what he had called "the absurd silence under which it lies buried" (EH III: CW 4).[4] With his name in her hands, however, worse fates soon befell it. First was the fulfillment of the fear Nietzsche articulated in *Ecce Homo*: "I have a terrible fear that one day I will be pronounced *holy*" (EH IV:1). Elisabeth contributed substantially to the development of a cult atmosphere around her brother, in part by withholding his last books from publication for years. By offering selected quotations from them and claiming to have in her possession Nietzsche's *magnum opus*, which was later published as *The Will to Power*,[5] she established herself as the main spokesperson for Nietzsche's work, as the one who knew the "real" Nietzsche.[6] Worse, perhaps, she subjected her brother to what he would have considered the ultimate indignity, often having the half-paralyzed and insane Nietzsche—dressed in ways that encouraged perceiving him as a kind of holy apparition—appear on the balcony of his residence to groups that gathered below in anticipation of such appearances. When death finally granted him escape, he was eulogized by one of his most steadfast friends, Peter Gast, with stress on the line, "Holy be thy name to all coming generations."

In fact, Nietzsche's name managed to escape this fate, because a much worse fate awaited it: Elisabeth, outliving her brother by several decades, helped link his name to the great horrors of the twentieth century: nationalism, anti-Semitism, and fascism. First she established ties to both the Nazis and the Italian fascists. Her correspondence with Mussolini and a photo of her with Hitler, who came to Weimar especially for one of her birthday celebrations, can now be seen on display at what was Nietzsche's residence in Weimar. Further, the same display shows that in

---

4. See Aschheim (1992) to get a sense of how widely known and variously interpreted Nietzsche had become soon after his breakdown. This was by no means due solely to Elisabeth's influence. For instance, Georg Brandes, the influential Danish critic, began delivering university lectures on Nietzsche's philosophy shortly before Nietzsche's breakdown.

5. This was actually not a book composed by Nietzsche, but one constructed by Elisabeth and her appointed editors. They made a selection from the notes and jottings found in Nietzsche's notebooks and organized them according to one of the many plans for such a book found in the same notebooks. Nietzsche usually composed his books from the material with which he filled his notebooks, and some of the passages published in *The Will to Power* are clearly rough drafts of passages he had already revised and published in his books. Some others were undoubtedly ones he would have discarded in his wastebasket if given a choice.

6. In the service of the same ends, she changed her name from Elisabeth Förster to Elisabeth Förster-Nietzsche in 1894.

her appeals for official funds to promote the work of the Nietzsche Archive, Elisabeth had no qualms about presenting her brother's philosophy as offering support for Nazi aspirations. She told Hitler that he was exactly what her brother meant by the *Übermensch* (the "overhuman," one who transcends the merely human). It was hardly surprising, therefore, that Nazi theoreticians read Nietzsche and tried to use him in support of their own program.

It is thus nothing short of amazing that at the end of the twentieth century, *On the Genealogy of Morality* stands as a widely acknowledged masterpiece. Many consider it indispensable reading for understanding the intellectual life of the twentieth century, and some (a smaller group certainly) consider it essential for anyone who is serious about understanding morality. In the United States, at least, the book is now often taught in standard ethics courses at some of the best colleges and universities. This is not to say that it enjoys universal acclaim, or that most philosophers agree with it. Quite the contrary, as the discussion below will indicate. But a major change has taken place, and it did not happen overnight. At the three-quarter century mark, Nietzsche's status was very different: The vast majority of philosophers at these same colleges and universities did not recognize him as a philosopher, much less take him seriously as one. His *Genealogy* was taught at some of these schools in general education or Western civilization courses, but if allowed into the philosophy curriculum at all, it was almost always confined to courses on existentialism. That, however, was a tremendous improvement over Nietzsche's status at mid-century, when his reputed connection to the Nazis still tainted his name beyond repair for the vast majority of academics and scholars. That was usually enough to dismiss any claim that his ideas deserved serious consideration.

In this context, the publication of Walter Kaufmann's 1950 book on Nietzsche can be seen as the major event of twentieth-century Nietzsche scholarship in the United States. For Kaufmann showed that the Nazi appropriation of Nietzsche involved a complete distortion, achieved by unscrupulously tearing a few of his words out of context and ignoring most of what he had written on the topics in question. In fact, Nietzsche had foreseen and spoken out against the dangers of German nationalism and anti-Semitism more clearly than anyone. By demonstrating this beyond a reasonable doubt, Kaufmann finally made it possible for academics in the English-speaking world to begin to take Nietzsche seriously, to look for the serious thinker behind the dazzling metaphors and dramatic formulations. Kaufmann was so successful that four editions of his book were published, and his interpretation of Nietzsche came to seem "almost completely dominant in America."[7] This is no longer the case. But his answer to the charge that Nietzsche's ideas supported Nazi aspirations is still widely accepted, and by providing it, he paved the way for the recent explosion of interest in Nietzsche's work in the United States, interest generated in large part by academics influenced by Heidegger, Derrida, and Foucault—important twentieth-century European philosophers who were influenced by Nietzsche but whose influence on Nietzsche interpretation Kaufmann would have abhorred.[8] For Kaufmann tried to establish Nietzsche as a serious thinker by showing that he fit into the great tradition of Western philosophy, that in fact Socrates was his true model and hero. More recent interpreters in the United States have been in a better position than Kaufmann was to take for granted Nietzsche's status as a serious thinker, hence to concern themselves with showing how revolutionary his thought is, how much of what others considered sacred—including the style and content of traditional philosophy—he questioned and attacked.

By the 1970s, Nietzsche's reputation had recovered sufficiently for many academics to recognize him as a serious thinker, and, morevoer, as someone who had deeply influenced many of the most important writers and thinkers of the century—among them, Freud, Jung, Oswald Spengler, André Gide, Thomas Mann, André Malraux, Rainer Maria Rilke, William Butler Yeats, George Bernard Shaw, Hermann Hesse, Paul Tillich, and Martin Buber. In fact, it was becoming difficult to see who besides Freud and Marx could rival Nietzsche's deep influence on so many different areas of twentieth-century culture. Yet his thought was still widely perceived as peripheral to philosophy. Although he had influenced Heidegger, Sartre, and Camus, they could be cordoned off from philosophy as "existentialists" and treated more as writers or poets than as thinkers who dealt with serious issues of philosophy. At the end of the twentieth century, in contrast, Nietzsche is widely perceived as a philosopher, and he is a widely read philosopher. His own books and books about his thought now sell extremely well, as can be confirmed by talking to any

7. See Conor Cruise O'Brien, p. 12.

8. Another major event of Nietzsche scholarship in the twentieth century was the publication of Heidegger's two-volume *Nietzsche* in 1961. Foucault and Derrida were both deeply influenced by Heidegger, but each arrived at his understanding and use of Nietzsche through serious confrontation with and rejection of much of Heidegger's interpretation of him.

academic publisher or by looking at the philosophy section in the major (high-end) chain bookstores. Few thinkers identified primarily as philosophers now generate the interest that Nietzsche does, perhaps especially among non-philosophers.

Among philosophers, on the other hand, a major distinction must be made. Nietzsche has become a major influence in one of the two main traditions of philosophy as it is practiced in this country, so-called "Continental" philosophy, which takes its bearings and inspiration from philosophers associated with Continental Europe.[9] Within this tradition Nietzsche is not only taken seriously as a philosopher, but his thought, whether one agrees with it or not, is seen as setting much of the context and agenda for philosophy as it now exists. Nietzsche occupies a quite different position in this country's other major tradition in philosophy, so-called "analytic" philosophy, which takes its bearings and style from philosophers associated with Britain rather than with Continental Europe. He is probably still not taken seriously by the majority of philosophers in this tradition. His style, which is often dramatic and emotion-laden rather than cool and analytic, is an impediment to appreciation within this tradition, and his reputation for often saying things that seem contradictory, idiosyncratic, or just plain outrageous may be enough to keep the majority of its practitioners from even reading him. But here too serious change has taken place. In the 1970s, people who taught ethics in the analytic tradition had virtually no interest in Nietzsche. And when their students applied for jobs, they certainly did not mention Nietzsche's *Genealogy* as one of the texts they would or could teach in a standard ethics course. A large number of candidates from analytic departments applying for ethics positions now do exactly that. Even if most analytic philosophers still have not read Nietzsche, many are interested in him, especially in relation to issues in ethics, and more are actually teaching his *Genealogy* in ethics courses. Finally, an increasing number of important analytic philosophers now

9. Here I use the vague term "associated" deliberately, for it is clear that a number of the most important philosophers in the analytical tradition are actually from Continental Europe. Analytical philosophy is a style of doing philosophy—one that stresses argumentative clarity and precision and is likely to be accompanied by a high regard for logic, mathematics, and the sciences—a style that is associated with Britain because of its genealogical connection to earlier British philosophers.

mention Nietzsche in print as importantly connected to their own work in philosophy.[10]

None of this means that Nietzsche's reputation will continue its ascent. For one thing, the Nazi charge, seemingly put to rest forever by Kaufmann, has reappeared. No one claims that Nietzsche actually called for the actions carried out by the Nazis, especially given his vehement and unambiguous denunciations of anti-Semitism and nationalism, but some think he is somehow still to blame for them.[11] And there are those in both philosophical traditions who consider Nietzsche's thought dangerous and destructive and are working against its continuing influence.[12] In short, despite the remarkable change in his reputation since mid-century, Nietzsche is far from being an uncontroversial figure. Indeed, he is one of the most controversial philosophers, a thinker who arouses very strong feelings both for and against. To understand why, Nietzsche's *Genealogy*

10. Bernard Williams is the most obvious example; the Nietzschean influence on his work in ethics and his understanding of morality is increasingly evident. Richard Rorty and Alasdair MacIntyre, both at least originally analytic philosophers, see Nietzsche as a major thinker who establishes much of the context for contemporary philosophy, though one who went wrong in important ways. Recently, Daniel Dennett and Christine Korsgaard have both expressed their admiration for Nietzsche's *Genealogy* in very strong terms, and Simon Blackburn pays homage to Nietzsche's early distinction between the "Apollonian" and the "Dionysian" by using it in his forthcoming book on metaethical issues. Finally, unlike a quarter-century ago, a number of philosophers are now saying things about morality that at least sound something like Nietzsche. For an analysis, see Brian Leiter's recent paper "Nietzsche and the Morality Critics," in *Ethics*. The publication of this paper in a major analytic journal is itself an indication that analytic philosophers are much more interested in Nietzsche than they used to be.

11. Steven Aschheim argues that Nietzsche's sensibility ("radically experimental, morality-challenging, tradition-shattering") and incendiary rhetoric made such acts *"conceivable in the first place,"* that his work thus "constitutes an important (if not the only) long-term enabling precondition" of the Holocaust. See "Nietzsche, Anti-Semitism, and the Holocaust," in Jacob Golomb (1997), p. 16. For views on other sides of this issue, see the other articles in this same volume, especially those by Weaver Santaniello and Yirmiyahu Yovel. Yovel's "Nietzsche, the Jews and *Ressentiment*" in Richard Schacht (1994) is also an important contribution on this issue. For instance, Charles Larmore (1996) and Luc Ferry and Alain Renaut (1997), the authors of *Why We Are Not Nietzscheans*, recently published in France and almost immediately translated into English. This book's title attests to both the influence Nietzsche is perceived as having and the perception of this influence as something to be fought.

is probably the best place to start. It is in any case essential reading if one wishes to understand Nietzsche's thought and the enthusiasm and controversy it has generated.

2. *Genealogy*'s Importance Among Nietzsche's Writings

On the Genealogy of Morality contains some of Nietzsche's most disturbing ideas and images: e.g., the "slave revolt" in morality, which he claims began with the Jews and has now triumphed, and the "blond beast" that must erupt, which he claims to find behind all civilizations. It is therefore a major source for understanding why "Nietzschean" ideas are controversial. Further, it is one of Nietzsche's most important books, a work of his maturity that shows him at the height of his powers both as a thinker and as an artist in the presentation of ideas. Nietzsche's writing career was relatively short: Only sixteen years separated his first book from the five books of his last productive year. As he makes clear in prefaces to his books, however, his ideas changed and developed considerably in that time. But since he usually leaves it to the reader to determine exactly where and how they changed,[13] it can be difficult to decide which of his earlier ideas he still accepts. Because *Genealogy* was published in his penultimate productive year, it can largely be taken as Nietzsche's "finished" thoughts on its major topics. During his final year, he himself called it "my touchstone of what belongs to me" (CW: Epilogue), thereby granting it the role of criterion for which of his earlier ideas still count as "Nietzschean." Finally, and above all, *Genealogy* is an ideal entry point for understanding Nietzsche's thought and the controversy it provokes because its topic is morality and it is Nietzsche's most extended discussion of this topic.

"Morality" is the best one-word answer to the question as to what Nietzsche is against. He repeatedly identifies himself as an "immoralist," that is, as one who opposes morality. It would be surprising if this self-identification did not arouse negative feelings in many, especially when one considers the horrific images *Genealogy* offers us of much that it claims underlies morality.[14] Philosophers and many others tend to regard the capacity for morality as a distinguishing mark of humanity, the

13. HA II:309 may offer an explanation for this.
14. As the previous note on Aschheim's view suggests, Nietzsche's opposition to morality is also a major source of the feeling that he is somehow responsible for the Nazi horrors.

source both of human dignity and of whatever stability and value human life has managed to achieve. In *The Birth of Tragedy*, Nietzsche suggests, in opposition, that morality is a "will to negate life," a "principle of decay," the "danger of dangers" (BT P:5). *Genealogy*'s preface repeats this suggestion (GM:P 5-6) and its analysis of morality culminates in the prediction that "morality will gradually *perish*: that great spectacle in a hundred acts that is reserved for Europe's next two centuries, the most terrible, most questionable, and perhaps also most hopeful of all spectacles" (GM III:27).

When Nietzsche wrote this a little over a century ago, it must have been difficult for anyone to take it seriously. After the horrors of the twentieth century, it is easier to find plausibility in the idea that morality is a veneer that might someday be completely stripped away. But it is difficult to believe that this might be a "hopeful" event, much less "the most hopeful of all spectacles." This is a major reason why Nietzsche's thought can seem so dangerous: He attacks and seems detemined to undermine what is plausibly seen as our best defense against barbarism, as well as our claim to dignity and respect. But the same set of claims can also help one begin to appreciate what many find attractive in his *Genealogy*: namely, that it can radically revise one's world view and enable one to question what has been considered unquestionable. For that, as Nietzsche makes clear in the preface, is precisely the status morality has enjoyed. How can one question or be against morality? What basis could one possibly have? Almost all of Nietzsche's books are relevant to *why* he opposes morality. To understand *why*, however, one needs to be careful about exactly *what* he opposes— what he means or refers to when he uses the word "morality." For this question, one book is relevant above all others, namely, *Genealogy*, for it is, among other things, an extended analysis of the concept of morality, a detailed and very original explanation of what morality is.

This important aspect of the book is obscured by Kaufmann's extremely influential translation of its title: *On the Genealogy of Morals*. Why did Kaufmann translate the final word of the title [*Moral*] as "morals," when he used "morality" for the same word almost everywhere else? From what he says in the introduction to his translation, the explanation seems to be that he perceived the book as concerned with "the origins of moral phenomena." The book has three main parts (treatises or essays), and Kaufmann saw each as an inquiry into the origin of a different phenomenon of morality: master and slave morality in the first, bad conscience in the second, and ascetic ideals in the third. But these three topics or phenomena leave out so much of morality (right and wrong, to begin with) that Kaufmann's way of looking at the book makes it almost impossible to see it as a genealogy or account of morality itself. He therefore used a somewhat looser word than "morality" in his translation of the title, a choice that unfortunately makes it more difficult for readers to see that this book offers us an account of what morality is, where it came from, and where it is going. That, in turn, makes it more difficult to appreciate what may be the book's chief importance at the end of the twentieth century: that it offers us a diagnosis of our current situation with respect to morality.

3. Morality and Nietzsche's Immoralism

It is clear that Nietzsche considers his attack on morality absolutely central to his philosophy. He locates its beginning in *Daybreak* (1881),[15] but finds signs of it even in his first book. Although *The Birth of Tragedy* had barely mentioned morality, fourteen years after its original publication and in the face of everything that now made it an "impossible book" for him, Nietzsche claimed that its ultimate importance lay in the fact "that it betrays a spirit who will one day fight at any risk whatsoever the *moral* interpretation and significance of existence" (BT P:5).

Nietzsche's immoralism is a complicated matter, but one point is clear: It is not intended to promote immorality, i.e., to encourage people to perform immoral actions. In explaining the sense in which he "denies morality" in *Daybreak*, he insists that "it goes without saying that I do not deny, presupposing I am no fool, that many actions called immoral ought to be avoided and resisted, or that many called moral ought to be done and encouraged—but *for different reasons than formerly*" (D 103). Thus, he does not claim that there are no good reasons for obeying the norms we in fact regard as moral norms—e.g., norms against murder, lying, and stealing—much less that we should violate these norms. In *Daybreak*,

---

15. It may seem strange that he does not locate it instead in *Human, All Too Human*, since this is the book he cites in *Genealogy*'s preface as giving his first published account of morality. A plausible explanation is that *Human, All Too Human*, written under the influence of La Rochefoucauld and Paul Rée (see End Notes 3:17 and 4:35) treated morality as mere veneer. It did not attack morality, but only the claim that morality actually existed in the human world, that people were actually guided by moral reasons. *Daybreak* begins a much more radical project: that of opposing morality, exposing it as something no longer worth holding onto. See the Introduction to Nietzsche's *Daybreak* by Maudemarie Clark and Brian Leiter (1997).

Nietzsche's denial of morality is rather a rejection of specifically *moral* reasons for obeying these norms, a denial that the reasons morality gives us for doing so are good reasons. By the time he wrote *Genealogy*, Nietzsche's position had changed. His ultimate problem with morality is no longer that it does not give us good reasons but, as he suggests in *Genealogy*'s preface, that it stands in the way of a kind of human perfection, that it blocks the realization of "a highest power and splendor of the human type" (GM P:6). But he never gives up *Daybreak*'s claim that there are, of course, often good reasons to act and to encourage actions in accord with norms that many in fact hold as *moral* norms and obey for *moral reasons*, and to avoid and discourage actions that violate these same norms.

A second point is that Nietzsche's immoralism is not a simplistic rejection of all claims of duty. In *Beyond Good and Evil*, he makes explicit that "*we immoralists*" are "human beings of duty."

> *We immoralists*...have been spun into a severe yarn and shirt of duties and *cannot* get out of that—in this we are "human beings of duty," we, too. Occasionally, it is true, we dance in our "chains" and between our "swords"; more often, that is no less true, we gnash our teeth and feel impatient with the secret harshness of our destiny. But we can do what we like—the dolts and appearances speak against us, saying: "these are human beings without duty." We always have the dolts and appearances against us (BGE 226).

This suggests that Nietzsche does reject what appears to be duty, the only thing the "dolts" recognize as duty, but that he sees himself as motivated by duty, perhaps even in the development of his immoralism. (Cf. End Note 2:28). But if Nietzsche agrees that certain actions are to be "done and encouraged" or "avoided and resisted," isn't he embracing a morality of his own? And if his immoralism does not even exclude considering himself bound by duty, what does it exclude?

A terminological distinction between "morality" and "ethics" may be a helpful beginning here. As Nietzsche explains elsewhere (BGE 32), the word "morality" can be used in both a wider and a narrower sense. In the wider sense, any internalized code of conduct or system of values that constrains behavior in relation to other people counts as a morality. The wider sense is thus equivalent to "ethic" or "ethics," as Bernard Williams uses these terms. We can, for instance, entertain the possibility that thieves and others who are beyond the pale of what we call "morality" live by an ethical code, perhaps a code of honor. This means that they may consider it important not to treat each other, or their victims, in certain ways, even when it would be convenient to do so, that they might actually be unable to live with themselves if they did. Tales and movies of the old American West that glorify outlaws and mercenaries provide good images of this possibility. Because such "heroes" are constrained by codes of conduct, we can say that they have a morality, but only if we are using the wide sense of the term. But we can also say that such men are guided by honor, not by morality. Their ethical codes are codes of honor, not of morality. Here we are using "morality" in the narrower sense. In this narrower sense, morality is only one of the possibilities for ethical life, i.e., for morality in the wider sense.

Some may resist the distinction between a wider and a narrower sense of "morality," for, as Nietzsche makes clear (BGE 32), the latter is the usual sense, "the sense morality has had until now (*Moral im bisherigen Sinne*)." He occasionally uses "morality" in its wider sense, as when he refers to "noble morality," or to "*higher* moralities, [which] arc, or ought to be, possible" (BGE 202). But he much more often follows common usage, which means that he uses "morality" in the narrower sense. When he calls himself an "immoralist" or commits himself to "the overcoming of morality," he is always using "morality" in the narrower sense. Morality in our usual sense, he is claiming, does not exhaust the possible forms of ethical life, although those who are committed to morality in that sense often assume that it does. It is this assumption that Nietzsche rejects with his assertion that "higher moralities" are or ought to be possible. Nietzsche does not, that is, oppose all forms of ethical life, all codes of conduct that place restraints on behavior, or that obligate human beings to others, but only the ones that are instances of "morality" in the narrower sense. This is why he can, without contradiction, oppose morality and yet say that certain actions are to be "resisted" and others "done and encouraged," and why he can even consider himself a person of duty: He opposes what we usually mean by "morality," but he does not think that this exhausts the possibilites for ethics or ethical life. He accepts some other ethical system in terms of which he considers himself "bound" or "pledged."

At this point, one would like to know exactly how Nietzsche defines "morality" in the narrower sense and characterizes his own "non-moral" ethic. But there are no quick and simple answers to these questions. In fact, as will be discussed, the whole of Nietzsche's *Genealogy* is an attempt to show us what is involved in the narrow sense of morality. One suggestion that would make things much easier is that Nietzsche's narrower sense of morality is simply Christian morality. There is some truth in this. At the very least, there is a special connection between the morality Nietzsche opposes and Christianity. At the end of *Genealogy*, he associates the perishing of morality with the overcoming of "Christianity *as morality*" (GM III:27). And in explaining why he chose to call himself an "immoralist," he writes: "What defines me, what sets me apart from the rest of humanity is that I *uncovered* Christian morality. That is why I needed a word that had the meaning of a provocation for everyone" (EH IV:7). The point here is not that his fight against morality is directed only against Christian morality, however, but that what we in the West, including those of us who do not accept or even reject Christianity, call "morality" is *in fact* Christian morality. What we want to know, therefore, is what Nietzsche thinks our idea of "morality" is, such that morality can in fact turn out to be "Christianity as morality" even though we do not recognize it as such.

Several points are already clear from Nietzsche's discussion of the two senses of "morality" in *Beyond Good and Evil* 32. First, Nietzsche thinks that our idea of morality captures only one of the possibilities for ethical life ("morality" in the wider sense). Further, we can divide possibilities for ethical life into the moral, the pre-moral, and the post-moral (in the narrower sense of "moral").[16] Therefore, although Nietzsche claims that the moral "must be overcome," this does not mean that he wants to go back to pre-moral forms of ethical life, as exemplified, for instance, by at

---

16. It may seem that *Beyond Good and Evil* 32 gives us an easy way of characterizing the narrower sense of "moral," namely, in terms of whether intentions play a role in the assessment of actions. During the "pre-moral period," Nietzsche suggests, the value or disvalue of an action was determined by its consequences, whereas "the sign of a period that one may call *moral* in the narrower sense" is that the origin of the action, in particular the intention that is taken to be its origin, determines its value. Nietzsche goes on to equate the normal or narrower sense of morality with the "morality of intention," and claims that this involves a "superstition," an overvaluation of the role of consciousness in action. But this is not as helpful as it may look for explaining the object of Nietzsche's fight against morality. For utilitarianism, with its emphasis on consequences, is as much an object of that fight as is Kant's morality of intention. Further, Nietzsche claims that morality in the narrower sense is "the unconscious after-effect of the rule of aristocratic values," a suggestion that is much further developed in his *Genealogy*, where the morality of intention is not mentioned by name or given a central role. It seems best to take the "morality of intention" as one of the major signs of the period Nietzsche calls "*moral* in the narrower sense," rather than as a strict definition or equivalent of

least some codes of honor (those, say, of Clint Eastwood's spaghetti Westerns). The passage makes clear that Nietzsche's hope is not to go back, but to go forward, to a period "that should be designated negatively, to begin with, as *non-moral*." But we can also call this period "post-moral." It is clear that its ethic or ethics would differ from any pre-moral ethical system since Nietzsche claims that it would result from the "overcoming of morality," indeed from its "self-overcoming." This means that a Nietzschean ethic must be a product of morality, as well as its overcoming. The "self-overcoming of morality," Nietzsche proclaims, "let this be the name for that long secret work that remains reserved for the most refined and honest, also the most malicious, consciences of today, as living touchstones of the soul" (BGE 32).

To begin to have a picture of what Nietzsche thinks this task involves and some understanding of why he speaks of it so reverentially here, one needs an account of what is to be overcome, i.e., of what morality is—using this word from now on always in the narrower sense. To provide such an account is one of the major tasks of Nietzsche's genealogy of morality, thus of the entire book under consideration. We all have a sense of what "morality" means, but Nietzsche claims that in the case of things that are products of a complicated history, as morality is, the "meaning" of the corresponding concept or word is the "crystallization" of that history, a synthesis of "meanings," which makes defining it impossible.[17] Nietzsche will therefore attempt to clarify and illuminate the concept of morality—our sense of what morality is—precisely by examining its genealogy.

4. Genealogy

To construct a genealogy is to map out ancestors or sets of parents from which an individual or family of individuals has come. Nietzsche's use of the word "genealogy" in the title of this work is a brilliant way for

---

morality in that sense. We might put it this way: The narrower sense of "morality" (our normal sense) is such that we are at least strongly tempted to evaluate actions in terms of their intentions, but we can overcome this temptation and still count as accepting morality in that sense.

17. One might wonder at this point why it was so easy to define the wider sense of morality. The answer is that the wider sense was basically a matter of stipulation, a concept we need in order to have any chance of gaining clarity concerning the sense of morality that is confusing to us precisely because it is a product of historical developments and not something we have simply stipulated.

him to suggest two major points about its approach to morality. First and foremost, its approach is *naturalistic*: It treats morality as a phenomenon of life, as a purely natural phenomenon, one whose existence is to be explained without any reference to a world beyond nature, a supernatural or metaphysical world. Nietzsche tells us that he first gave public expression to hypotheses about the origins of morality in *Human, All Too Human*, which was published in 1878, nine years before *Genealogy* (GM P:4). The earlier book was also his first attempt to contribute to the establishment of a naturalistic perspective. His first two books, *The Birth of Tragedy* and *Unfashionable Observations*, had accepted much of Schopenhauer's metaphysical picture of reality, and had seen at least some human capacities and activities as putting us in contact with a higher level of reality than the empirical or natural world. In *Human, All Too Human*, by contrast, he examines the typical traits and activities that are taken as indications of our "higher" nature, hence of an essential break between humanity and other animal species, and argues that these can all be explained as sublimations of traits and activities that are easily recognized as "lower," as continuous with those of other animals. The point was to demonstrate that traditional religious or metaphysical explanations of distinctive human accomplishments are superfluous and thus have no cognitive basis. Writing *Genealogy* nine years later, he is no longer concerned to establish his naturalistic perspective against competitors, but takes it for granted, just as he takes for granted that human "sinfulness" is not a fact but only the interpretation of a fact from "a moral-religious perspective that is no longer binding on us" (GM III:16). We are no longer "bound" to a perspective that interprets suffering as punishment for sin because it has become clear how much we can explain from an alternative naturalistic perspective. In fact, Nietzsche clearly believes something stronger than this, namely, that the naturalistic perspective has moved to a position where it is now "binding" on those who seek knowledge, whereas explanations based on a moral-religious perspective have "the conscience *against* it" (GM III:27).

The project of a genealogy of morality is thus to explain in purely naturalistic terms, without appeal to the voice of God or an immortal soul in touch with eternal values, the origins of morality: how it came about that human beings are guided by morality. The question is not why we are morally good, but why it is that human animals accept (hence act on the basis of) specifically *moral* reasons or values.

Naturalism is not, however, the distinguishing characteristic of *Genealogy*'s account of morality. British moral philosophers had been explaining morality in terms of human psychology and without resorting to God or metaphysics for more than two hundred years before Nietzsche. These are the "English psychologists" he discusses at the very beginning of the first treatise. Nietzsche thus opens his genealogy of morality by telling us something about his own genealogy: the "English psychologists" are his intellectual ancestors, the only ones who have previously attempted "to produce a history of the genesis of morality." Whereas other thinkers took morality for granted as a necessary part of humanity's existence and a sign of its "higher" origins, the "English psychologists" tried to give a naturalistic account of its genesis.

What Nietzsche believes distinguishes him from his "English" ancestors is the historical spirit he claims they lack: They have no sense of the second point Nietzsche suggests in calling the book a "genealogy," that morality has ancestors. The "English psychologists" simply collect the facts regarding *current* moral valuations and look for a theory that will explain them. Thus David Hume (1711–76), probably Nietzsche's greatest "English" ancestor, finds it evident that "the benevolent or softer affections are **Estimable**; and, wherever they appear, engage the approbation, and good will of mankind. The epithets *sociable, good-natured, humane, merciful, grateful, friendly, generous, beneficent*, or their equivalents, are known in all languages, and universally express the highest merit, which human nature is capable of attaining."[18] Given the assumption that these "softer affections" are useful to those to whom they are directed, Hume can explain fairly easily why human beings universally esteem them: that we praise and approve of what furthers either our own self-interest or the self-interest of those with whom we sympathize. This requires him to posit at the origin of morality an inborn sympathy with our fellow human beings and with societal aims. He must also make the assumption, one which Nietzsche explicitly attributes to the "English psychologists," that moral qualities are praised as "good" or "virtuous" from the viewpoint of those to whom they are useful.

Nietzsche would undoubtedly see a lack of historical sense in Hume's belief that the softer affections that we now equate with virtue "express the highest merit which human nature is capable of attaining" in all human cultures. His methodological objection would be to Hume's move

18. David Hume, *An Enquiry Concerning the Principles of Morals* (Indianapolis: Hackett Publishing Co., 1983), pp. 16–17. Hume was actually Scottish, which may begin to give some sense of how loosely Nietzsche intends "English" to be understood.

from the usefulness of *current* valuations directly to a theory of human nature and psychology that explains why these valuations exist. Such a move violates the major point of "historical method" laid down at *Genealogy*'s midpoint: The purpose served by a thing does not explain its origin; rather, the cause of its coming into being and "its final usefulness, its actual employment and integration into a system of purposes," lie worlds apart (GM II:12). Nietzsche's prime example of a violation of this principle is the assumption that the eye was made to see, the hand to grasp. This suggests that his principle of historical method is inspired by Darwin's theory of evolution, according to which the eye's usefulness does not explain why it originally came into existence, but only why, having somehow or other come into existence, it had a greater chance of surviving and being passed on to heirs. To explain how the eye came into existence would be to trace it back through a whole series of previous forms, and transformations of these forms by means of new variations, to something that lies "worlds apart" from it, say a simple nerve that is particularly sensitive to light.

Nietzsche's *Genealogy* applies the same principle to human history. Questions of origin and purpose are to be separated; the purpose served by a practice or custom does not explain how it came into existence. Instead, something that somehow or other already existed came to be "interpreted" differently; that is, it came to be seen as serving a different purpose. To explain why a custom or practice exists would be to trace it back through the series of past forms and transformations of its "meaning" from which it emerged in its present form, suitable for serving the purpose it is now taken to serve. If it is the case, as Hume claims, that moral valuation of actions is now directed towards praising and encouraging actions that are seen as *useful* to oneself and others, this does not mean that it functioned in this way originally, much less that it came into existence in order to serve this purpose. Instead, if Nietzsche's approach is correct, one will find that a practice of valuation with a very different "meaning" was already there, a practice that was not perceived to have anything to do with utility. This practice was then "taken over" by having a series of new functions imposed on it, which is to say that it was interpreted as serving a variety of functions, ultimately the function of praising useful actions. This imposition of a series of new "meanings" transformed the practice itself until it arrived at its current state, seemingly designed by nature to serve the purpose of praising and encouraging "useful" actions. Nietzsche's alternative to the "English" account of the origin of morality thus takes the form of a genealogy: He attempts to show how morality emerged from its ancestors, previous valuations and practices that had meanings different from those morality is now taken to have.

One might wonder, however, why morality's ancestors are of such concern. If we know that morality now serves a certain purpose, why is it so important that it emerged from something that serves a different purpose? Nietzsche's answer is that otherwise too much will remain hidden for us to understand morality's present character. This point follows from the important discussion of concepts that Nietzsche places squarely at the midpoint of *Genealogy*. That discussion implies about the concept of morality what it says about the concept of punishment: in a late state of culture, it no longer has a single meaning but instead represents "an entire synthesis of 'meanings': the previous history of punishment in general, the history of its exploitation for the most diverse purposes, finally crystallizes into a kind of unity that is difficult to dissolve, difficult to analyze and—one must emphasize—is completely and utterly *undefinable*." Nietzsche adds in parentheses: "only that which has no history is definable" (GM II:13).

Anglo-American philosophers who also regard Nietzsche's "English psychologists" as their ancestors once considered it their business to clarify concepts by formulating necessary and sufficient conditions for the use of the corresponding terms. The concept of morality was to be clarified by specifying the characteristics that are both necessary and sufficient to qualify a code of conduct as "a morality." This procedure is now out of fashion, never having delivered great clarification, and Nietzsche's discussion of concepts explains why that is what we should expect. It suggests that our concepts need clarification precisely because they are products of a complicated historical development, a development that synthesizes various elements of its meaning into such a tight unity that they seem inseparable and are no longer visible as elements. We are therefore deprived of a clear view of the concept's structure.

Borrowing from Wittgenstein, we might say that a concept influenced by history is constituted and held together like a rope, by the intertwining of its strands rather than by a core strand running through it. To analyze or clarify such a concept is not to isolate a core strand, as one tries to do by finding necessary and sufficient conditions for a term's use, but to disentangle a number of its strands so that we can see what is actually involved in it. History can play an important role in conceptual clarification because it can help us to separate out the strands that have become so tightly intertwined that they seem inseparable. Nietzsche tells us that at earlier stages the synthesis of "meanings" that constitutes the concept will appear "more soluble, also more capable of shifts; one can still perceive in each individual case how the elements of the synthesis change their valence and rearrange themselves accordingly, so that now this, now that element comes to the fore" (GM II:13).

I want now to offer a hypothesis concerning the overall structure of *Genealogy* that fits with this account of the connection between concepts and history. I suggest that Nietzsche incorporates into *Genealogy*'s structure much of the conceptual clarification of morality that history has offered him: His historical investigations, many of them prior to *Genealogy*, have led him to conclude that our concept of morality involves the intertwining of at least three major strands, which are morality's answer to three different questions. First, goodness or virtue, morality's answer to the question: What are the qualities or traits of a good or virtuous person? Second, duty or obligation, morality's answer to the question: What is my duty? What do I owe others? Third, the ideal, morality's answer to the question: What is the ultimate point and value of human life? My proposal is that each of the book's three treatises focuses on the development of one of these strands or answers without paying attention to the other two, even though the actual development of each took place in interaction with the others. The point of treating them in isolation, in abstraction from their actual interaction, is to emphasize that they are separable aspects—for morality's intertwining of them makes that point very difficult to appreciate. Nietzsche's account demonstrates their separability by appealing to historical factors: ideas of virtue and ideas of duty, for instance, turn out to have very different origins.

In each treatise a clearly *moral* version of one of the strands is traced back to non-moral factors—in the first two treatises, to a version of the strand that can easily be recognized as pre-moral. These two treatises present an account of the historical development that led from pre-moral versions of virtue and duty, respectively, to clearly moral versions of these strands. This kind of historical analysis will not make it possible to specify the exact point at which, for instance, the non-moral version of debt or guilt becomes the specifically *moral* version, but it will give us a means of specifying what makes a version more or less distant from the clearly moral version. To see this, however, readers must be willing to piece together the accounts given in the three treatises. For although Nietzsche treats morality's three major strands separately to stress their separability, it is actually only through their interaction—which hovers in the background of each treatise rather than being brought to the fore—that he thinks morality came to be.

If we come to recognize "morality" as a particular interweaving of these strands, however, it becomes possible to begin to recognize possibilities for re-weaving the strands, i.e., for reconstituting ethical life in a new form. This is the major upshot of the framework I have provided for understanding this book. The one image Nietzsche gives us of a "post-moral" ethical form, I suggest, is his portrait of the philosopher near the beginning of the third treatise. This portrait gives us Nietzsche's image of a post-moral version of the particular aspect of morality under consideration in this treatise: the ideal. What notions of virtue and duty would be compatible with this non-moral ideal is not a question Nietzsche takes up here. But if one understands the structure of the book in accord with the framework I have offered, this can be seen as one of the central questions Nietzsche leaves readers to ask and answer for themselves. Likewise, I must leave it to readers to test for themselves the hypothesis I have offered concerning the book's framework, a test that can be conducted by considering how well it illuminates the whole of the work and fits with the details that Nietzsche actually provides in each treatise. I will, however, attempt to make my hypothesis a little more concrete in the two sections below by looking at a few of the details of the first and third treatises of *Genealogy* and suggesting how they fit into the framework I have offered.

5. *Genealogy* I: The "Slave Revolt" in Morality

In *Genealogy*'s first and most famous treatise, Nietzsche locates the origins of judgments of moral goodness or virtue in the ideas of goodness he claims to find among politically superior groups in the ancient world, ideas of goodness that seem obvious cases of non-moral ones. The members of such groups, the ancient nobles, called themselves "the good," Nietzsche claims, but this was equivalent to "noble" or "superior" in the political sense; the contrasting term "bad" was equivalent to "plebeian," "common," or "inferior"—not to "evil," which Nietzsche uses as equivalent to "morally bad." Over time, the nobles developed a sense of the qualities that constituted their goodness or virtue, but these were simply the qualities they perceived as distinguishing them from the common people: originally wealth, power, and military distinction; later, character traits such as truthfulness and loyalty. When the nobility declined, Nietzsche claims, "good" remained as "the term for *noblesse* of soul";

that is, it came to represent a kind of nobility that is independent of political status.

Nietzsche seems right that many of the words now used to refer to moral goodness and its opposite originally had a non-moral meaning, for instance, that the Greek words for "good" and "virtuous" were originally equivalent to "noble" in the political sense, and that the German word for "bad" is a transformation of the word for "simple" or "plain." And a reading of Homer and other early Greek literature also seems to support Nietzsche's hypothesis that judgments of goodness and virtue originally had little to do with what we mean by "morality."[19] But suppose we agree that the ancient nobles originally picked out as virtues rougher and tougher traits than the humane virtues of modern human beings. Need we reject Hume's theory concerning the relation between utility and morality? Can we not argue that rougher times require rougher virtues, thus that precisely the usefulness of such traits for the well-being of society as it existed in those days explains why they were recognized as virtues?

Nietzsche's answer seems to be that while the ancient nobles may well have recognized the traits that constituted their virtue as useful to themselves or society, this does not explain *why* they accorded them the status of virtues, the "meaning" of virtue to them. The pride these men took in being virtuous and the esteem they accorded virtue and the virtuous simply cannot be explained in terms of a concern for utility. In a sense, Nietzsche agrees with Kant against the "English psychologists," that goodness or virtue represents for us a kind of worth that simply cannot be reduced to being useful to others. Kant claimed that the morally good will is not only good in itself, apart from any consideration of its effects, but unconditionally good and a condition of the goodness of any other good in the human world. We can make sense of such a value, he argued further, only if the human will is autonomous, meaning that it is subject only to laws it gives itself, and that it therefore transcends nature and nature's laws. Nietzsche denies that anything human transcends nature, but his criticism of the theory attributed to the English psychologists (GM I:3)

19. Although he seems not to be aware of Nietzsche and would have little sympathy for his point of view, A. W. H. Adkins's examination of early Greek literature provides significant evidence in support of Nietzsche's suggestion that the Greeks of the Homeric age lived in a basically "non-moral" ethical universe, that morality is a later development. See Williams (1993) for a critique of Adkins's attempt to show that this non-moral ethical universe involved an inadequate notion of responsibility.

suggests that he wants to be able to explain naturalistically how human beings could come to feel about virtue as Kant did. His answer is that the origin of such a feeling is ultimately the esteem that belonged to virtue in the ancient world, when it was seen as a mark of distinction. Virtue, Nietzsche suggests, is originally what distinguishes, what separates one from and places one above common human beings.

To explain how this pre-moral idea of virtue was transformed into a more modern conception, how virtue came to be associated with Hume's "softer affections," Nietzsche postulates what he infamously calls the "slave revolt in morality." He claims that this revolt brought about a revaluation of the nobles' values, so that the persons and characteristics established as "good" (elevated or superior) by the noble manner of valuation were declared inferior. As a result, the distinguishing characteristics of noble, proud, and self- and life-affirming human animals were devalued, and the more "humane" traits of people whose position in life forced them to be quiet, patient, and humble were elevated to the status of virtue.

It is difficult to assess the plausibility of this account; I will limit myself here to stating briefly several interpretive points that can be used to answer some of the more obvious objections to it. First, the "slave revolt" was not a discrete historical event, but a development that took place over a very long period of time, perhaps thousands of years. (This development was also not a Jewish conspiracy, contrary to what a careless reading of GM I:8 might suggest.) Second, "slave revolt" is a misleading phrase because it leads some readers to suppose that the revolt was led by slaves or common people who finally decided that they could be good too. Nietzsche's "slave revolt" was led by priests, not by slaves. He claims that spiritual leaders whose own mode of valuation was originally a noble one—i.e., one that distinguished "good" from "bad" or "common," not from "evil"—began a process that overthrew the noble way of evaluating goodness and replaced it with one in which traits that are particularly useful to slaves and others in dependent positions became virtues. These traits did gain the status of virtue, but not because anyone—the priests or the people—esteemed them or came to recognize them as admirable or intrinsically valuable. They could only come to be regarded as admirable, Nietzsche suggests, with the help of the illusion that they were deliberately chosen, an expression of free will (GM I:13).[20] But why did anyone

---

20. This is the same free will that Nietzsche thinks was needed to make sense of the idea that the nobles deserved eternal punishment for being "birds of prey"

want to regard them as virtues? The answer depends on whether one is asking about the spiritual leaders or the people. This much is clear: The priests' concern, according to Nietzsche, was not to help the people fight oppression or gain self-esteem. What the priests wanted was *revenge*, revenge against the nobles, their rivals for power and prestige. Nietzsche claims that the priests transformed the noble idea of goodness into moral goodness precisely in order to use it against their rivals, to take a kind of "spiritual revenge" against them when they could not get the other kind, to "bring them down," if only (initially at least) in their own imagination. Think of the priests' condemnation of the nobles, the judgment that they are "evil," as a spiritualized version of burning someone in effigy.

A final point about the "slave revolt" is that it does not explain, and is not intended to explain, how violence and other unacceptable actions of human birds of prey came to be regarded as *wrong*. In particular, Nietzsche is not claiming that these actions came to be regarded as wrong because slaves or commoners resented being treated that way. The job of the "slave revolt" is to explain the transformation of a pre-moral notion of *goodness* into a specifically moral one; it is not directly concerned with right and wrong. This follows from the intrepretive framework offered earlier. The first treatise deals with only one major aspect of morality, the idea of goodness in the sense of virtue. In reality, of course, ideas of goodness developed in concert and interaction with ideas of right and wrong.[21]

(GM I:13). The idea of free will involved is the idea that one is a *causa sui*, the ultimate cause of what one is, which Nietzsche calls "the best self-contradiction that has been conceived so far" (BGE 21). In GM II:4, Nietzsche makes clear that ideas of responsibility for actions and desert of punishment developed quite independently of this idea of free will, which BGE 21 calls the idea of "freedom of the will in the superlative metaphysical sense."

21. It is easy to overlook the suggestion in GM I:11 that the instincts of "reaction and *ressentiment*" that helped to overthrow noble ideals are actually "instruments of culture." That culture is something Nietzsche himself values is made clear in this passage by the fact that Nietzsche immediately proceeds to deny at length that the "bearers of these instincts" thereby represent culture. But why consider the instinct that led to the "slave revolt" an instrument of culture if the revolt has nothing to do with civilizing human standards of right and wrong, but only with overthrowing a certain idea of goodness? I assume Nietzsche's point here is that by overthrowing the noble idea of goodness, the "slave revolt" eventually made it possible for the realm and rule of right, which the nobles extended only to members of their own group, to be extended to all. If this interpretation of the passage

But each treatise abstracts from this interaction between aspects to focus on one of them. Once we see that the first treatise abstracts from questions regarding right and wrong to focus on ideas of goodness and virtue, we can see more clearly that noble values are the ancestors of only one aspect of morality, the idea of moral virtue, and that Nietzsche appeals to the "slave revolt" to explain one major point: namely, how this noble idea of virtue was transformed into our idea of specifically *moral* virtue.

In the second treatise, Nietzsche focuses on the aspect of morality I have claimed he abstracts from in the first: the realm of right, which includes ideas of right and wrong, duty and obligation, fairness and justice. This may be obscured by the fact that the centerpiece of the second treatise is a striking account of the sense of guilt, one that obviously influenced Freud's later account. But guilt plays a major role in Nietzsche's genealogy of morality, I will only suggest here, because he sees it as the focal point for the transformation of pre-moral notions of right into specifically *moral* ones. The clearest example of such a pre-moral notion is the idea of debt. Nietzsche's account of how this pre-moral notion of owing was transformed into a moral notion of guilt is at the same time an attempt to show that the whole world of moral notions of right and wrong, obligation and duty, justice and fairness developed as transformations of a set of pre-moral ideas and practices. The development Nietzsche sketches in the second treatise is complicated, but it is easier to follow if one recognizes that it begins much earlier than and interacts with the development he describes in the first treatise, and that Nietzsche largely leaves it to the reader to make explicit the details of that interaction.

6. *Genealogy* III: The Ascetic Ideal

The third treatise concerns ascetic ideals, all of which turn out to be variations on *the* ascetic ideal, the priestly ideal according to which the life of self-denial, the monkish life, is the highest human life. Nietzsche claims that this priestly ideal is the only ideal human beings have had so far. But even if that is true, what does it have to do with morality? If each treatise deals with a central aspect of morality, as my framework suggests, Nietzsche must believe that the ascetic ideal is central to morality. But that seems highly implausible. How can ascetic ideals be central to morality when, as Hume says about the "monkish virtues," they are "every

---

is correct, Nietzsche takes for granted that this extension of the realm of right to all is a condition of higher culture, and that it is a good upshot of the "slave revolt."

where rejected by men of sense ... because they serve to no manner of purpose"? They can be regarded as virtues, Hume adds, only by the "delirious and dismal"; the rest of us perceive the priestly valuation of these traits as a perversion of "natural sentiments."[22] Nietzsche seems largely to agree with Hume on this point. For he claims that the ascetic ideal and its devaluation of life are motivated by a "*ressentiment* without equal" and "power-will" (GM III:11) By devaluing life, the ascetic priest attempts to gain a sense of power over life (in much the same way that the priests of the first treatise gain a sense of revenge against the nobles by condemning them). This certainly sounds like a strategy of the "delirious and dismal." Further, Nietzsche finds only one place where the ascetic ideal is still alive and well—among the philosophers in whom he finds the will to truth—and he believes its continuing strength there depends on a failure to recognize it for what it is. But how can he think that the ascetic ideal is central to morality if he thinks it is largely dead?

The answer, I suggest, is that he believes that morality is also largely dead. This is why he tells us at the end of the third treatise that morality will "gradually perish" once those with a will to truth recognize that they are in fact the last and latest expression of the ascetic ideal. This can seem crazy—how can Nietzsche possibly believe that what a few ascetic philosophers figure out about their own will to truth will bring about the destruction of morality? It makes sense only if he believes that the ascetic ideal is central to morality, hence that its destruction means the destruction of morality.

Nietzsche's point, I suggest, is that the particular transformations of pre-moral practices into moral ones described in the first two treatises took place by means of the ascetic ideal. If we apply to morality his distinction between practices and meaning (GM II:13), we can say that he sees morality as involving not merely a set of evaluative practices and associated feelings, but also an "interpretation" of these practices and feelings, an understanding of their ultimate purpose and value. I take his point to be that the ascetic ideal of self-denial provided the interpetation that, over time, transformed the practices of judging the right and the virtuous, practices that were already in place quite apart from the priest and his ascetic ideal, into our recognizably moral practices. Both the slave revolt and the transformation of pre-moral notions of debt, obligation, and duty into specifically moral notions, Nietzsche implies, were brought about by means of the ascetic ideal and its understanding of the ultimate

22. Hume, 73-74.

point and value of human life. This explains why Nietzsche claims repeatedly that morality "denies" or "negates" life: Morality is an ascetic interpretation of ethical life, which means that how far a form of ethical life is from morality depends on the extent to which an ascetic (hence, life-devaluing) interpretation is woven into its basic evaluative practices.

This suggests something of how Nietzsche would diagnose the current situation of morality. At the end of the twentieth century in the United States, morality does not seem in good shape. Relativism is rampant and many people feel that some kind of breakdown has occurred, that morality is no longer firmly under our feet. To be sure, something is there, but something is also missing. Nietzsche's analysis suggests that the evaluative practices and feelings that we associate with morality are still there. What is missing is the interpretation, the ascetic meaning that was imposed on the practices, a meaning that ultimately made the practices into a great instrument for the transformation of human beings.

When Nietzsche says that the ascetic ideal is the only ideal human beings have had so far, I take him to mean that this ideal embodies the only understanding of the point of human life that has in fact prompted human beings to raise their sights beyond goods external to the self and to focus on making over the self, making the self into something more than it was originally. As such, the ascetic ideal has been the "guts" and meaning behind morality. Without its interpretation of the value and point of human life, the practices and associated feelings remain, at least for a while, and they do some kind of work; but they lose their ability to inspire and transform human lives.[23]

23. Important remnants of the ascetic ideal certainly remain, including the continued teaching of the ideal of self-denial in moderated form in some religions. Still, if one looks, for instance, at the culture of the United States at the end of the twentieth century, it is difficult to believe that the ascetic ideal has much real purchase in it. The American ideal is now surely the "good life," and that does not mean the life of self-denial. Americans certainly admired Mother Teresa, but no one really wanted to be like her. Politicians still get some mileage out of the ascetic ideal, of course, but this is now largely a hypocritical and obvious screen for self-interest. Beyond that, there are many remnants of the ideal both in ascetic practices that still abound, though now often given an aesthetic interpretation (excessive dieting and exercise as necessary for the life of success, money, and happiness), and in many people's understanding of ethical practices. I think Nietzsche's point is that despite all of this, the ascetic ideal no longer goes deep enough to do much serious work, that the practices are no longer informed and inspired by the ideal, except in the case of philosophers who exhibit the will to truth.

Genealogy's project is not to undermine morality, therefore, but to show that and how it has already been undermined—by the breakdown of faith in the ascetic ideal. Nietzsche does seek to contribute to this ideal's final overcoming by exposing it in its one remaining stronghold, among "we knowers" (GM P:1), the group whose will to truth has led to the development of a completely naturalistic understanding of reality. The "filtering down" of their naturalism (of the scientific view of things) is precisely what Nietzsche thinks has undermined the ascetic ideal elsewhere, making it impossible to defend it against Hume's type of contempt. But Nietzsche is not simply "jumping on the bandwagon," kicking morality and its ascetic ideal when they are already down. His point is to bring out what is lost by the demise of this ideal: the inspiration for all of the greatest human cultural achievements. These include not only art and philosophy, but also the great self-overcomings with which Nietzsche particularly identifies, namely, atheism and immoralism. But these great cultural achievements also include, perhaps above all else, morality. It is not that Nietzsche thinks we can just let it go and say "good riddance." His point is to show us what we had, so that we can see what we now need. My own suggestion is that he thinks we need a new ideal (or new ideals), new interpretations and meanings for our ethical practices. He attempts to destroy the last stronghold of the ascetic ideal precisely because those hiding in it are the ones who are best suited to understand what is needed in a new ideal, and thus to have a chance of providing it. Under the influence of the old ideal, however, they see their job as that of simply telling us the truth about reality, and evade what Nietzsche thinks is an equally or even more important task: the creation of new meaning, a "creation" that is not *ex nihilo*, but is a matter of providing new interpretations of practices and fragments of ethical life that are already there, seeing and presenting their ultimate value in new ways.

Maudemarie Clark

Selected Bibliography

A brief overview of Nietzsche's life and the development of his thought can be found in the "Nietzsche" entry by M. Clark in E. Craig (ed.), *The Routledge Encyclopedia of Philosophy* (1998). For detailed accounts of Nietzsche's life, see R. J. Hollingdale, *Nietzsche: The Man and His Philosophy* (1965) or R. Hayman, *Nietzsche: A Critical Life* (1980). An English translation of the standard German biography of Nietzsche, a three-volume work by C. P. Janz (1978), is underway, but has not yet appeared.

G. Morgen, *What Nietzsche Means* (1941), is still a valuable and very accessible introduction to Nietzsche's thought. For a more comprehensive and philosophically up-to-date treatment of all of the major themes of Nietzsche's philosophy, see R. Schacht, *Nietzsche* (1983). A. Nehamas, *Nietzsche: Life as Literature* (1985), is an important and influential attempt to relate Nietzsche's philosophical views to the ways in which he writes, and, in effect, to show how Nietzsche's writings create new ethical "meanings" by creating a certain kind of character. W. Kaufmann, *Nietzsche: Philosopher, Psychologist, Antichrist*, fourth edition (1974), offers an important and widely accepted defense of Nietzsche against the charge that he supported Nazi aspirations and a wealth of information about various aspects of Nietzsche's life and the reception of his thought. For an introduction to interpretations that departed from Kaufmann's views when his was still the dominant interpretation of Nietzsche in the United States, especially those inspired by Continental European thinkers, see D. Allison (ed.), *The New Nietzsche* (1977).

For more information on Nietzsche's views of the topics discussed in *On the Genealogy of Morality* (1887), the best sources are Nietzsche's other books, especially *Beyond Good and Evil* (1886); *Genealogy* was intended as a "supplement and clarification" of it. Nietzsche's brief analysis of *Genealogy* in the third part of the *Ecce Homo* is also illuminating. The most relevant of Nietzsche's other books are those in the series of so-called "aphoristic" works that lead up to *Beyond Good and Evil* and *Genealogy*: the two volumes of *Human, All Too Human* (1878–80), *Daybreak* (1881), and *The Gay Science* (1882; fifth part and new preface, 1887). These are the works in which Nietzsche developed the naturalistic perspective on morality that lies behind *Genealogy*, and they often fill in gaps in the latter's presentation of it. Because Nietzsche's views changed considerably as he worked out and refined his naturalistic account, however, *Genealogy*'s claims about morality often differ from those of the earlier books; in doing so, they also provide valuable information about the process of thinking from which *Genealogy* emerged. *Twilight of the Idols* and *The Antichrist*, both written during Nietzsche's final productive year (1888), also contain a number of passages that function as helpful clarifications and supplements to *Genealogy*.

Helpful secondary sources on Nietzsche's claims about morality include the chapters on morality or ethics in the books cited above. No helpful book-length study has yet appeared. R. Schacht (ed.), *Nietzsche, Genealogy, Morality* (1994) offers an important collection of papers on various aspects of the views presented in *Genealogy*. Criticisms of Nietzsche's views are developed in several of these papers, including P. Foot's well-known article "Nietzsche's Immoralism." See also Foot's paper "Nietzsche: The Revaluation of Values," in R. Solomon (ed.), *Nietzsche: A Collection of Critical Essays* (1973). M. Clark's paper in the Schacht volume is a response to Foot; it also fills in more of the details of the framework offered in the Introduction to the present book. For a contrasting framework, see B. Leiter, "Morality in the Pejorative Sense: On the Logic of Nietzsche's Critique of Morality," *British Journal for the History of Philosophy* 3 (1995), pp. 113–45. Also see Leiter's "Beyond Good and Evil," *History of Philosophy Quarterly* 10 (1993), pp. 261–70, and F. Bergmann, "Nietzsche's Critique of Morality," R. Solomon and K. Higgens (eds.), *Reading Nietzsche* (1988). John Wilcox, "What Aphorism Does Nietzsche Explicate in *Genealogy of Morals*, Essay III?," *Journal of the History of Philosophy* 4 (1997), establishes the aphorism that the third treatise explicates based on a careful reading of that treatise. Chapter 6 of M. Clark's *Nietzsche on Truth and Philosophy* (1990), "The Ascetic Ideal," also a reading of the third treatise, concentrates on the ascetic ideal and its relation to the will to truth.

M. Foucault, "Nietzsche, Genealogy, History," in *Language, Counter-Memory, Practice* (1977), is a very influential interpretation of Nietzsche's idea of genealogy. For an alternative interpretation based on Nietzsche's use of genealogy in his *Genealogy*, see Raymond Geuss, "Nietzsche and Genealogy," *European Journal of Philosophy* 2 (1994). G. Deleuze, *Nietzsche and Philosophy*, translated by Hugh Tomlinson (1983), is the most important book by a Continental European philosopher in terms of its influence on readings of specific passages in Nietzsche's *Genealogy*.

For the background of Nietzsche's own thought, Schopenhauer is the most important source, especially *The World as Will and Representation* and *On the Basis of Morality.* For a short introduction to Schopenhauer, see C. Janaway, *Schopenhauer* (1994). For essays on Schopenhauer and Nietzsche, see C. Janaway (ed.), *Willing and Nothingness: Schopenhauer as Nietzsche's Educator* (1998).

Works Cited

Translations of Nietzsche's books cited in the Introduction and End Notes are based on the *Kritische Studienausgabe* (KSA), edited by G. Colli and M. Montinari, 15 volumes (Berlin: de Gruyter, 1980). N's letters cited in the End Notes are from *Kritische Gesamtausgabe: Briefwechsel,* edited by C. Colli and M. Montinari, 24 volumes (Berlin: de Gruyter, 1975–84). Nietzsche's books are listed below in the order in which he finished them, followed by the year in which they were first published and preceded by the acronyms used to cite them in the Introduction and End Notes. The books are always cited by main part and section number, which are the same in all editions, not by page number. "P" always stands for the preface to the work cited. Sometimes shortened forms of the book's name are used instead of the acronyms, e.g., "*Human*" for "*Human, All Too Human.*"

BT   = *The Birth of Tragedy* (1872); P=new preface of 1886

UO   = *Unfashionable Observations* (1873-76); also translated as *Untimely Meditations* and as *Unmodern Observations*

HA   = *Human, All Too Human,* 2 vols. (1878-80)

D   = *Daybreak* (1881); also translated as *Dawn* and as *Dawn of Day*

GS   = *The Gay Science* (1882; new preface and fifth part, 1887). Also translated as *Joyful Wisdom*

Z   = *Thus Spoke Zarathustra* (1883-85)

BGE = *Beyond Good and Evil* (1886)

GM   = *On the Genealogy of Morality* (1887); also translated as *On the Genealogy of Morals*

CW   = *The Case of Wagner* (1889)

TI   = *Twilight of the Idols* (1889)

A   = *The Antichrist* (1895); sometimes referred to as *The Antichrist(ian)*

EH   = *Ecce Homo* (1908)

NW   = *Nietzsche Contra Wagner* (1895)

Other Works Cited in the Introduction

Adkins, Arthur W.H. *Merit and Responsibility: A Study in Greek Values*. Oxford: Oxford University Press, 1960.

Aschheim, Steven E. *The Nietzsche Legacy in Germany 1890-1990*. Berkeley: University of California Press, 1992.

Clark, Maudemarie and Brian Leiter. "Introduction" to Nietzsche's *Daybreak*. Cambridge: Cambridge University Press, 1997.

Dennett, Daniel. "Friedrich Nietzsche's Just So Stories." In *Darwin's Dangerous Idea*. New York: Simon and Schuster, 1996.

Ferry, Luc and Alain Renaut. *Why We Are Not Nietzscheans*. Trans. Robert de Loaiza. Chicago: The University of Chicago Press, 1997.

Golomb, Jacob (ed). *Nietzsche and Jewish Culture*. New York: Routledge, 1997.

Heidegger, Martin. *Nietzsche*, 2 vols. Pfullingen: Neske, 1961. Trans. David F. Krell. 4 vols. New York: Harper & Row, 1979–84.

Hume, David. *An Enquiry Concerning the Principles of Morals*. Edited by J.B. Schneewind. Indianapolis: Hackett Publishing Co., 1983.

Korsgaard, Christine. *The Sources of Normativity*. Cambridge: Cambridge University Press, 1996.

Larmore, Charles. "The Nietzsche Legacy." In *The Morals of Modernity*. Cambridge: Cambridge University Press, 1996.

Leiter, Brian. "Nietzsche and the Morality Critics." *Ethics* 107 (1997), pp. 250–85.

MacIntyre, Alasdair. *After Virtue: A Study of Moral Theory*. Notre Dame, Ind.: University of Notre Dame, 1981.

———. *Three Rival Versions of Moral Enquiry: Encyclopedia, Genealogy, and Tradition*. Notre Dame, Ind.: University of Notre Dame Press, 1990.

O'Brien, Conor Cruise, "The Gentle Nietzscheans," *The New York Review of Books*. Nov. 5, 1970, pp. 12–16.

Rorty, Richard. *Contingency, Irony, and Solidarity*. Cambridge: Cambridge University Press, 1989.

Schaberg, William H. *The Nietzsche Canon: A Publication History and Bibliography*. Chicago: The University of Chicago Press, 1995.

Schacht, Richard (ed.). *Nietzsche, Genealogy, Morality*. Berkeley: University of California, 1994.

Williams, Bernard. *Moral Luck*. Cambridge: Cambridge University Press, 1981.

———. *Ethics and the Limits of Philosophy*. Cambridge, Mass.: Harvard University Press, 1985.

———. "Nietzsche's Minimalist Moral Psychology," *European Journal of Philosophy* 1 (1993), pp. 1–14.

———. *Shame and Necessity*. Berkeley: University of California Press, 1993.

Translators' Note and Acknowledgments

We began this translation of *On the Genealogy of Morality* from the now standard edition by C. Colli and M. Montinari, which both of us used initially in its paperback edition, the *Kritische Studienausgabe*. The final version has been informed by a comparison of that text with several editions, especially with the first edition and with the manuscript, which is kept in the *Nietzsche-Archiv* now administered by the *Goethe-Schiller-Archiv* in Weimar, Germany.

Alan Swensen did all of this work with the other editions and the printer's manuscript. He also did the initial rough version of the translation. The two of us then discussed it at length and debated what sometimes seemed like every word, often on many different occasions and over several years, until we arrived at a version of the whole that both of us could accept. The final version has also been informed by very conscientious readers' reports and by the choices made in three other English translations of the text, those of Walter Kaufmann, Carol Diethe (edited by K. Ansell-Pearson), and Douglas Smith (the last two of which appeared while we were working on our translation).

This final version of the translation involved some compromises on both our parts. We have no remaining disagreements concerning Nietzsche's meaning, but it would be surprising if two individuals, especially two from very different disciplines, agreed in every case about the best way to convey Nietzsche's meaning in English. We are in complete agreement about the goal, however, which is (as Paul Guyer and Allen Wood have recently formulated it in their translation of Kant's *Critique of Pure Reason*) "to give the reader of the translation an experience as close as possible to that of the reader of the German original."

This goal dictated a number of commitments: wherever possible, to translate every occurrence of a potentially significant word with the same English word, to use that word for only one German word, to translate all words deriving from a common German root with words deriving from a common English root, and to avoid collapsing German synonyms into a single English term. We also attempted to preserve certain striking features of Nietzsche's style that are often sacrificed in translations. For instance, Nietzsche's punctuation is idiosyncratic and frequently has a significant expressive function. In particular, he makes heavy use of punctuation suggesting incompleteness or elision ("—" and "..."). He also uses final sentence punctuation ("!" and "?") in mid-sentence—at the end of section 6 of the preface, for example. Here he splits the expression "what if" such that it combines the expression of surprise (or disbelief) "What?" with the introduction of a hypothetical observation "what if." This is as odd in German as it is in English. Nietzsche's use of the colon also fits neither German nor English usage, and we have accordingly left them as he used them—trusting that the reader will develop a sense for their function in his prose. The ideal is to make available to the reader of the English translation all of the possibilities for interpreting the text and appreciating its subtleties that are available to the reader of the German text.

Nietzsche's text contains only one note (at the end of the first treatise) and no note numbers. As the End Notes to this translation show, this was not because his book involved no scholarship. We have therefore chosen not to impose note numbers on Nietzsche's text. Words, phrases, and passages that occur in a language other than German in the original are left in that language; translations are provided at the bottom of the page. We follow the standard convention for English of italicizing all foreign words, but we also use italics for Nietzsche's emphasis. To preserve his emphases of foreign words, we put these in bold. End Notes are given by page and line number at the back of the book. The acronyms for Nietzsche's works used in the Introduction and throughout the End Notes are listed in the Selected Bibliography. The text of GM and other end notes are usually also cited by page and line number in the End Notes.

The End Notes are largely devoted to four sorts of matters: providing information concerning Nietzsche's references and sources, identifying passages in his other books or letters that may throw light on specific passages, explaining translation choices that may seem controversial or in violation of principles we otherwise follow, and sketching the views of philosophers and other thinkers to whom Nietzsche refers (including his own earlier self) that form the most important background for understanding the views he develops in this book. The sometimes detailed sketches of other philosophers' views may provide a useful supplement to the Introduction, which offers a general interpretive framework for understanding Nietzsche's views.

Alan Swensen did all of the work on the footnotes to the translation and the majority of work on the End Notes, including the initial version of most of them. Maudemarie Clark's contribution is found in the philosophical material and the notes on intellectual history, especially when these have a bearing on translation choices or are particularly related to Nietzsche's philosophy or its development. In preparing the notes, Alan consulted the *Kritische Studienausgabe*, the Kaufmann and Diethe translations (the latter's notes are by Raymond Geuss), and the French, Italian, and Spanish translations. David S. Thatcher's detailed annotations—in *Nietzsche-Studien* 18 (1989), pp. 587-600—were also helpful. Use of their information is indicated in the notes.

Alan Swensen is greatly indebted to a number of native speakers who patiently allowed him to probe the boundaries of various terms or expressions. In particular he wishes to thank his colleagues Jürgen Meyer-Wendt, Dierk Hoffman, and also visiting colleagues from the University of Freiburg, Martin Baltes, Heide Schilk, and Harald Zils. Maudemarie Clark thanks her colleagues in philosophy, at Colgate and elsewhere, for many discussions over the years on philosophical issues concerning translation and various translation choices and their philosophical implications. We owe a great deal of thanks to Connie Jones and Susan Schoonmaker, who read and proofread the manuscript on numerous occasions.

We both spent time in Weimar working at the *Nietzsche-Archiv* and at the *Anna Amalia Bibliothek* where Nietzsche's personal library is now kept. We wish to thank the staff of both institutions for the assistance they gave us—they made it a pleasure to work there. Alan especially wishes to thank Dr. Roswitha Wollkopf and the staff of the *Goethe-Schiller-Archiv* for the generous assistance he received while he was working on the manuscripts.

Preface

1

We are unknown to ourselves, we knowers: and for a good reason. We have never sought ourselves—how then should it happen that we *find* ourselves one day? It has rightly been said: "where your treasure is, there will your heart be also"; *our* treasure is where the beehives of our knowledge stand. We are forever underway toward them, as born winged animals and honey-gatherers of the spirit, concerned with all our heart about only one thing—"bringing home" something. As for the rest of life, the so-called "experiences"—who of us even has enough seriousness for them? Or enough time? In such matters I'm afraid we were never really "with it": we just don't have our heart there—or even our ear! Rather, much as a divinely distracted, self-absorbed person into whose ear the bell has just boomed its twelve strokes of noon suddenly awakens and wonders, "what did it actually toll just now?" so we rub our ears *afterwards* and ask, completely amazed, completely disconcerted, "what did we actually experience just now?" still more: "who *are* we actually?" and count up, afterwards, as stated, all twelve quavering bellstrokes of our experience, of our life, of our *being*—alas! and miscount in the process ... We remain of necessity strangers to ourselves, we do not understand ourselves, we *must* mistake ourselves, for us the maxim reads to all eternity: "each is furthest from himself,"—with respect to ourselves we are not "knowers" ...

2

—My thoughts on the *origins* of our moral prejudices—for that is what this polemic is about—found their first, economical, and preliminary expression in the collection of aphorisms that bears the title *Human, All Too Human: A Book for Free Spirits,* the writing of that was begun in Sorrento during a winter that permitted me to pause, as a traveler pauses, and look out over the broad and dangerous land through which my spirit had thus far traveled. This occurred in the winter of 1876-77; the thoughts themselves are older. In essentials they were already the same thoughts which I now take up again in the treatises at hand: let us hope that the long period in between has been good for them, that they have become more mature, brighter, stronger, more perfect! That I still hold fast to them

1

today, that they themselves have, in the meantime, held to each other ever
more firmly, indeed have grown into each other and become intermeshed,
strengthens within me the cheerful confidence that they came about not
singly, not arbitrarily, not sporadically, but rather from the beginning arose
out of a common root, out of a *basic will* of knowledge which commands
from deep within, speaking ever more precisely, demanding something
ever more precise. For this alone is fitting for a philosopher. We have no
right to be *single* in anything: we may neither err singly nor hit upon the
truth singly. Rather, with the necessity with which a tree bears its fruit our
thoughts grow out of us, our values, our yes's and no's and if's and
whether's—the whole lot related and connected among themselves, witnesses to one will, one health, one earthly kingdom, one sun.—And do
they taste good *to you*, these fruits of ours?—But of what concern is that to
the trees! Of what concern is that *to us*, us philosophers! ...

3

Given a skepticism that is characteristic of me, to which I reluctantly
admit—for it is directed towards *morality*, towards everything on earth that has
until now been celebrated as morality—a skepticism that first appeared so early
in my life, so spontaneously, so irrepressibly, so much in contradiction to my
environment, age, models, origins, that I almost have the right to call it my "*a
priori*"—it was inevitable that early on my curiosity and my suspicion as well
would stop at the question: *what*, in fact, is the *origin* of our good and evil? In
fact, the problem of the origin of evil haunted me as a thirteen-year-old lad: at
an age when one has "half child's play, half God in one's heart," I devoted my
first literary child's play to it, my first philosophic writing exercise—and as to
my "solution" to the problem back then, well, I gave the honor to God, as is fitting, and made him the *father* of evil. Was *this* what my "a priori" wished of me?
that new, immoral, at least immoralistic "a priori" and the, alas! so anti-Kantian,
so mysterious "categorical imperative" speaking through it, to which I have
since increasingly lent my ear, and not just my ear? ... Fortunately I learned
early on to distinguish theological from moral prejudice and no longer sought
the origin of evil *behind* the world. A little historical and philological schooling,
combined with an innate sense of discrimination in all psychological questions,
soon transformed my problem into a different one: under what conditions did
man invent those value judgments good and evil? *and what value do they them-*

"*a priori*"] nonempirical or independent of experience; literally: from what is
before.

selves have? Have they inhibited or furthered human flourishing up until now? Are they a sign of distress, of impoverishment, of the degeneration of life? Or, conversely, do they betray the fullness, the power, the will of life, its courage, its confidence, its future?—In response I found and ventured a number of answers; I distinguished ages, peoples, degrees of rank among individuals; I   5
divided up my problem; out of the answers came new questions, investigations, conjectures, probabilities: until I finally had a land of my own, a ground of my own, an entire unspoken growing blossoming world, secret gardens as it were, of which no one was permitted even an inkling ... O how we are *happy*, we knowers, provided we simply know how to be silent long enough! ...   10

4

The first impetus to divulge something of my hypotheses on the origin of morality came to me from a clear, tidy, and smart, even overly smart little book in which for the first time I was clearly confronted by the reverse and perverse sort of genealogical hypotheses, the specifically *English* sort, and this book attracted me—with that power of attraction exerted by   15
everything contrary, everything antipodal. The title of the little book was *The Origin of Moral Sensations*; its author, Dr. Paul Rée; the year of its publication, 1877. I may never have read anything to which I so emphatically said "no" as I did to this book, proposition by proposition, conclusion by conclusion: and yet entirely without vexation or impatience. In the   20
previously named volume on which I was then working, I made occasional and occasionally inopportune reference to the propositions of that book, not that I refuted them—what have I to do with refutations!—but rather, as befits a positive spirit, putting in place of the improbable the more probable, sometimes in place of one error another one. It was then, as   25
mentioned, that I brought into the light of day those hypotheses concerning origins to which these treatises are devoted, clumsily, as I wish last of all to conceal from myself—still unfree, still without a language of my own for these things of my own, and with many a relapse and wavering. In particular, compare what I say in *Human, All Too Human* 45, on the dual pre-   30
history of good and evil (namely out of the sphere of the nobles and that of the slaves); likewise section 136, on the value and origins of ascetic morality; likewise 96, 99, and volume II, 89, on the "morality of custom," that much older and more original kind of morality that is removed *toto caelo*   35
from the altruistic manner of valuation (which Dr. Rée, like all English

---

toto caelo] by a tremendous distance; literally: by all of heaven.

genealogists of morality, sees as the moral manner of valuation *in itself*);
likewise volume I, 92; *Wanderer,* section 26; *Daybreak,* 112, on the origins
of justice as a settlement between approximately equal powers (equilibrium as presupposition of all contracts, accordingly of all law); likewise
Wanderer 22 and 33, on the origins of punishment, for which the purpose
of terrorizing is neither essential nor present at the beginning (as Dr. Rée
believes:—rather this was inserted into it, under specific circumstances,
and always as something incidental, as something additional).

5

Actually there was something much more important on my mind just
then than my own or anyone else's hypothesizing about the origin of
morality (or, more precisely: the latter concerned me solely for the sake of
an end to which it is one means among many). The issue for me was the
value of morality—and over this I had to struggle almost solely with my
great teacher Schopenhauer, to whom that book, the passion and the
secret contradiction of that book, is directed, as if to a contemporary
(—for that book, too, was a "polemic"). In particular the issue was the
value of the unegoistic, of the instincts of compassion, self-denial, self-
sacrifice, precisely the instincts that Schopenhauer had gilded, deified,
and made otherworldly until finally they alone were left for him as the
"values in themselves," on the basis of which he *said "no"* to life, also to
himself. But against precisely *these* instincts there spoke from within me
an ever more fundamental suspicion, an ever deeper-delving skepticism!
Precisely here I saw the *great* danger to humanity, its most sublime lure
and temptation—and into what? into nothingness?—precisely here I saw
the beginning of the end, the standstill, the backward-glancing tiredness,
the will turning *against* life, the last sickness gently and melancholically
announcing itself: I understood the ever more widely spreading morality
of compassion—which seized even the philosophers and made them
sick—as the most uncanny symptom of our now uncanny European culture, as its detour to a new Buddhism? to a Buddhism for Europeans?
to—*nihilism*? ... For this preferential treatment and overestimation of
compassion on the part of modern philosophers is something new: until
this point philosophers had agreed precisely on the *worthlessness* of compassion. I name only Plato, Spinoza, La Rochefoucauld, and Kant, four
spirits as different from each other as possible, but united on one point:
their low regard for compassion.—

6

This problem of the *value* of compassion and of the morality of compassion (—I am an opponent of the disgraceful modern softening of feelings—) appears at first to be only an isolated matter, a lone question mark; whoever sticks here for once, however, and *learns* to ask questions here, will fare as I have fared:—an immense new vista opens up to him, a possibility takes hold of him like a dizziness, every sort of mistrust, suspicion, fear springs forth, the belief in morality, in all morality totters,—finally a new challenge is heard. Let us speak it aloud, this *new challenge*: we need a *critique* of moral values, *for once the value of these values must itself be called into question*—and for this we need a knowledge of the conditions and circumstances out of which they have grown, under which they have developed and shifted (morality as consequence, as symptom, as mask, as Tartuffery, as sickness, as misunderstanding; but also morality as cause, as medicine, as stimulus, as inhibitor, as poison), knowledge of a kind that has neither existed up until now nor even been desired. One has taken the *value* of these "values" as given, as a fact, as beyond all calling-into-question; until now one has not had even the slightest doubt or hesitation in ranking "the good" as of higher value than "the evil," of higher value in the sense of its furtherance, usefulness, beneficiality—with respect to man *in general* (taking into account the future of man). What? if the opposite were true? What? if a symptom of regression also lay in the "good," likewise a danger, a temptation, a poison, a narcotic through which perhaps the present were living *at the expense of the future*? Perhaps more comfortably, less dangerously, but also in a reduced style, on a lower level? ... So that precisely morality would be to blame if a *highest power and splendor* of the human type—in itself possible—were never attained? So that precisely morality were the danger of dangers? ...

7

Suffice it to say that once this prospect opened up to me, I myself had reasons for looking about for learned, bold, and industrious comrades (I am still doing so today). It is a matter of traveling the vast, distant, and so concealed land of morality—of the morality which has really existed, really been lived—with a completely new set of questions and as it were with new eyes: and is this not virtually to *discover* this land for the first time? ... If in the process I thought of, among others, the above named Dr. Rée, this happened because I had no doubt that he would be pushed by the very nature of his questions to a more correct method of attaining answers. Did I deceive myself in this? My wish, in any case, was to turn so sharp and disinterested an eye in a better direction, the direction of the real *history of morality* and to warn him while there was still time against such English hypothesizing *into the blue*. It is of course obvious which color must be a hundred times more important to a genealogist of morality than blue: namely *gray*, which is to say, that which can be documented, which can really be ascertained, which has really existed, in short, the very long, difficult-to-decipher hieroglyphic writing of the human moral past! *This* was unknown to Dr. Rée; but he had read Darwin:—and thus in his hypothesizing we have, in a manner that is at least entertaining, the Darwinian beast politely joining hands with the most modern, unassuming moral milquetoast who "no longer bites"—the latter with an expression of a certain good-natured and refined indolence on his face, into which is mixed even a grain of pessimism, of weariness: as if there weren't really any reward for taking all these things—the problems of morality—so seriously. To me it seems that, on the contrary, there are no things which would *reward* one more for taking them seriously; to which reward belongs, for example, that one might perhaps some day gain permission to take them *cheerfully*. For cheerfulness, or to say it in my language, *gay science*—is a reward: a reward for a long, brave, industrious, and subterranean seriousness that is admittedly not for everyone. On that day, however, when we say from a full heart: "Onward! even our old morality belongs *in comedy*!" we will have discovered a new complication and possibility for the Dionysian drama of the "Destiny of the Soul"—: and he will certainly make use of it, one can bet on that, he, the great old eternal comic poet of our existence! ...

8

—If this book is unintelligible to anyone and hard on the ears, the fault, as I see it, does not necessarily lie with me. It is clear enough, presupposing, as I do, that one has first read my earlier writings and has not spared some effort in the process: these are in fact not easily accessible. As far as my *Zarathustra* is concerned, for example, I count no one an authority on it who has not at sometime been deeply wounded and at sometime deeply delighted by each of its words: for only then may he enjoy the privilege of reverent participation in the halcyon element out of which the work was born, in its sunny brightness, distance, expanse, and certainty. In other cases the aphoristic form creates a difficulty—it lies in the fact that we don't attach *enough weight* to this form today. An aphorism honestly coined and cast has not been "deciphered" simply because it has been read through; rather its *interpretation* must now begin, and for this an art of interpretation is needed. In the third treatise of this book I have offered a sample of what I call "interpretation" in such a case:—an aphorism is placed before this treatise, the treatise itself is a commentary on it. Admittedly, to practice reading as an *art* in this way one thing above all is necessary, something which these days has been unlearned better than anything else—and it will therefore be a while before my writings are "readable"—something for which one must almost be a cow and in any case *not* a "modern man": *ruminating* ...

Sils-Maria, Upper Engadine, in July 1887.

First Treatise: "Good and Evil," "Good and Bad"

1

—These English psychologists whom we also have to thank for the only attempts so far to produce a history of the genesis of morality—they themselves are no small riddle for us; I confess, in fact, that precisely as riddles in the flesh they have something substantial over their books— *they themselves are interesting!* These English psychologists—what do they actually want? One finds them, whether voluntarily or involuntarily, always at the same task, namely of pushing the *partie honteuse* of our inner world into the foreground and of seeking that which is actually effective, leading, decisive for our development, precisely where the intellectual pride of man would least of all *wish* to find it (for example in the *vis inertiae* of habit or in forgetfulness or in a blind and accidental interlacing and mechanism of ideas or in anything purely passive, automatic, reflexive, molecular, and fundamentally mindless)—what is it actually that always drives these psychologists in precisely *this* direction? Is it a secret, malicious, base instinct to belittle mankind, one that perhaps cannot be acknowledged even to itself? Or, say, a pessimistic suspicion, the mistrust of disappointed, gloomy idealists who have become poisonous and green? Or a little subterranean animosity and rancor against Christianity (and Plato) that has perhaps not yet made it past the threshold of consciousness? Or even a lascivious taste for the disconcerting, for the painful-par- adoxical, for the questionable and nonsensical aspects of existence? Or finally—a little of everything, a little meanness, a little gloominess, a little anti-Christianity, a little tickle and need for pepper? ... But I am told that they are simply old, cold, boring frogs who creep and hop around on human beings, into human beings, as if they were really in their element there, namely in a *swamp.* I resist this, still more, I don't believe it; and if one is permitted to wish where one cannot know, then I wish from my heart that the reverse may be the case with them—that these explorers

partie honteuse] shameful part (in the plural, this expression is the equivalent of the English "private parts").
vis inertiae] force of inactivity. In Newtonian physics, this term denotes the resis- tance offered by matter to any force tending to alter its state of rest or motion.

and microscopists of the soul are basically brave, magnanimous, and
proud animals who know how to keep a rein on their hearts as well as their
pain and have trained themselves to sacrifice all desirability to truth, to
every truth, even plain, harsh, ugly, unpleasant, unchristian, immoral
truth ... For there are such truths.——

2

Hats off then to whatever good spirits may be at work in these historians of morality! Unfortunately, however, it is certain that they lack the
historical spirit itself, that they have been left in the lurch precisely by all
the good spirits of history! As is simply the age-old practice among philosophers, they all think *essentially* ahistorically; of this there is no
doubt. The ineptitude of their moral genealogy is exposed right at the
beginning, where it is a matter of determining the origins of the concept
and judgment "good." "Originally"—so they decree—"unegoistic
actions were praised and called good from the perspective of those to
whom they were rendered, hence for whom they were *useful*; later one
forgot this origin of the praise and, simply because unegoistic actions
were *as a matter of habit* always praised as good, one also felt them to be
good—as if they were something good in themselves." One sees immediately: this first derivation already contains all the characteristic traits
of the idiosyncrasy of English psychologists—we have "usefulness,"
"forgetting," "habit," and in the end "error," all as basis for a valuation
of which the higher human being has until now been proud as if it were
some kind of distinctive prerogative of humankind. This pride *must* be
humbled, this valuation devalued: has this been achieved? ... Now in the
first place it is obvious to me that the actual genesis of the concept
"good" is sought and fixed in the wrong place by this theory: the judgment "good" does *not* stem from those to whom "goodness" is rendered!
Rather it was "the good" themselves, that is the noble, powerful, higher-
ranking, and high-minded who felt and ranked themselves and their
doings as good, which is to say, as of the first rank, in contrast to everything base, low-minded, common, and vulgar. Out of this *pathos of distance* they first took for themselves the right to create values, to coin
names for values: what did they care about usefulness! The viewpoint of
utility is as foreign and inappropriate as possible, especially in relation to
so hot an outpouring of highest rank-ordering, rank-distinguishing
value judgments: for here feeling has arrived at an opposite of that low
degree of warmth presupposed by every calculating prudence, every

assessment of utility—and not just for once, for an hour of exception, but rather for the long run. As was stated, the pathos of nobility and distance, this lasting and dominant collective and basic feeling of a higher ruling nature in relation to a lower nature, to a "below"—*that* is the origin of the opposition "good" and "bad." (The right of lords to give names goes so far that we should allow ourselves to comprehend the origin of language itself as an expression of power on the part of those who rule: they say "this *is* such and such," they seal each thing and happening with a sound and thus, as it were, take possession of it.) It is because of this origin that from the outset the word "good" does *not* necessarily attach itself to "unegoistic" actions—as is the superstition of those genealogists of morality. On the contrary, only when aristocratic value judgments begin to *decline* does this entire opposition "egoistic" "unegoistic" impose itself more and more on the human conscience—to make use of my language, it is *the herd instinct* that finally finds a voice (also *words*) in this opposition. And even then it takes a long time until this instinct becomes dominant to such an extent that moral valuation in effect gets caught and stuck at that opposition (as is the case in present-day Europe: today the prejudice that takes "moral," "unegoistic," *"désintéressé"* to be concepts of equal value already rules with the force of an *"idée fixe"* and sickness in the head).

3

In the second place, however: quite apart from the historical untenability of that hypothesis concerning the origins of the value judgment "good," it suffers from an inherent psychological absurdity. The usefulness of the unegoistic action is supposed to be the origin of its praise, and this origin is supposed to have been *forgotten*:—how is this forgetting even *possible*? Did the usefulness of such actions cease at some point? The opposite is the case: this usefulness has been the everyday experience in all ages, something therefore that was continually underscored anew; accordingly, instead of disappearing from consciousness, instead of becoming forgettable, it could not help but impress itself upon consciousness with ever greater clarity. How much more reasonable is that opposing theory (it is not therefore truer—) advocated for example by Herbert Spencer—which ranks the concept "good" as essentially identi-

désintéressé] disinterested, unselfish, selfless.
"idée fixe"] obsession; literally: a fixed idea.

cal with the concept "useful," "purposive," so that in the judgments
"good" and "bad" humanity has summed up and sanctioned its *unforgot-
ten* and *unforgettable* experiences concerning what is useful-purposive,
what is injurious-nonpurposive. Good, according to this theory, is what-
5   ever has proved itself as useful from time immemorial: it may thus claim
validity as "valuable in the highest degree," as "valuable in itself." This
path of explanation is also false, as noted above, but at least the explanation is in itself reasonable and psychologically tenable.

4

    —The pointer to the *right* path was given to me by the question: what
10   do the terms coined for "good" in the various languages actually mean
from an etymological viewpoint? Here I found that they all lead back to
the *same conceptual transformation*—that everywhere the basic concept is
"noble," "aristocratic" in the sense related to the estates, out of which
"good" in the sense of "noble of soul," "high-natured of soul," "privi-
15   leged of soul" necessarily develops: a development that always runs parallel to that other one which makes "common," "vulgar," "base" pass over
finally into the concept "bad." The most eloquent example of the latter is
the German word *"schlecht"* [bad] itself: which is identical with *"schlicht"*
[plain, simple]—compare *"schlechtweg," "schlechterdings"* [simply or
20   downright]—and originally designated the plain, the common man, as yet
without a suspecting sideward glance, simply in opposition to the noble
one. Around the time of the Thirty-Years' War, in other words late
enough, this sense shifts into the one now commonly used.—With
respect to morality's genealogy this appears to me to be an *essential*
25   insight; that it is only now being discovered is due to the inhibiting influence that democratic prejudice exercises in the modern world with regard
to all questions of origins. And this influence extends all the way into that
seemingly most objective realm of natural science and physiology, as I
shall merely hint at here. But the nonsense that this prejudice—once
30   unleashed to the point of hate—is able to inflict, especially on morality
and history, is shown by Buckle's notorious case; the *plebeianism* of the
modern spirit, which is of English descent, sprang forth there once again
on its native ground, vehemently like a muddy volcano and with that
oversalted, overloud, common eloquence with which until now all volca-
35   noes have spoken.—

5

With regard to *our* problem—which can for good reasons be called a *quiet* problem and which addresses itself selectively to but few ears—it is of no small interest to discover that often in those words and roots that designate "good" that main nuance still shimmers through with respect to which the nobles felt themselves to be humans of a higher rank. To be sure, they may name themselves in the most frequent cases simply after their superiority in power (as "the powerful," "the lords," "the commanders") or after the most visible distinguishing mark of this superiority, for example as "the rich," "the possessors," (that is the sense of *arya*; and likewise in Iranian and Slavic). But also after a *typical character trait*: and this is the case which concerns us here. They call themselves for example "the truthful"—led by the Greek nobility, whose mouthpiece is the Megarian poet Theognis. The word coined for this, *esthlos*, means according to its root one who *is*, who possesses reality, who is real, who is true; then, with a subjective turn, the true one as the truthful one: in this phase of the concept's transformation it becomes the by- and catchword of the nobility and passes over completely into the sense of "aristocratic," as that which distinguishes from the *lying* common man as Theognis understands and depicts him—until finally, after the demise of the nobility, the word remains as the term for *noblesse* of soul and becomes as it were ripe and sweet. In the word *kakos* as well as in *deilos* (the plebeian in contrast to the *agathos*) cowardliness is underscored: perhaps this gives a hint in which direction one should seek the etymological origins of *agathos*, which can be interpreted in many ways. In the Latin *malus* (beside which I place *melas*), the common man could be characterized as the dark-colored, above all as the black-haired ("*hic niger est*—"), as the pre-Aryan occupant of Italian soil, who by his color stood out most clearly from the blonds who had become the rulers, namely the Aryan conqueror-race; at any rate Gaelic offered me an exactly corresponding

arya] Sanskrit: noble.
esthlos] good, brave, noble.
kakos] bad, ugly, ill-born, base, cowardly, ignoble.
deilos] cowardly, worthless, low-born, miserable, wretched.
agathos] good, well-born, noble, brave, capable.
malus] bad, evil.
melas] black, dark.
hic niger est] he is black. Horace's *Satires*, I. 4, line 85.

case—*fin* (for example in the name Fin-Gal), the distinguishing word of
the nobility, in the end, the good, noble, pure one, originally the blond-
headed one, in contrast to the dark, black-haired original inhabitants. The
Celts, incidentally, were by all means a blond race; it is wrong to associate
5   those tracts of an essentially dark-haired population, which are noticeable
on the more careful ethnographic maps of Germany, with any Celtic origins or blood mixtures, as even Virchow does: rather it is the *pre-Aryan*
population of Germany that comes to the fore in these places. (The same
is true for almost all of Europe: in essence, the subjected race has in the
10   end regained the upper hand there, in color, shortness of skull, perhaps
even in intellectual and social instincts—who will guarantee us that modern democracy, the even more modern anarchism, and in particular that
inclination toward the "commune," the most primitive form of society—
an inclination now common to all of Europe's socialists—does not signify,
15   on the whole, a tremendous *atavism*—and that the *race of lords* and conquerors, that of the Aryans, is not in the process of succumbing physiologically as well? ...) I believe I may interpret the Latin *bonus* as "the
warrior": assuming that I am correct in tracing *bonus* back to an older *duonus* (compare *bellum* = *duellum* = *duen-lum*, in which that *duonus* seems to
20   me to be preserved). *Bonus* accordingly as man of strife, of division (*duo*),
as man of war—one sees what it was about a man that constituted his
"goodness" in ancient Rome. Our German "*gut*" [good] itself: wasn't it
supposed to mean "the godly one," the man "of godly race"? And to be
identical with the name for the nation (originally for the nobility) of the
25   Goths? The reasons for this supposition do not belong here.—

6

To this rule that the concept of superiority in politics always resolves
itself into a concept of superiority of soul, it is not immediately an exception (although it provides occasion for exceptions) when the highest caste
is at the same time the *priestly* caste and hence prefers for its collective
30   name a predicate that recalls its priestly function. Here, for example,
"pure" and "impure" stand opposite each other for the first time as marks
of distinction among the estates; and here, too, one later finds the devel-

---

fin] Gaelic: white, bright.
bonus] good.
duonus] earlier form of *bonus*.
bellum ... *duen-lum*] war; the latter two are older, poetic forms.

opment of a "good" and a "bad" in a sense no longer related to the estates. Incidentally, let one beware from the outset of taking these concepts "pure" and "impure" too seriously, too broadly, or even too symbolically: rather all of earlier humanity's concepts were initially understood in a coarse, crude, superficial, narrow, straightforward, and above all *unsymbolic* manner, to an extent that we can hardly imagine. The "pure one" is from the beginning simply a human being who washes himself, who forbids himself certain foods that bring about skin diseases, who doesn't sleep with the dirty women of the baser people, who abhors blood—nothing more, at least not much more! On the other hand the entire nature of an essentially priestly aristocracy admittedly makes clear why it was precisely here that the valuation opposites could so soon become internalized and heightened in a dangerous manner; and indeed through them gulfs were finally torn open between man and man across which even an Achilles of free-spiritedness will not be able to leap without shuddering. From the beginning there is something *unhealthy* in such priestly aristocracies and in the habits ruling there, ones turned away from action, partly brooding, partly emotionally explosive, habits that have as a consequence the intestinal disease and neurasthenia that almost unavoidably clings to the priests of all ages; but what they themselves invented as a medicine against this diseasedness of theirs—must we not say that in the end it has proved itself a hundred times more dangerous in its aftereffects than the disease from which it was to redeem them? Humanity itself still suffers from the aftereffects of these priestly cure naïvetés! Think, for example, of certain dietary forms (avoidance of meat), of fasting, of sexual abstinence, of the flight "into the wilderness" (Weir-Mitchellian isolation, admittedly without the ensuing fattening diet and over-feeding, which constitutes the most effective antidote for all the hysteria of the ascetic ideal): in addition, the whole anti-sensual metaphysics of priests, which makes lazy and overrefined, their self-hypnosis after the manner of the fakir and Brahmin—brahma used as glass pendant and *idée fixe*—and the final, only too understandable general satiety along with its radical cure, *nothingness* (or God—the longing for a *unio mystica* with God is the longing of the Buddhist for nothingness, Nirvâna—and nothing more!) With priests *everything* simply becomes more dangerous, not only curatives and healing arts, but also arrogance, revenge, acuity, excess, love, lust to rule, virtue, disease;—though with some fairness one could also add that it was on the soil of this *essentially dangerous* form of human existence, the

unio mystica] mystical union.

priestly form, that man first became *an interesting animal*, that only here
did the human soul acquire *depth* in a higher sense and become *evil*—and
these are, after all, the two basic forms of the previous superiority of man
over other creatures! ...

7

5   —One will already have guessed how easily the priestly manner of valuation can branch off from the knightly-aristocratic and then develop into
its opposite; this process is especially given an impetus every time the
priestly caste and the warrior caste confront each other jealously and are
unable to agree on a price. The knightly-aristocratic value judgments have
10   as their presupposition a powerful physicality, a blossoming, rich, even
overflowing health, together with that which is required for its preservation: war, adventure, the hunt, dance, athletic contests, and in general
everything which includes strong, free, cheerful-hearted activity. The
priestly-noble manner of valuation—as we have seen—has other presup-
15   positions: too bad for it when it comes to war! Priests are, as is well
known, the *most evil enemies*—why is that? Because they are the most powerless. Out of their powerlessness their hate grows into something enormous and uncanny, into something most spiritual and most poisonous.
The truly great haters in the history of the world have always been priests,
20   also the most ingenious haters:—compared with the spirit of priestly
revenge all the rest of spirit taken together hardly merits consideration.
Human history would be much too stupid an affair without the spirit that
has entered into it through the powerless:—let us turn right to the greatest example. Of all that has been done on earth against "the noble," "the
25   mighty," "the lords," "the power-holders," nothing is worthy of mention
in comparison with that which the *Jews* have done against them: the Jews,
that priestly people who in the end were only able to obtain satisfaction
from their enemies and conquerors through a radical revaluation of their
values, that is, through an act of *spiritual revenge*. This was the only way
30   that suited a priestly people, the people of the most suppressed priestly
desire for revenge. It was the Jews who in opposition to the aristocratic
value equation (good = noble = powerful = beautiful = happy = beloved
of God) dared its inversion, with fear-inspiring consistency, and held it
fast with teeth of the most unfathomable hate (the hate of powerlessness),
35   namely: "the miserable alone are the good; the poor, powerless, lowly
alone are the good; the suffering, deprived, sick, ugly are also the only
pious, the only blessed in God, for them alone is there blessedness,—

whereas you, you noble and powerful ones, you are in all eternity the evil, the cruel, the lustful, the insatiable, the godless, you will eternally be the wretched, accursed, and damned!" ... We know *who* inherited this Jewish revaluation ... In connection with the enormous and immeasurably doom-laden initiative provided by the Jews with this most fundamental of all declarations of war, I call attention to the proposition which I arrived at on another occasion ("Beyond Good and Evil" section 195)—namely, that with the Jews *the slave revolt in morality* begins: that revolt which has a two-thousand-year history behind it and which has only moved out of our sight today because it—has been victorious ...

8

—But you don't understand that? You don't have eyes for something that has taken two thousand years to achieve victory? ... There is nothing to wonder at in this: all *lengthy* things are difficult to see, to see in their entirety. *This* however is what happened: out of the trunk of that tree of revenge and hate, Jewish hate—the deepest and most sublime hate, namely an ideal-creating, value-reshaping hate whose like has never before existed on earth—grew forth something just as incomparable, a *new love*, the deepest and most sublime of all kinds of love:—and from what other trunk could it have grown? ... But by no means should one suppose it grew upwards as, say, the true negation of that thirst for revenge, as the opposite of Jewish hate! No, the reverse is the truth! This love grew forth out of it, as its crown, as the triumphant crown unfolding itself broadly and more broadly in purest light and sunny fullness, reaching out, as it were, in the realm of light and of height, for the goals of that hate—for victory, for booty, for seduction—with the same drive with which the roots of that hate sunk themselves ever more thoroughly and greedily down into everything that had depth and was evil. This Jesus of Nazareth, as the embodied Gospel of Love, this "Redeemer" bringing blessedness and victory to the poor, the sick, the sinners—was he not precisely seduction in its most uncanny and irresistible form, the seduction and detour to precisely those *Jewish* values and reshapings of the ideal? Has not Israel reached the final goal of its sublime desire for revenge precisely via the detour of this "Redeemer," this apparent adversary and dissolver of Israel? Does it not belong to the secret black art of a truly *great* politics of revenge, of a far-seeing, subterranean, slow-working and precalculating revenge, that Israel itself, before all the world, should deny as its mortal enemy and nail to the cross the actual tool of its revenge, so that

"all the world," namely all the opponents of Israel, could take precisely
this bait without thinking twice? And, out of all sophistication of the
spirit, could one think up any more *dangerous* bait? Something that in its
enticing, intoxicating, anesthetizing, destructive power might equal that
5   symbol of the "holy cross," that gruesome paradox of a "god on the
cross," that mystery of an inconceivable, final, extreme cruelty and self-
crucifixion of God *for the salvation of man*? ... What is certain, at least, is
that *sub hoc signo* Israel, with its revenge and revaluation of all values, has
thus far again and again triumphed over all other ideals, over all *more noble*
10   ideals.— —

9

—"But why are you still talking about *nobler* ideals! Let's submit to the
facts: the people were victorious—or 'the slaves,' or 'the mob,' or 'the
herd,' or whatever you like to call them—if this happened through the
Jews, so be it! then never has a people had a more world-historic mission.
15   'The lords' are cast off; the morality of the common man has been victorious. One may take this victory to be at the same time a blood poisoning (it
mixed the races together)—I won't contradict; in any event it is beyond
doubt that this toxication *succeeded*. The 'redemption' of the human race
(namely from 'the lords') is well under way; everything is jewifying or
20   christifying or mobifying as we watch (what do the words matter!). The
progress of this poisoning through the entire body of humanity appears
unstoppable, from now on its tempo and step may even be slower, more
refined, less audible, more thoughtful—one has time after all ... Does the
church today still have a *necessary* task in this scheme, still a right to exist-
25   ence at all? Or could one do without it? *Quaeritur*. It seems more likely
that it inhibits and holds back this progress instead of accelerating it?
Well, even that could be its usefulness ... By now it is certainly something
coarse and peasant-like, which repels a more delicate intelligence, a truly
modern taste. Shouldn't it at least become somewhat refined? ... Today it
30   alienates more than it seduces ... Which of us indeed would be a free
spirit if there were no church? The church, *not* its poison, repels us ...
Leaving the church aside, we, too, love the poison ..."—This, the epilogue of a "free spirit" to my speech, an honest animal, as he has richly
betrayed, moreover a democrat; he had listened to me up until then and

sub hoc signo] under this sign.
Quaeritur] one asks, i.e., that is the question.

couldn't stand to hear me be silent. For at this point I have much to be
silent about.—

10

The slave revolt in morality begins when *ressentiment* itself becomes
creative and gives birth to values: the *ressentiment* of beings denied the
true reaction, that of the deed, who recover their losses only through an   5
imaginary revenge. Whereas all noble morality grows out of a triumphant
yes-saying to oneself, from the outset slave morality says "no" to an "outside," to a "different," to a "not-self": and *this* "no" is its creative deed.
This reversal of the value-establishing glance—this *necessary* direction
toward the outside instead of back onto oneself—belongs to the very   10
nature of *ressentiment*: in order to come into being, slave-morality always
needs an opposite and external world; it needs, psychologically speaking,
external stimuli in order to be able to act at all,—its action is, from the
ground up, reaction. The reverse is the case with the noble manner of valuation: it acts and grows spontaneously, it seeks out its opposite only in   15
order to say "yes" to itself still more gratefully and more jubilantly—its
negative concept "low" "common" "bad" is only an after-birth, a pale
contrast-image in relation to its positive basic concept, saturated through
and through with life and passion: "we noble ones, we good ones, we
beautiful ones, we happy ones!" When the noble manner of valuation lays   20
a hand on reality and sins against it, this occurs relative to the sphere with
which it is *not* sufficiently acquainted, indeed against a real knowledge of
which it rigidly defends itself: in some cases it forms a wrong idea of the
sphere it holds in contempt, that of the common man, of the lower people; on the other hand, consider that the affect of contempt, of looking   25
down on, of the superior glance—assuming that it does *falsify* the image
of the one held in contempt—will in any case fall far short of the falsifica-
tion with which the suppressed hate, the revenge of the powerless, lays a
hand on its opponent—in effigy, of course. Indeed there is too much
carelessness in contempt, too much taking-lightly, too much looking-   30
away and impatience mixed in, even too much of a feeling of cheer in oneself, for it to be capable of transforming its object into a real caricature
and monster. Do not fail to hear the almost benevolent nuances that, for
example, the Greek nobility places in all words by which it distinguishes
the lower people from itself; how they are mixed with and sugared by a   35
kind of pity, considerateness, leniency to the point that almost all words
that apply to the common man ultimately survive as expressions for

"unhappy" "pitiful" (compare *deilos, deilaios, poneros, mochtheros,* the latter two actually designating the common man as work-slave and beast of
burden)—and how, on the other hand, to the Greek ear "bad" "low"
"unhappy" have never ceased to end on the same note, with a tone color
5   in which "unhappy" predominates: this as inheritance of the old, nobler
aristocratic manner of valuation that does not deny itself even in its contempt (let philologists be reminded of the sense in which *oizyros, anolbos,
tlemon, dystychein, xymphora* are used). The "well-born" simply *felt* themselves to be the "happy"; they did not first have to construct their happi-
10   ness artificially by looking at their enemies, to talk themselves into it, to
lie themselves into it (as all human beings of *ressentiment* tend to do); and as
full human beings, overloaded with power and therefore *necessarily* active,
they likewise did not know how to separate activity out from happiness,—
for them being active is of necessity included in happiness (whence *eu
15   prattein* takes its origins)—all of this very much in opposition to "happiness" on the level of the powerless, oppressed, those festering with poisonous and hostile feelings, in whom it essentially appears as narcotic,
anesthetic, calm, peace, "Sabbath," relaxation of mind and stretching of
limbs, in short, *passively.* While the noble human being lives with himself
20   in confidence and openness (*gennaios* "noble-born" underscores the
nuance "sincere" and probably also "naive") the human being of *ressentiment* is neither sincere, nor naive, nor honest and frank with himself.
His soul *looks obliquely* at things; his spirit loves hiding places, secret passages and backdoors, everything hidden strikes him as *his* world, *his* secu-
25   rity, *his* balm; he knows all about being silent, not forgetting, waiting,
belittling oneself for the moment, humbling oneself. A race of such
human beings of *ressentiment* in the end necessarily becomes *more prudent*
than any noble race, it will also honor prudence in an entirely different
measure: namely as a primary condition of existence. With noble human

---

deilos, deilaios, poneros, mochtheros] *deilos:* cowardly, worthless, low-born, miserable, wretched; *deilaios:* wretched, sorry, paltry; *poneros:* wretched, oppressed by
toils, worthless, base, cowardly; *mochtheros:* wretched, suffering hardship, miserable, worthless, knavish.
oizyros, anolbos, tlemon, dystychein, xymphora] *oizyros:* woeful, pitiable, miserable,
sorry, poor; *anolbos:* unblest, wretched, luckless, poor; *tlemon:* suffering, endur-
ing; hence: "steadfast, stouthearted," but also "wretched, miserable"; *dystychein:*
to be unlucky, unhappy, unfortunate; *xymphora:* originally "chance," then usually
in a bad sense, that is, "misfortune."
eu prattein] to do well, to fare well, or to do good.
gennaios] high-born, noble, high-minded.

beings, in contrast, prudence is likely to have a refined aftertaste of luxury and sophistication about it:—here it is not nearly as essential as the
complete functional reliability of the regulating *unconscious* instincts or
even a certain imprudence, for example the gallant making-straight-for-
it, be it toward danger, be it toward the enemy, or that impassioned sud-   5
denness of anger, love, reverence, gratitude, and revenge by which noble
souls in all ages have recognized each other. For the *ressentiment* of the
noble human being, when it appears in him, runs its course and exhausts
itself in an immediate reaction, therefore it does not *poison*—on the other
hand it does not appear at all in countless cases where it is unavoidable in   10
all the weak and powerless. To be unable for any length of time to take his
enemies, his accidents, his *misdeeds* themselves seriously—that is the
sign of strong, full natures in which there is an excess of formative,
reconstructive, healing power that also makes one forget (a good example
of this from the modern world is Mirabeau, who had no memory for   15
insults and base deeds committed against him and who was only unable
to forgive because he—forgot). Such a human is simply able to shake off
with a single shrug a collection of worms that in others would dig itself
in; here alone is also possible—assuming that it is at all possible on
earth—the true *"love* of one's enemies." What great reverence for his   20
enemies a noble human being has!—and such reverence is already a
bridge to love ... After all, he demands his enemy for himself, as his distinction; he can stand no other enemy than one in whom there is nothing
to hold in contempt and *a very great deal* to honor! On the other hand,
imagine "the enemy" as the human being of *ressentiment* conceives of   25
him—and precisely here is his deed, his creation: he has conceived of
"the evil enemy," *"the evil one,"* and this indeed as the basic concept,
starting from which he now also thinks up, as reaction and counterpart, a
"good one"—himself! ...

11

Precisely the reverse, therefore, of the case of the noble one, who con-   30
ceives the basic concept "good" in advance and spontaneously, starting
from himself that is, and from there first creates for himself an idea of
"bad"! This "bad" of noble origin and that "evil" out of the brewing
cauldron of unsatiated hate—the first, an after-creation, something on
the side, a complementary color; the second, in contrast, the original, the   35
beginning, the true *deed* in the conception of a slave morality—how differently the two words "bad" and "evil" stand there, seemingly set in

opposition to the same concept "good"! But it is *not* the same concept "good": on the contrary, just ask yourself *who* is actually "evil" in the sense of the morality of *ressentiment*. To answer in all strictness: *precisely* the "good one" of the other morality, precisely the noble, the powerful,
5   the ruling one, only recolored, only reinterpreted, only reseen through the poisonous eye of *ressentiment*. There is one point we wish to deny least of all here: whoever encounters those "good ones" only as enemies encounters nothing but *evil enemies*, and the same humans who are kept so strictly within limits *inter pares*, by mores, worship, custom, gratitude,
10 still more by mutual surveillance, by jealousy, and who on the other hand in their conduct towards each other prove themselves so inventive in consideration, self-control, tact, loyalty, pride, and friendship,—they are not much better than uncaged beasts of prey toward the outside world, where that which is foreign, the foreign world, begins. There they enjoy
15 freedom from all social constraint; in the wilderness they recover the losses incured through the tension that comes from a long enclosure and fencing-in within the peace of the community; they step *back* into the innocence of the beast-of-prey conscience, as jubilant monsters, who perhaps walk away from a hideous succession of murder, arson, rape, tor-
20 ture with such high spirits and equanimity that it seems as if they have only played a student prank, convinced that for years to come the poets will again have something to sing and to praise. At the base of all these noble races one cannot fail to recognize the beast of prey, the splendid *blond beast* who roams about lusting after booty and victory; from time to
25 time this hidden base needs to discharge itself, the animal must get out, must go back into the wilderness: Roman, Arab, Germanic, Japanese nobility, Homeric heroes, Scandinavian Vikings—in this need they are all alike. It is the noble races who have left the concept "barbarian" in all their tracks wherever they have gone; indeed from within their highest
30 culture a consciousness of this betrays itself and even a pride in it (for example when Pericles says to his Athenians in that famous funeral oration, "to every land and sea our boldness has broken a path, everywhere setting up unperishing monuments in good *and bad*"). This "boldness" of noble races—mad, absurd, sudden in its expression; the unpredict-
35 able, in their enterprises even the improbable—Pericles singles out for distinction the *rhathymia* of the Athenians—their indifference and contempt toward all security, body, life, comfort; their appalling light-

inter pares] among equals; here, "among themselves."
rhathymia] easiness of temper; indifference, rashness. Thucydides 2. 39.

heartedness and depth of desire in all destruction, in all the delights of victory and of cruelty—all was summed up for those who suffered from it in the image of the "barbarian," of the "evil enemy," for example the "Goth," the "Vandal." The deep, icy mistrust that the German stirs up as soon as he comes into power, today once again—is still an atavism of that inextinguishable horror with which Europe has for centuries watched the raging of the blond Germanic beast (although there is hardly a conceptual, much less a blood-relationship between the ancient Teutons and us Germans). I once called attention to Hesiod's embarrassment as he was devising the succession of the cultural ages and attempted to express it in terms of gold, silver, bronze: he knew of no other way to cope with the contradiction posed by the glorious but likewise so gruesome, so violent world of Homer, than by making one age into two, which he now placed one after the other—first the age of the heroes and demigods of Troy and Thebes, as this world had remained in the memory of the noble dynasties who had their own ancestors there; then the bronze age, which was that same world as it appeared to the descendants of the downtrodden, plundered, mistreated, dragged-off, sold-off: an age of bronze, as stated—hard, cold, cruel, without feeling or conscience, crushing everything and covering it with blood. Assuming it were true, that which is now in any case believed as "truth," that the *meaning of all culture* is simply to breed a tame and civilized animal, a *domestic animal*, out of the beast of prey "man," then one would have to regard all those instincts of reaction and *ressentiment*, with the help of which the noble dynasties together with their ideals were finally brought to ruin and overwhelmed, as the actual *tools of culture*; which is admittedly not to say that the *bearers* of these instincts themselves at the same time also represent culture. On the contrary, the opposite would not simply be probable—no! today it is *obvious*! These bearers of the oppressing and retaliation-craving instincts, the descendants of all European and non-European slavery, of all pre-Aryan population in particular—they represent the *regression* of humankind! These "tools of culture" are a disgrace to humanity, and rather something that raises a suspicion, a counter-argument against "culture" in general! It may be entirely justifiable if one cannot escape one's fear of the blond beast at the base of all noble races and is on guard: but who would not a hundred times sooner fear if he might at the same time admire, than *not* fear but be unable to escape the disgusting sight of the deformed, reduced, atrophied, poisoned? And is that not *our* doom? What causes *our* aversion to "man"?— for we *suffer* from man, there is no doubt. —*Not* fear; rather that we have

nothing left to fear in man; that the worm "man" is in the foreground
and teeming; that the "tame man," this hopelessly mediocre and unin-
spiring being, has already learned to feel himself as the goal and pinnacle,
as the meaning of history, as "higher man"—indeed that he has a certain
right to feel this way, insofar as he feels himself distanced from the pro-
fusion of the deformed, sickly, tired, worn-out of which Europe today is
beginning to stink; hence as something that is at least relatively well-
formed, at least still capable of living, that at least says "yes" to life ...

12

—At this point I will not suppress a sigh and a final confidence. What
is it that I in particular find utterly unbearable? That with which I cannot
cope alone, that causes me to suffocate and languish? Bad air! Bad air!
That something deformed comes near me; that I should have to smell the
entrails of a deformed soul! ... How much can one not otherwise bear of
distress, deprivation, foul weather, infirmity, drudgery, isolation? Basically one deals with everything else, born as one is to a subterranean and
fighting existence; again and again one reaches the light, again and again
one experiences one's golden hour of victory,—and then one stands
there as one was born, unbreakable, tensed, ready for something new,
something still more difficult, more distant, like a bow that any distress
simply pulls tauter still. —But from time to time grant me—assuming
that there are heavenly patronesses beyond good and evil—a glimpse,
grant me just one glimpse of something perfect, completely formed,
happy, powerful, triumphant, in which there is still something to fear! Of
a human being who justifies man *himself;* a human being who is a stroke
of luck, completing and redeeming man, and for whose sake one may
hold fast to *belief in man!* ... For things stand thus: the reduction and
equalization of the European human conceals *our* greatest danger, for
this sight makes tired ... We see today nothing that wishes to become
greater, we sense that things are still going downhill, downhill—into
something thinner, more good-natured, more prudent, more comfortable, more mediocre, more apathetic, more Chinese, more Christian—
man, there is no doubt, is becoming ever "better" ... Precisely here lies
Europe's doom—with the fear of man we have also forfeited the love of
him, the reverence toward him, the hope for him, indeed the will to him.
The sight of man now makes tired—what is nihilism today if it is not
that? ... We are tired of *man* ...

13

—But let us come back: the problem of the *other* origin of "good," of the good one as conceived by the man of *ressentiment*, demands its conclusion. —That the lambs feel anger toward the great birds of prey does not strike us as odd: but that is no reason for holding it against the great birds of prey that they snatch up little lambs for themselves. And when the lambs say among themselves "these birds of prey are evil; and whoever is as little as possible a bird of prey but rather its opposite, a lamb,—isn't he good?" there is nothing to criticize in this setting up of an ideal, even if the birds of prey should look on this a little mockingly and perhaps say to themselves: "*we* do not feel any anger towards them, these good lambs, as a matter of fact, we love them: nothing is more tasty than a tender lamb."— To demand of strength that it *not* express itself as strength, that it *not* be a desire to overwhelm, a desire to cast down, a desire to become lord, a thirst for enemies and resistances and triumphs, is just as nonsensical as to demand of weakness that it express itself as strength. A quantum of power is just such a quantum of drive, will, effect—more precisely, it is nothing other than this very driving, willing, effecting, and only through the seduction of language (and the basic errors of reason petrified therein), which understands and misunderstands all effecting as conditioned by an effecting something, by a "subject," can it appear otherwise. For just as common people separate the lightning from its flash and take the latter as a *doing*, as an effect of a subject called lightning, so popular morality also separates strength from the expressions of strength as if there were behind the strong an indifferent substratum that is free to express strength—or not to. But there is no such substratum; there is no "being" behind the doing, effecting, becoming; "the doer" is simply fabricated into the doing—the doing is everything. Common people basically double the doing when they have the lightning flash; this is a doing-doing: the same happening is posited first as cause and then once again as its effect. Natural scientists do no better when they say "force moves, force causes," and so on—our entire science, despite all its coolness, its freedom from affect, still stands under the seduction of language and has not gotten rid of the changelings slipped over on it, the "subjects" (the atom, for example, is such a changeling, likewise the Kantian "thing in itself"): small wonder if the suppressed, hiddenly glowing affects of revenge and hate exploit this belief and basically even uphold no other belief more ardently than this one, that *the strong one is free* to be weak, and the bird of prey to be a lamb:—they thereby gain for themselves the right to hold the bird of prey

accountable for being a bird of prey ... When out of the vengeful cunning
of powerlessness the oppressed, downtrodden, violated say to themselves:
"let us be different from the evil ones, namely good! And good is what
everyone is who does not do violence, who injures no one, who doesn't
5   attack, who doesn't retaliate, who leaves vengeance to God, who keeps
himself concealed, as we do, who avoids all evil, and in general demands
very little of life, like us, the patient, humble, righteous"—it means, when
listened to coldly and without prejudice, actually nothing more than: "we
weak ones are simply weak; it is good if we do nothing *for which we are not*
10 *strong enough*"—but this harsh matter of fact, this prudence of the lowest
order, which even insects have (presumably playing dead when in great
danger in order not to do "too much"), has, thanks to that counterfeiting
and self-deception of powerlessness, clothed itself in the pomp of
renouncing, quiet, patiently waiting virtue, as if the very weakness of the
15 weak—that is to say, his *essence*, his effecting, his whole unique, unavoidable, undetachable reality—were a voluntary achievement, something
willed, something chosen, a *deed*, a *merit*. This kind of human *needs* the
belief in a neutral "subject" with free choice, out of an instinct of self-
preservation, self-affirmation, in which every lie tends to hallow itself. It is
20 perhaps for this reason that the subject (or, to speak more popularly, the
soul) has until now been the best article of faith on earth, because it made
possible for the majority of mortals, the weak and oppressed of every kind,
that sublime self-deception of interpreting weakness itself as freedom, of
interpreting their being-such-and-such as a *merit*.

14

25 Would anyone like to go down and take a little look into the secret of
how they *fabricate ideals* on earth? Who has the courage to do so? ... Well
then! The view into these dark workplaces is unobstructed here. Wait just
a moment, Mr. Wanton-Curiosity and Daredevil: your eyes must first get
used to this falsely shimmering light ... So! Enough! Now speak! What's
30 going on down there? Tell me what you see, man of the most dangerous
curiosity—now *I* am the one listening.—
—"I don't see anything, but I hear all the more. There is a cautious
malicious quiet whispering and muttering-together out of all corners and
nooks. It seems to me that they are lying; a sugary mildness sticks to each
35 sound. Weakness is to be lied into a *merit*, there is no doubt about it—it is
just as you said."—
—Go on!

—"and the powerlessness that does not retaliate into kindness; fearful baseness into 'humility'; subjection to those whom one hates into 'obedience' (namely to one whom they say orders this subjection—they call him God). The inoffensiveness of the weak one, cowardice itself, which he possesses in abundance, his standing-at-the-door, his unavoidable having-to-wait, acquires good names here, such as 'patience,' it is even called virtue *itself*; not being able to avenge oneself is called not wanting to avenge oneself, perhaps even forgiveness ('for *they* know not what they do—we alone know what *they* do!'). They also talk of 'love of one's enemies'—and sweat while doing so."

—Go on!

—"They are miserable, there is no doubt, all of these whisperers and nook-and-cranny counterfeiters, even if they are crouching together warmly—but they tell me that their misery is a distinction and election from God, that one beats the dogs one loves the most; perhaps this misery is also a preparation, a test, a schooling, perhaps it is still more—something for which there will one day be retribution, paid out with enormous interest in gold, no! in happiness. This they call 'blessedness'."

—Go on!

—"Now they are giving me to understand that they are not only better than the powerful, the lords of the earth, whose saliva they must lick (*not out of fear, not at all out of fear! but rather because God commands that they honor all authority*)—that they are not only better, but that they are also 'better off,' at least will be better off one day. But enough! enough! I can't stand it anymore. Bad air! Bad air! This workplace where they *fabricate ideals*—it seems to me it stinks of sheer lies."

—No! A moment more! You haven't said anything about the masterpiece of these artists of black magic who produce white, milk, and innocence out of every black:—haven't you noticed what the height of their sophistication is, their boldest, finest, most ingenious, most mendacious artistic stroke? Pay attention! These cellar animals full of revenge and hate—what is it they make precisely out of this revenge and hate? Did you ever hear these words? Would you guess, if you trusted their words alone, that those around you are all humans of *ressentiment*? ...

—"I understand, I'll open my ears once again (oh! oh! oh! and *close* my nose). Now for the first time I hear what they have said so often: 'We good ones—*we are the just*'—what they demand they call not retaliation but rather 'the triumph of *justice*'; what they hate is not their enemy, no! they hate '*injustice*,' 'ungodliness'; what they believe and hope for is not the hope for revenge, the drunkenness of sweet revenge (—already Homer

called it 'sweeter than honey'), but rather the victory of God, of the *just*
God over the ungodly; what is left on earth for them to love are not their
brothers in hate but rather their 'brothers in love,' as they say, all the good
and just on earth."

5   —And what do they call that which serves them as comfort against all
the sufferings of life—their phantasmagoria of the anticipated future
blessedness?

        —"What? Did I hear right? They call that 'the last judgment,' the
coming of *their* kingdom, of the 'kingdom of God'—*meanwhile*, however,
10   they live 'in faith,' 'in love,' 'in hope.'"

        —Enough! Enough!

15

        In faith in what? In love of what? In hope of what? —These weak ones—
someday *they* too want to be the strong ones, there is no doubt, someday
their "kingdom" too shall come—among them it is called "the kingdom of
15   God" pure and simple, as was noted: they are of course so humble in all
things! Even to experience *that* they need to live long, beyond death—
indeed they need eternal life so that in the 'kingdom of God' they can also
recover eternally the losses incurred during that earth-life "in faith, in love,
in hope." Recover their losses for what? Recover their losses through what?
20   ... It was a gross blunder on Dante's part, it seems to me, when, with ter-
ror-instilling ingenuousness, he placed over the gate to his hell the inscription "I, too, was created by eternal love":—in any case, over the gate of the
Christian paradise and its "eternal blessedness" there would be better justification for allowing the inscription to stand "I, too, was created by eternal
25   *hate*"—assuming that a truth may stand above the gate to a lie! For *what* is
the blessedness of that paradise? ... We would perhaps guess it already; but
it is better that it is expressly documented for us by an authority not to be
underestimated in such matters, Thomas Aquinas, the great teacher and
saint. "*Beati in regno coelestia,*" he says meekly as a lamb, "*videbunt poenas*
30   *damnatorum, ut beatitudo illis magis complaceat.*" Or would you like to
hear it in a stronger key, for instance from the mouth of a triumphant
church father who counseled his Christians against the cruel pleasures of
the public spectacles—and why? "Faith offers us much more,"—he says,

Beati in ... magis complaceat] "The blessed in the kingdom of heaven will see the
punishments of the damned, *in order that their bliss be more delightful to them.*"
Summa Theologica III *Supplementum* Q. 94, Art. 1.

De spectac. c. 29 ss.—*"something much stronger;* thanks to salvation there are entirely different joys at our disposal; in place of the athletes we have our martyrs; if we desire blood, well, we have the blood of Christ ... But what awaits us above all on the day of his return, of his triumph!"—and now he continues, the enraptured visionary: *"At enim supersunt alia spectacula, ille* 5
ultimus et perpetuus judicii dies, ille nationibus insperatus, ille derisus, cum tanta saeculi vetustas et tot ejus nativitates uno igne haurientur. Quae tunc spectaculi latitudo! **Quid admirer! Quid rideam! Ubi gaudeam! Ubi exultem,** *spect-ans tot et tantos reges, qui in coelum recepti nuntiabantur, cum ipso Jove et ipsis suis testibus in imis tenebris congemescentes! Item praesides* (the provincial gov- 10
ernor) *persecutores dominici nominis saevioribus quam ipsi flammis saevierunt insultantibus contra Christianos liquescentes! Quos praeterea sapientes illos philosophos coram discipulis suis una conflagrantibus erubescentes, quibus nihil ad deum pertinere suadebant, quibus animas aut nullas aut non in pristina cor-pora redituras affirmabant! Etiam poëtàs non ad Rhadamanti nec ad Minois,* 15
sed ad inopinati Christi tribunal palpitantes! Tunc magis tragoedi audiendi, magis scilicet vocales (in better voice, even more awful screamers) *in sua pro-pria calamitate; tunc histriones cognoscendi, solutiores multo per ignem; tunc spectandus auriga in flammea rota totus rubens, tunc xystici contemplandi non in gymnasiis, sed in igne jaculati, nisi quod ne tunc quidem illos velim vivos, ut qui malim ad eos potius conspectum* **insatiabilem** *conferre, qui in dominum desaevi-* 20
erunt. 'Hic est ille, dicam, fabri aut quaestuariae filius* (as everything that fol-lows shows, and in particular this well-known designation from the Talmud for the mother of Jesus, from here on Tertullian means the Jews), *sabbati destructor, Samarites et daemonium habens. Hic est, quem a Juda redemistis, hic* 25
est ille arundine et colaphis diverberatus, sputamentis dedecoratus, felle et aceto potatus. Hic est, quem clam discentes subripuerunt, ut resurrexisse dicatur vel hortulanus detraxit, ne lactucae suae frequentia commeantium laederentur.' Ut talia spectes, **ut talibus exultes,** *quis tibi praetor aut consul aut quaestor aut sacerdos de sua liberalitate praestabit? Et tamen haec jam habemus quodammodo* 30
per fidem spiritu imaginante repraesentata. Ceterum qualia illa sunt, quae nec oculus vidit nec auris audivit nec in cor hominis ascenderunt? (1 Cor. 2:9) *Credo circo et utraque cavea* (first and fourth tiers, or, according to others, comic and tragic stages) *et omni stadio gratiora."—Per fidem:* thus it is written.

"At enim supersunt ... omni stadio gratiora."] "But indeed there are still other sights, that last and eternal day of judgment, that day unlooked for by the nations, that day they laughed at, when the world so great with age and all its generations shall be consumed by one fire. What variety of sights then! *What should I admire! What Per fidem*] by [my] faith.

16

Let us conclude. The two *opposed* values 'good and bad,' 'good and evil,' have fought a terrible millennia-long battle on earth; and as certainly as the second value has had the upper hand for a long time, even so there is still no shortage of places where the battle goes on, undecided. One could even say that it has in the meantime been borne up ever higher and precisely thereby become ever deeper, ever more spiritual: so that today there is perhaps no more decisive mark of the "*higher nature*," of the more

---

should I laugh at! In which should I feel joy! In which should I exult, seeing so many and great *kings* who were reported to have been received into heaven, now groaning in deepest darkness with Jove himself and those who testified of their reception into heaven! Likewise the praesides *(the provincial governor)*, persecutors of the name of the Lord, being liquefied by flames fiercer than those with which they themselves raged against the Christians! What wise men besides, those very philosophers reddening before their disciples as they blaze together, the disciples to whom they suggested that nothing was of any concern to God; to whom they asserted that our souls are either nothing or they will not return to their former bodies! And also the poets, trembling before the judgment seat, not of Rhadamanthys or Minos but of the Christ, whom they did not expect! Then the great tragedians will be heard, in great voice, no doubt *(in better voice, even more awful screamers)*, in their own calamities; then the actors will be recognized, made a great deal more limber by the fire; then the charioteer will be seen, all red on a flaming wheel; then the athletes will be observed, not in their gymnasiums but cast in the fire—were it not for the fact that not even then would I wish to see them since I would much rather bestow my *insatiable* gaze on those who raged against the Lord. 'This is he,' I shall say, 'the son of the carpenter or the prostitute *(as everything that follows shows, and in particular also this well-known designation from the Talmud for the mother of Jesus, from here on Tertullian means the Jews)*, the Sabbath-breaker, the Samaritan, the one possessed of a devil. This is he whom you bought from Judas, this is the one struck by reed and fist, defiled by spit, given gall and vinegar to drink. This is he whom the disciples secretly stole away that it might be said he had risen, or perhaps the gardener dragged him away so that his lettuce would not be damaged by the crowd of those coming and going.' That you may see such things, *that you may exult in such things*—what praetor or consul or quaestor or priest will, out of his generosity, see to this? And yet even now we have them in a way, *by faith*, represented through the imagining spirit. On the other hand, what are those things which eye hath not seen nor ear heard, nor have ever entered into the heart of man? *(1 Cor. 2: 9)* I believe they are more pleasing than circus and both theaters *(first and fourth tiers, or, according to others, comic and tragic stages)* and any stadium."

spiritual nature, than to be conflicted in that sense and still a real battle-
ground for those opposites. The symbol of this battle, written in a script
that has so far remained legible across all of human history, is "Rome
against Judea, Judea against Rome":—so far there has been no greater
event than *this* battle, *this* formulation of the problem, *this* mortally hostile   5
contradiction. Rome sensed in the Jew something like anti-nature itself,
its antipodal monstrosity as it were; in Rome the Jew was held to have
been "*convicted* of hatred against the entire human race": rightly so, insofar as one has a right to tie the salvation and the future of the human race
to the unconditional rule of aristocratic values, of Roman values. What the   10
Jews on the other hand felt towards Rome? One can guess it from a thousand indications; but it will suffice to recall again the Johannine Apoca-
lypse, that most immoderate of all written outbursts that revenge has on
its conscience. (Do not underestimate, by the way, the profound consistency of the Christian instinct when it gave precisely this book of hate the   15
name of the disciple of love, the same one to whom it attributed that
enamored-rapturous gospel—: therein lies a piece of truth, however
much literary counterfeiting may have been needed for this purpose.) The
Romans were after all the strong and noble ones, such that none stronger
and nobler have ever existed, ever even been dreamt of; everything that   20
remains of them, every inscription thrills, supposing that one can guess
what is doing the writing there. The Jews, conversely, were that priestly
people of *ressentiment* par excellence, in whom there dwelt a popular-
moral genius without parallel: just compare the peoples with related tal-
ents—for instance the Chinese or the Germans—with the Jews in order   25
to feel what is first and what fifth rank. Which of them has been victorious
in the meantime, Rome or Judea? But there is no doubt at all: just consider before whom one bows today in Rome itself as before the quintes-
sence of all the highest values—and not only in Rome, but over almost
half the earth, everywhere that man has become tame or wants to become   30
tame,—before *three Jews*, as everyone knows, and *one Jewess* (before Jesus
of Nazareth, the fisher Peter, the carpet-weaver Paul, and the mother of
the aforementioned Jesus, called Mary). This is very remarkable: Rome
has succumbed without any doubt. To be sure, in the Renaissance there
was a brilliant-uncanny reawakening of the classical ideal, of the noble   35
manner of valuing all things: Rome itself moved like one awakened from
apparent death, under the pressure of the new Judaized Rome built above
it, which presented the appearance of an ecumenical synagogue and was
called "church": but immediately Judea triumphed again, thanks to that
thoroughly mobbish (German and English) *ressentiment* movement called   40

the Reformation, and that which had to follow from it, the restoration of
the church—also the restoration of the old sepulchral sleep of classical
Rome. In an even more decisive and more profound sense than before,
Judea once again achieved a victory over the classical ideal with the
5   French Revolution: the last political nobleness there was in Europe, that
of the seventeenth and eighteenth *French* centuries, collapsed under the
instincts of popular *ressentiment*—never on earth has a greater jubilation,
a noisier enthusiasm been heard! It is true that in the midst of all this the
most enormous, most unexpected thing occurred: the classical ideal itself
10   stepped *bodily* and with unheard of splendor before the eyes and conscience of humanity—and once again, more strongly, more simply, more
penetratingly than ever, the terrible and thrilling counter-slogan "the
privilege of the few" resounded in the face of the old lie-slogan of *ressentiment*, "the privilege of the majority," in the face of the will to lowering, to
15   debasement, to leveling, to the downward and evening-ward of man! Like
a last sign pointing to the *other* path, Napoleon appeared, that most individual and late-born human being there ever was, and in him the incarnate problem of the *noble ideal in itself*—consider well, *what* kind of
problem it is: Napoleon, this synthesis of an *inhuman* and a *superhuman* ...

17

20   —Was that the end of it? Was that greatest of all conflicts of ideals
thus placed *ad acta* for all time? Or just postponed, postponed for a long
time? ... Won't there have to be a still much more terrible, much more
thoroughly prepared flaming up of the old fire someday? Still more:
wouldn't precisely *this* be something to desire with all our might? even to
25   will? even to promote? ... Whoever starts at this point, like my readers, to
ponder, to think further, will hardly come to an end any time soon—reason enough for me to come to an end myself, assuming that it has long
since become sufficiently clear what I *want*, what I want precisely with
that dangerous slogan that is so perfectly tailored to my last book:
30   "*Beyond Good and Evil*" ... At the very least this does *not* mean "Beyond
Good and Bad."—

Note. I take advantage of the opportunity that this treatise gives me
to express publicly and formally a wish that until now I have
expressed only in occasional conversations with scholars: namely

ad acta] shelved, filed away; literally: to the documents.

that some philosophical faculty might do a great service for the promotion of *moral-historical* studies through a series of academic essay contests:—perhaps this book will serve to give a forceful impetus in just such a direction. With respect to a possibility of this sort let me suggest the following question: it merits the attention of philologists and historians as much as that of those who are actual scholars of philosophy by profession.

> *"What clues does the study of language, in particular etymological research, provide for the history of the development of moral concepts?"*

—On the other hand it is admittedly just as necessary to win the participation of physiologists and physicians for these problems (of the *value* of previous estimations of value): it may be left to the professional philosophers to act as advocates and mediators in this individual case as well, after they have succeeded in reshaping in general the relationship between philosophy, physiology, and medicine—originally so standoffish, so mistrustful—into the friendliest and most fruit-bearing exchange. Indeed every value table, every "thou shalt," of which history or ethnological research is aware, needs *physiological* illumination and interpretation first of all, in any case before the psychological; all of them likewise await a critique on the part of medical science. The question: what is the *value* of this or that value table or "morality"? demands to be raised from the most diverse perspectives; for this "value relative *to what end?*" cannot be analyzed too finely. Something, for example, that clearly had value with regard to the greatest possible longevity of a race (or to a heightening of its powers of adaptation to a specific climate, or to the preservation of the greatest number), would by no means have the same value if it were an issue of developing a stronger type. The welfare of the majority and the welfare of the few are opposing value viewpoints: to hold the former one to be of higher value already *in itself,* this we will leave to the naïveté of English biologists ... *All* sciences are henceforth to do preparatory work for the philosopher's task of the future: understanding this task such that the philosopher is to solve the *problem of value,* that he is to determine the *order of rank among values.*—

Second Treatise: "Guilt," "Bad Conscience," and Related Matters

1

To breed an animal that *is permitted to promise*—isn't this precisely the paradoxical task nature has set for itself with regard to man? isn't this the true problem *of* man? ... That this problem has been solved to a high degree must appear all the more amazing to one who can fully appreciate the force working in opposition, that of *forgetfulness*. Forgetfulness is no mere *vis inertiae* as the superficial believe; rather, it is an active and in the strictest sense positive faculty of suppression, and is responsible for the fact that whatever we experience, learn, or take into ourselves enters just as little into our consciousness during the condition of digestion (one might call it "inanimation") as does the entire thousand-fold process through which the nourishing of our body, so-called "incorporation," runs its course. To temporarily close the doors and windows of consciousness; to remain undisturbed by the noise and struggle with which our underworld of subservient organs works for and against each other; a little stillness, a little *tabula rasa* of consciousness so that there is again space for new things, above all for the nobler functions and functionaries, for ruling, foreseeing, predetermining (for our organism is set up oligarchically)—that is the use of this active forgetfulness, a doorkeeper as it were, an upholder of psychic order, of rest, of etiquette: from which one can immediately anticipate the degree to which there could be no happiness, no cheerfulness, no hope, no pride, no *present* without forgetfulness. The human being in whom this suppression apparatus is damaged and stops functioning is comparable to a dyspeptic (and not just comparable—) he can't "process" anything ... Precisely this necessarily forgetful animal in whom forgetting represents a force, a form of *strong* health, has now bred in itself an opposite faculty, a memory, with whose help forgetfulness is disconnected for certain cases,—namely for those cases where a promise is to be made: it is thus by no means simply a passive no-longer-being-able-to-get-rid-of the impression once it has been inscribed, not simply indigestion from a once-pledged word over which one cannot regain control, but rather an active no-longer-wanting-to-get-rid-of, a willing on

and on of something one has once willed, a true *memory of the will*: so that
a world of new strange things, circumstances, even acts of the will may be
placed without reservation between the original "I want," "I will do," and
the actual discharge of the will, its *act*, without this long chain of the will
5   breaking. But how much this presupposes! In order to have this kind of
command over the future in advance, man must first have learned to separate the necessary from the accidental occurrence, to think causally, to see
and anticipate what is distant as if it were present, to fix with certainty
what is end, what is means thereto, in general to be able to reckon, to cal-
10   culate,—for this, man himself must first of all have become *calculable*, *regular*, *necessary*, in his own image of himself as well, in order to be able to
vouch for himself *as future*, as one who promises does!

2

Precisely this is the long history of the origins of *responsibility*. As we
have already grasped, the task of breeding an animal that is permitted to
15   promise includes, as condition and preparation, the more specific task of
first *making* man to a certain degree necessary, uniform, like among like,
regular, and accordingly predictable. The enormous work of what I have
called "morality of custom" (cf. *Daybreak* 9, 14, 16)—the true work of man
on himself for the longest part of the duration of the human race, his entire
20   *prehistoric* work, has in this its meaning, its great justification—however
much hardness, tyranny, mindlessness, and idiocy may be inherent in it:
with the help of the morality of custom and the social straightjacket man
was *made* truly calculable. If, on the other hand, we place ourselves at the
end of the enormous process, where the tree finally produces its fruit,
25   where society and its morality of custom finally brings to light that *to which*
it was only the means: then we will find as the ripest fruit on its tree the
sovereign individual, the individual resembling only himself, free again from
the morality of custom, autonomous and supermoral (for "autonomous"
and "moral" are mutually exclusive), in short, the human being with his
30   own independent long will, the human being who *is permitted to promise*—
and in him a proud consciousness, twitching in all his muscles, of *what* has
finally been achieved and become flesh in him, a true consciousness of
power and freedom, a feeling of the completion of man himself. This being
who has become free, who is really *permitted* to promise, this lord of the *free*
35   will, this sovereign—how could he not know what superiority he thus has
over all else that is not permitted to promise and vouch for itself, how much
trust, how much fear, how much reverence he awakens—he *"earns"* all
three—and how this mastery over himself also necessarily brings with it

mastery over circumstances, over nature and all lesser-willed and more unreliable creatures? The "free" human being, the possessor of a long, unbreakable will, has in this possession his *standard of value* as well: looking from himself toward the others, he honors or holds in contempt; and just as necessarily as he honors the ones like him, the strong and reliable (those who are *permitted* to promise),—that is, everyone who promises like a sovereign, weightily, seldom, slowly, who is stingy with his trust, who *conveys a mark of distinction* when he trusts, who gives his word as something on which one can rely because he knows himself to be strong enough to uphold it even against accidents, even "against fate"—: just as necessarily he will hold his kick in readiness for the frail dogs who promise although they are not permitted to do so, and his switch for the liar who breaks his word already the moment it leaves his mouth. The proud knowledge of the extraordinary privilege of *responsibility*, the consciousness of this rare freedom, this power over oneself and fate, has sunk into his lowest depth and has become instinct, the dominant instinct:—what will he call it, this dominant instinct, assuming that he feels the need to have a word for it? But there is no doubt: this sovereign human being calls it his *conscience* ...

3

His conscience? ... One can guess in advance that the concept "conscience," which we encounter here in its highest, almost disconcerting form, already has behind it a long history and metamorphosis. To be permitted to vouch for oneself, and with pride, hence to be *permitted to say "yes"* to oneself too—that is, as noted, a ripe fruit, but also a *late* fruit:— how long this fruit had to hang on the tree harsh and sour! And for a still much longer time one could see nothing of such a fruit,—no one could have promised it, however certainly everything on the tree was prepared and in the process of growing towards it!—"How does one make a memory for the human animal? How does one impress something onto this partly dull, partly scattered momentary understanding, this forgetfulness in the flesh, so that it remains present?" ... As one can imagine, the answers and means used to solve this age-old problem were not exactly delicate; there is perhaps nothing more terrible and more uncanny in all of man's prehistory than his *mnemo-technique*. "One burns something in so that it remains in one's memory: only what does not cease *to give pain* remains in one's memory"—that is a first principle from the most ancient (unfortunately also longest) psychology on earth. One might even say that everywhere on earth where there is still solemnity, seriousness, secrecy, gloomy colors in the life of man and of a people, something of

that terribleness *continues to be felt* with which everywhere on earth one
formerly promised, pledged, vowed: the past, the longest deepest hardest
past, breathes on us and wells up in us when we become "serious."
Whenever man considered it necessary to make a memory for himself it
was never done without blood, torment, sacrifice; the most gruesome sacrifices and pledges (to which sacrifices of firstborn belong), the most
repulsive mutilations (castrations, for example), the cruelest ritual forms
of all religious cults (and all religions are in their deepest foundations systems of cruelties)—all of this has its origin in that instinct that intuited in
pain the most powerful aid of mnemonics. In a certain sense the entirety
of asceticism belongs here: a few ideas are to be made indelible, omni-
present, unforgettable, "fixed," for the sake of hypnotizing the entire nervous and intellectual system with these "fixed ideas"—and the ascetic
procedures and forms of life are means for taking these ideas out of competition with all other ideas in order to make them "unforgettable." The
worse humanity was "at memory" the more terrible is the appearance of
its practices; the harshness of penal laws in particular provides a measuring stick for the amount of effort it took to achieve victory over forgetfulness and to keep a few primitive requirements of social co-existence
present for these slaves of momentary affect and desire. We Germans certainly do not regard ourselves as a particularly cruel and hard-hearted
people, still less as particularly frivolous or living-for-the-day; but one
need only look at our old penal codes to discover what amount of effort it
takes to breed a "people of thinkers" on earth (that is to say: *the* people of
Europe, among whom one still finds even today the maximum of confidence, seriousness, tastelessness, and matter-of-factness, qualities which
give it a right to breed every type of European mandarin). Using terrible
means these Germans have made a memory for themselves in order to
become master over their mobbish basic instincts and the brutal heavy-
handedness of the same: think of the old German punishments, for
example of stoning (—even legend has the millstone fall on the head of
the guilty one), breaking on the wheel (the most characteristic invention
and specialty of German genius in the realm of punishment!), casting
stakes, having torn or trampled by horses ("quartering"), boiling the
criminal in oil or wine (as late as the fourteenth and fifteenth centuries),
the popular flaying (*"Riemenschneiden"*), cutting flesh from the breast;
also, no doubt, that the evil-doer was smeared with honey and abandoned

"Riemenschneiden"] literally: "strap-cutting," a medieval trade equivalent to saddle
or harness-making.

to the flies under a burning sun. With the help of such images and processes one finally retains in memory five, six "I will nots," in connection
with which one has given one's *promise* in order to live within the advantages of society,—and truly! with the help of this kind of memory one
finally came "to reason"!—Ah, reason, seriousness, mastery over the   5
affects, this entire gloomy matter called reflection, all these prerogatives
and showpieces of man: how dearly they have been paid for! how much
blood and horror there is at the base of all "good things"! ...

4

But how then did that other "gloomy thing," the consciousness of
guilt, the entire "bad conscience" come into the world?—And thus we   10
return to our genealogists of morality. To say it once more—or haven't I
said it at all yet?—they aren't good for anything. Their own five-span-
long, merely "modern" experience; no knowledge, no will to knowledge of
the past; still less an instinct for history, a "second sight" necessary precisely here—and nonetheless doing history of morality: this must in all   15
fairness end with results that stand in a relation to truth that is not even
flirtatious. Have these previous genealogists of morality even remotely
dreamt, for example, that that central moral concept "guilt" had its origins in the very material concept "debt"? Or that punishment as *retribution* developed completely apart from any presupposition concerning   20
freedom or lack of freedom of the will?—and to such a degree that in fact
a *high* level of humanization is always necessary before the animal "man"
can begin to make those much more primitive distinctions "intentional,"
"negligent," "accidental," "accountable," and their opposites, and to take
them into account when measuring out punishment. The thought, now so   25
cheap and apparently so natural, so unavoidable, a thought that has even
had to serve as an explanation of how the feeling of justice came into being
at all on earth—"the criminal has earned his punishment *because* he could
have acted otherwise"—is in fact a sophisticated form of human judging
and inferring that was attained extremely late; whoever shifts it to the   30
beginnings lays a hand on the psychology of older humanity in a particularly crude manner. Throughout the greatest part of human history punishment was definitely *not* imposed *because* one held the evil-doer
responsible for his deed, that is, *not* under the presupposition that only
the guilty one is to be punished:—rather, as parents even today punish   35
their children, from anger over an injury suffered, which is vented on the
agent of the injury—anger held within bounds, however, and modified

through the idea that every injury has its *equivalent* in something and can really be paid off, even if only through the *pain* of its agent. Whence has this age-old, deeply-rooted, perhaps now no longer eradicable idea taken its power—the idea of an equivalence between injury and pain? I have
5   already given it away: in the contractual relationship between *creditor* and *debtor*, which is as old as the existence of "legal subjects" and in turn points back to the basic forms of purchase, sale, exchange, trade, and commerce.

5

Calling to mind these contract relationships admittedly awakens vari-
10   ous kinds of suspicion and resistance toward the earlier humanity that created or permitted them, as is, after the preceding remarks, to be expected from the outset. Precisely here there are *promises* made; precisely here it is a matter of *making* a memory for the one who promises; precisely here, one may suspect, will be a place where one finds things that are
15   hard, cruel, embarrassing. In order to instill trust in his promise of repay-ment, to provide a guarantee for the seriousness and the sacredness of his promise, to impress repayment on his conscience as a duty, as an obliga-tion, the debtor—by virtue of a contract—pledges to the creditor in the case of non-payment something else that he "possesses," over which he
20   still has power, for example his body or his wife or his freedom or even his life (or, under certain religious conditions, even his blessedness, the salva-tion of his soul, finally even his peace in the grave: as in Egypt where the corpse of the debtor found no rest from the creditor, even in the grave—and indeed there was something to this rest, precisely among the Egyp-
25   tians.) Above all, however, the creditor could subject the body of the debtor to all manner of ignominy and torture, for example cutting as much from it as appeared commensurate to the magnitude of the debt:—and everywhere and early on there were exact assessments of value devel-oped from this viewpoint—some going horribly into the smallest detail—
30   *legally* established assessments of the individual limbs and areas on the body. I take it already as progress, as proof of a freer, more grandly calcu-lating, *more Roman* conception of the law when the Twelve Tables legisla-tion of Rome decreed it was of no consequence how much or how little the creditors cut off in such a case, *"si plus minusve secuerunt, ne fraude*
35   *esto."* Let us make clear to ourselves the logic of this whole form of com-

"si plus ... fraude esto."] If they have secured more or less, let that be no crime.

pensation: it is foreign enough. The equivalence consists in this: that in place of an advantage that directly makes good for the injury (hence in place of a compensation in money, land, possession of any kind) the creditor is granted a certain *feeling of satisfaction* as repayment and compensation,—the feeling of satisfaction that comes from being permitted to vent his power without a second thought on one who is powerless, the carnal delight *"de faire le mal pour le plaisir de le faire,"* the enjoyment of doing violence: which enjoyment is valued all the higher the lower and baser the creditor's standing in the social order and can easily appear to him as a most delectable morsel, indeed as a foretaste of a higher status. Through his "punishment" of the debtor the creditor participates in a *right of lords*: finally he, too, for once attains the elevating feeling of being permitted to hold a being in contempt and maltreat it as something "beneath himself"—or at least, if the actual power of punishment, the execution of punishment has already passed over into the hands of the "authorities," of *seeing* it held in contempt and maltreated. The compensation thus consists in a directive and right to cruelty.—

6

In *this* sphere, in contract law that is, the moral conceptual world "guilt," "conscience," "duty," "sacredness of duty" has its genesis—its beginning, like the beginning of everything great on earth, was thoroughly and prolongedly drenched in blood. And might one not add that this world has in essence never again entirely lost a certain odor of blood and torture? (not even in old Kant: the categorical imperative smells of cruelty ...) It was likewise here that that uncanny and perhaps now inextricable meshing of ideas, "guilt and suffering," was first knitted. Asking once again: to what extent can suffering be a compensation for "debts"? To the extent that *making*-suffer felt good, and in the highest degree; to the extent that the injured one exchanged for what was lost, including the displeasure over the loss, an extraordinary counter-pleasure: *making*-suffer,—a true *festival*, something that, as stated, stood that much higher in price, the more it contradicted the rank and social standing of the creditor. This stated as conjecture: for it is difficult to see to the bottom of such subterranean things, not to mention that it is embarrassing; and whoever clumsily throws the concept of "revenge" into the middle of it all has covered and obscured his insight into the matter rather than making it easier

"de faire ... plaisir de le faire,"] to do evil for the pleasure of doing it.

(—revenge simply leads back to the same problem: "how can making-suffer be a satisfaction?). It seems to me that it is repugnant to the delicacy,
even more to the Tartuffery of tame domestic animals (which is to say
modern humans, which is to say us) to imagine in all its force the degree
to which *cruelty* constitutes the great festival joy of earlier humanity,
indeed is an ingredient mixed in with almost all of their joys; how naïvely,
on the other hand, how innocently its need for cruelty manifests itself,
how universally they rank precisely "disinterested malice" (or, to speak
with Spinoza, *sympathia malevolens*) as a *normal* quality of man—: thus as
something to which the conscience heartily says "*yes*"! Perhaps even
today there is enough of this oldest and most pervasive festival joy of man
for a more profound eye to perceive; in *Beyond Good and Evil* 229 (even
earlier in *Daybreak* 18, 77, 113), I pointed with a cautious finger to the
ever-growing spiritualization and "deification" of cruelty that runs
though the entire history of higher culture (and in a significant sense even
constitutes it). In any case it has not been all that long since one could not
imagine royal marriages and folk festivals in the grandest style without
executions, torturings, or perhaps an *auto-da-fé*, likewise no noble household without beings on whom one could vent one's malice and cruel teasing without a second thought (—think for example of Don Quixote at the
court of the Duchess: today we read the entire *Don Quixote* with a bitter
taste on our tongue, almost with anguish, and would as a result appear
very strange, very puzzling to its author and his contemporaries—they
read it with the very clearest conscience as the most lighthearted of books,
they practically laughed themselves to death over it). Seeing-suffer feels
good, making-suffer even more so—that is a hard proposition, but a central one, an old powerful human-all-too-human proposition, to which, by
the way, even the apes might subscribe: for it is said that in thinking up
bizarre cruelties they already abundantly herald and, as it were, "prelude"
man. Without cruelty, no festival: thus teaches the oldest, longest part of
man's history—and in punishment too there is so much that is *festive*!—

7

—With these thoughts, incidentally, it is by no means my intent to
help our pessimists to new grist for their discordant and creaking mills of
life-weariness; on the contrary they are meant expressly to show that back

sympathia malevolens] ill-willing sympathy.

then, when humanity was not yet ashamed of its cruelty, life on earth was more lighthearted than it is now that there are pessimists. The darkening of the heavens over man has always increased proportionally as man has grown ashamed *of man*. The tired pessimistic glance, the mistrust toward the riddle of life, the icy "no" of disgust at life—these are not the distin-   *5* guishing marks of the *most evil* ages of the human race: rather, being the swamp plants they are, they first enter the light of day when the swamp to which they belong appears,—I mean the diseased softening and moraliza- tion by virtue of which the creature "man" finally learns to be ashamed of all of his instincts. Along the way to "angel" (to avoid using a harsher   *10* word here) man has bred for himself that upset stomach and coated tongue through which not only have the joy and innocence of the animal become repulsive but life itself has become unsavory:—so that he at times stands before himself holding his nose and, along with Pope Innocent the Third, disapprovingly catalogues his repulsive traits ("impure begetting,   *15* disgusting nourishment in the womb, vileness of the matter out of which man develops, revolting stench, excretion of saliva, urine, and feces"). Now, when suffering is always marshalled forth as the first among the arguments *against* existence, as its nastiest question mark, one would do well to remember the times when one made the reverse judgment because   *20* one did not wish to do without *making*-suffer and saw in it an enchant- ment of the first rank, an actual seductive lure *to* life. Perhaps back then— to the comfort of delicate souls—pain didn't yet hurt as much as it does today; at least such a conclusion will be permissible for a physician who has treated Negroes (taken as representatives of prehistorical man—) for   *25* cases of serious internal infection that would almost drive even the best constituted European to despair;—in Negroes they do *not* do this. (Indeed the curve of human capacity for feeling pain appears to sink extraordinarily and almost abruptly as soon as one gets beyond the upper ten thousand or ten million of the highest level of culture; and I, for my   *30* part, do not doubt that when held up against one painful night of a single hysterical educated female the combined suffering of all the animals thus far questioned with the knife to obtain scientific answers simply isn't worth considering.) Perhaps one may even be allowed to admit the possi- bility that this pleasure in cruelty needn't actually have died out: but, in   *35* the same proportion as the pain hurts more today, it would need a certain sublimation and subtilization, namely it would have to appear translated into the imaginative and inward, adorned with all kinds of names so harmless that they arouse no suspicion, not even in the most delicate, most hypocritical conscience ("tragic pity" is such a name; another is *"les*   *40*

nostalgies de la croix"). What actually arouses indignation against suffering is not suffering in itself, but rather the senselessness of suffering; but neither for the Christian, who has interpreted into suffering an entire secret salvation machinery, nor for the naive human of older times, who knew
5   how to interpret all suffering in terms of spectators or agents of suffering, was there any such *meaningless* suffering at all. So that concealed, undiscovered, unwitnessed suffering could be banished from the world and honestly negated, one was almost compelled back then to invent gods and intermediate beings of all heights and depths, in short, something that
10 also roams in secret, that also sees in the dark, and that does not easily let an interesting painful spectacle escape it. For with the help of such inventions life back then was expert at the trick at which it has always been expert, of justifying itself, of justifying its "evil"; today it would perhaps need other auxiliary inventions for this (for example life as riddle, life as
15 epistemological problem). "Every evil is justified, the sight of which edifies a god": thus went the prehistoric logic of feeling—and, really, was it only the prehistoric? The gods, conceived of as friends of *cruel* spectacles—oh how far this age-old conception extends even into our humanized Europe! on this point one may consult with Calvin and Luther for
20 instance. It is certain in any case that the *Greeks* still knew of no more pleasant offering with which to garnish the happiness of their gods than the joys of cruelty. With what sort of eyes then do you think Homer had his gods look down on the fates of humans? What was the ultimate meaning of Trojan wars and similar tragic horrors? There can be no doubt at
25 all: they were meant as *festival games* for the gods: and, insofar as the poet is in this respect more "godlike" than other humans, probably also as festival games for the poets ... The moral philosophers of Greece later imagined the eyes of the gods no differently, still glancing down at the moral struggle, at the heroism and the self-torture of the virtuous: the "Heracles
30 of duty" was on a stage, he also knew he was on it; virtue without witnesses was something entirely inconceivable for this people of spectacles. Wasn't that philosophers' invention, so audacious, so fateful, which was first devised for Europe back then—that of "free will," of the absolute spontaneity of man in good and evil—devised above all in order to create
35 a right to the idea that the interest of the gods in man, in human virtue, *could never be exhausted*? On this stage, the earth, there would never be a shortage of truly new things, of truly unheard-of tensions, complications, catastrophes: a world conceived as completely deterministic would have

---

"*les nostalgies de la croix*"] the nostalgias of the cross.

been predictable for the gods and accordingly soon tiring—reason enough
for these *friends of the gods*, the philosophers, not to expect their gods to be
able to deal with such a deterministic world! In antiquity all of humanity
is full of tender considerations for "the spectator," as an essentially public,
essentially visible world that could not imagine happiness without specta-   5
cles and festivals.—And, as already mentioned, in great *punishment* too
there is so much that is festive! ...

8

The feeling of guilt, of personal obligation—to take up the train of our
investigation again—had its origin, as we have seen, in the oldest and
most primitive relationship among persons there is, in the relationship   10
between buyer and seller, creditor and debtor: here for the first time person stepped up against person, here for the first time a person *measured
himself* by another person. No degree of civilization however low has yet
been discovered in which something of this relationship was not already
noticeable. Making prices, gauging values, thinking out equivalents,   15
exchanging—this preoccupied man's very first thinking to such an extent
that it is in a certain sense thinking *itself*: here that oldest kind of acumen
was bred, here likewise we may suspect the first beginnings of human
pride, man's feeling of pre-eminence with respect to other creatures. Perhaps our word "man" (*manas*) still expresses precisely something of this   20
self-esteem: man designated himself as the being who measures values,
who values and measures, as the "appraising animal in itself." Purchase
and sale, together with their psychological accessories, are older than
even the beginnings of any societal associations and organizational forms:
it was out of the most rudimentary form of personal legal rights that the   25
budding feeling of exchange, contract, guilt, right, obligation, compensation first *transferred* itself onto the coarsest and earliest communal complexes (in their relationship to similar complexes), together with the habit
of comparing, measuring, and calculating power against power. The eye
was simply set to this perspective: and with that clumsy consistency   30
characteristic of earlier humanity's thinking—which has difficulty moving but then continues relentlessly in the same direction—one arrived
straightaway at the grand generalization "every thing has its price;
everything can be paid off"—at the oldest and most naive moral canon of

(*manas*)] Sanskrit: mind; understanding or the conscious will.

justice, at the beginning of all "good-naturedness," all "fairness," all "good will," all "objectivity" on earth. Justice at this first stage is the good will among parties of approximately equal power to come to terms with one another, to reach an "understanding" again by means of a settlement—and in regard to less powerful parties, to *force* them to a settle-ment among themselves.—

9

Always measured by the standard of an earlier time (which earlier time is, by the way, at all times present or again possible): the community, too, thus stands to its members in that important basic relationship, that of the creditor to his debtor. One lives in a community, one enjoys the advantages of a community (oh what advantages! we sometimes underes-timate this today), one lives protected, shielded, in peace and trust, free from care with regard to certain injuries and hostilities to which the human *outside*, the "outlaw," is exposed—a German understands what "Elend," *êlend* originally means—, since one has pledged and obligated oneself to the community precisely in view of these injuries and hostili-ties. What happens *in the other case*? The community, the deceived credi-tor, will exact payment as best it can, one can count on that. Here it is least of all a matter of the direct injury inflicted by the injuring party; quite apart from this, the criminal is above all a "breaker," one who breaks his contract and word *with the whole*, in relation to all goods and conveniences of communal life in which he has until this point had a share. The criminal is a debtor who not only fails to pay back the advan-tages and advances rendered him, but also even lays a hand on his credi-tor: he therefore not only forfeits all of these goods and advantages from now on, as is fair,—he is also now reminded *how much there is to these goods*. The anger of the injured creditor, of the community, gives him back again to the wild and outlawed condition from which he was previ-ously protected: it expels him from itself,—and now every kind of hostil-ity may vent itself on him. At this level of civilization "punishment" is simply the copy, the *mimus* of normal behavior toward the hated, dis-armed, defeated enemy, who has forfeited not only every right and pro-tection, but also every mercy; in other words, the law of war and the

"*Elend*," *êlend*] The New High German *Elend* (misery) derives from the Old High German adjective *elilenti* (in another land or country; banished) via the shortened Middle High German *ellende* or *êlend* (foreign, miserable).

victory celebration of *vae victis!* in all their ruthlessness and cruelty:—
which explains why war itself (including the warlike cult of sacrifice) has
supplied all the *forms* in which punishment appears in history.

10

As its power grows, a community no longer takes the transgressions of
the individual so seriously because they can no longer count as dangerous   5
and subversive for the continued existence of the whole to the same extent
as formerly: the evildoer is no longer "made an outlaw" and cast out; the
general anger is no longer allowed to vent itself in the same unbridled
manner as formerly—rather, from now on, the evildoer is carefully
defended against this anger, particularly that of the ones directly injured,   10
and taken under the protection of the whole. Compromise with the anger
of the one immediately affected by the misdeed; a striving to localize the
case and prevent a further or indeed general participation and unrest;
attempts to find equivalents and to settle the entire affair (the *compositio*);
above all the increasingly more resolute will to understand every offense   15
as in some sense *capable of being paid off,* hence, at least to a certain extent,
to *isolate* the criminal and his deed from each other—these are the traits
that are imprinted with increasing clarity onto the further development of
penal law. If the power and the self-confidence of a community grow, the
penal law also always becomes milder; every weakening and deeper   20
endangering of the former brings the latter's harsher forms to light again.
The "creditor" has always become more humane to the degree that he has
become richer; finally the amount of injury he can bear without suffering
from it even becomes the *measure* of his wealth. It would not be impossible to imagine a *consciousness of power* in society such that society might   25
allow itself the noblest luxury there is for it—to leave the one who injures
it *unpunished.* "What concern are my parasites to me?" it might then say.
"Let them live and prosper: I am strong enough for that!" ... The justice
that began with "everything can be paid off, everything must be paid off,"
ends by looking the other way and letting the one unable to pay go free,—   30
it ends like every good thing on earth, by *cancelling itself.* This self-cancellation of justice: we know what pretty name it gives itself—*mercy*; as goes

vae victis!] Woe to the conquered! Livy, *Ab urbe condita*, Book V, 48, 9.
compositio] term from Roman law referring to the settlement in a case of injury or
damage caused by an illegal act.

without saying, it remains the privilege of the most powerful, better still,
his beyond-the-law.

11

—Here a word in opposition to recent attempts to seek the origin of
justice on an entirely different ground,—namely that of *ressentiment*.
First, for the ears of psychologists, supposing they should have the desire
to study *ressentiment* itself up close for once: this plant now blooms most
beautifully among anarchists and anti-Semites—in secret, incidentally, as
it has always bloomed, like the violet, albeit with a different scent. And as
like must necessarily always proceed from like, so it will not surprise us to
see proceeding again from just such circles attempts like those often
made before—compare above, section 14—to hallow *revenge* under the
name of *justice*—as if justice were basically only a further development of
the feeling of being wounded—and retroactively to raise to honor along
with revenge the *reactive* affects in general and without exception. At the
latter I would least take offense: with respect to the entire biological
problem (in relation to which the value of these affects has thus far been
underestimated) it would even appear to me to be a *merit*. I call attention
only to the circumstance that it is from the spirit of *ressentiment* itself that
this new nuance of scientific fairness (in favor of hate, envy, ill will, suspicion, rancor, revenge) grows forth. For this "scientific fairness" immediately shuts down and makes room for accents of mortal hostility and
prejudice as soon as it is a matter of another group of affects that are, it
seems to me, of still much higher biological value than those reactive
ones, and accordingly deserve all the more to be *scientifically* appraised
and esteemed: namely the truly *active* affects like desire to rule, greed,
and the like. (E. Dühring, *Value of Life*; *Course in Philosophy*; basically
everywhere.) So much against this tendency in general: as for Dühring's
particular proposition that the homeland of justice is to be sought on the
ground of reactive feeling, one must, for love of the truth, pit against it in
stark reversal this alternative proposition: the *last* ground conquered by
the spirit of justice is the ground of reactive feeling! If it really happens
that the just man remains just even toward those who injure him (and not
merely cold, moderate, distant, indifferent: being just is always a *positive*
way of behaving), if the high, clear objectivity—that sees as deeply as it
does generously—of the just eye, the *judging* eye, does not cloud even
under the assault of personal injury, derision, accusation, well, then that
is a piece of perfection and highest mastery on earth—what is more,

something one would be prudent not to expect here, in which one in any case should not all too easily *believe*. Even with the most righteous persons it is certain that a small dose of attack, malice, insinuation is, on the average, already enough to chase the blood into their eyes and the fairness *out*. The active, the attacking, encroaching human is still located a hundred paces nearer to justice than the reactive one; he simply has no need to appraise his object falsely and with prejudice as the reactive human does, must do. Therefore in all ages the aggressive human, as the stronger, more courageous, more noble one, has in fact also had the *freer* eye, the *better* conscience on his side: conversely one can already guess who actually has the invention of the "bad conscience" on his conscience,—the human being of *ressentiment*! Finally, just look around in history: in which sphere has the entire administration of justice, also the true need for justice, thus far been at home on earth? Perhaps in the sphere of the reactive human? Absolutely *not*: rather in that of the active, strong, spontaneous, aggressive. Considered historically, justice on earth represents—let it be said to the annoyance of the above-named agitator (who himself once confessed: "the doctrine of revenge runs through all my works and efforts as the red thread of justice")—precisely the battle *against* reactive feelings, the war against them on the part of active and aggressive powers that have used their strength in part to call a halt to and impose measure on the excess of reactive pathos and to force a settlement. Everywhere justice is practiced and upheld one sees a stronger power seeking means to put an end to the senseless raging of *ressentiment* among weaker parties subordinated to it (whether groups or individuals), in part by pulling the object of *ressentiment* out of the hands of revenge, in part by setting in the place of revenge the battle against the enemies of peace and order, in part by inventing, suggesting, in some cases imposing compensations, in part by raising certain equivalents for injuries to the status of a norm to which *ressentiment* is henceforth once and for all restricted. But the most decisive thing the highest power does and forces through against the predominance of counter- and after-feelings—which it always does as soon as it is in any way strong enough to do so—is the establishment of the *law*, the imperative declaration of what in general is to count in its eyes as permitted, as just, what as forbidden, as unjust: after it has established the law, it treats infringements and arbitrary actions of individuals or entire groups as wanton acts against the law, as rebellion against the highest power itself, thereby diverting the feeling of its subjects away from the most immediate injury caused by such wanton acts and thus achieving in the long run the opposite of what all revenge

5

10

15

20

25

30

35

40

wants, which sees only the viewpoint of the injured one, allows only it to count—from now on the eye is trained for an ever *more impersonal* appraisal of deeds, even the eye of the injured one himself (although this last of all, as was mentioned at the start).—Accordingly, only once the law has been established do "justice" and "injustice" exist (and *not* as Dühring would have it, beginning with the act of injuring). To talk of justice and injustice *in themselves* is devoid of all sense; *in itself* injuring, doing violence, pillaging, destroying naturally cannot be "unjust," insofar as life acts *essentially*—that is, in its basic functions—in an injuring, violating, pillaging, destroying manner and cannot be *thought* at all without this character. One must even admit to oneself something still more problematic: that, from the highest biological standpoint, conditions of justice can never be anything but *exceptional conditions*, as partial restrictions of the true will of life—which is out after power—and subordinating themselves as individual means to its overall end: that is, as means for creating *greater* units of power. A legal system conceived of as sovereign and universal, not as a means in the battle of power complexes, but rather as means *against* all battle generally, say in accordance with Dühring's communist cliché that every will must accept every other will as equal, would be a principle *hostile to life*, a destroyer and dissolver of man, an attempt to kill the future of man, a sign of weariness, a secret pathway to nothingness.—

12

Yet a word on the origin and purpose of punishment—two problems that fall out or ought to fall out separately: unfortunately they are usually lumped together. How do the previous genealogists of morality carry on in this case? Naively, as they have always carried on—: they discover some "purpose" or other in punishment, for example revenge or deterrence, then innocently place this purpose at the beginning as *causa fiendi* of punishment, and—are done. The "purpose in law," however, is the last thing that is usable for the history of the genesis of law: on the contrary, for history of every kind there is no more important proposition than that one which is gained with such effort but also really *ought to be* gained,— namely, that the cause of the genesis of a thing and its final usefulness, its actual employment and integration into a system of purposes, lie *toto caelo* apart; that something extant, something that has somehow or other

causa fiendi] cause of the coming into being.

come into being, is again and again interpreted according to new views,
monopolized in a new way, transformed and rearranged for a new use by
a power superior to it; that all happening in the organic world is an *overpowering, a becoming-lord-over*; and that, in turn, all overpowering and
becoming-lord-over is a new interpreting, an arranging by means of   5
which the previous "meaning" and "purpose" must of necessity become
obscured or entirely extinguished. However well one has grasped the
utility of some physiological organ (or of a legal institution, a social custom, a political practice, a form in the arts or in religious cult), one has
still not comprehended anything regarding its genesis: as uncomfortable   10
and unpleasant as this may sound to earlier ears,—for from time immemorial one had thought that in comprehending the demonstrable purpose, the usefulness of a thing, a form, an arrangement, one also
comprehended the reason for its coming into being—the eye as made to
see, the hand as made to grasp. Thus one also imagined punishment as   15
invented for punishing. But all purposes, all utilities, are only *signs* that a
will to power has become lord over something less powerful and has
stamped its own functional meaning onto it; and in this manner the
entire history of a "thing," an organ, a practice can be a continuous sign-
chain of ever new interpretations and arrangements, whose causes need   20
not be connected even among themselves—on the contrary, in some cases
only accidentally follow and replace one another. The "development" of a
thing, a practice, an organ is accordingly least of all its *progressus* toward a
goal, still less a logical and shortest *progressus*, reached with the smallest
expenditure of energy and cost,—but rather the succession of more or less   25
profound, more or less independent processes of overpowering that play
themselves out in it, including the resistances expended each time against
these processes, the attempted changes of form for the purpose of defense
and reaction, also the results of successful counter-actions. The form is
fluid but the "meaning" is even more so ... Even in the individual organ-   30
ism things are no different: with each essential growth of the whole the
"meaning" of the individual organs shifts as well,—in some cases their
partial destruction, their reduction in number (for example through
destruction of the intermediate members), can be a sign of growing
strength and perfection. I wanted to say: even the partial *loss of utility*,   35
atrophying and degenerating, the forfeiture of meaning and purposive-
ness, in short death, belongs to the conditions of true *progressus*: which
always appears in the form of a will and way to *greater power* and is always
pushed through at the expense of numerous smaller powers. The magnitude of a "progress" is even *measured* by the mass of all that had to be   40

sacrificed for it; humanity as mass sacrificed for the flourishing of a single *stronger* species of human being—that *would be* progress ...—I empha-size this main viewpoint of historical methodology all the more because it basically goes against the presently ruling instincts and taste of the times,

5   which would rather learn to live with the absolute randomness, indeed the mechanistic senselessness of all happening than with the theory of a *power-will* playing itself out in all happening. The democratic idiosyn-crasy against everything that rules and desires to rule, the modern *mis-archism* (to create a bad word for a bad thing) has gradually transformed

10   and disguised itself into something spiritual, most spiritual, to such an extent that today it is already penetrating, is *allowed* to penetrate, step by step into the most rigorous, apparently most objective sciences; indeed it appears to me already to have become lord over the whole of physiology and the doctrine of life—to its detriment, as goes without saying—by

15   removing through sleight of hand one of its basic concepts, that of true *activity*. Under the pressure of that idiosyncrasy one instead places "adaptation" in the foreground, that is to say an activity of second rank, a mere reactivity; indeed life itself is defined as an ever more purposive inner adaptation to external circumstances (Herbert Spencer). In so

20   doing, however, one mistakes the essence of life, its *will to power*; in so doing one overlooks the essential pre-eminence of the spontaneous, attacking, infringing, reinterpreting, reordering, and formative forces, upon whose effect the "adaptation" first follows; in so doing one denies the lordly role of the highest functionaries in the organism itself, in

25   which the will of life appears active and form-giving. One recalls that for which Huxley reproached Spencer—his "administrative nihilism": but it is a matter of *more* than just "administering" ...

13

     —To return to our topic, namely to *punishment*, one must then distin-guish in it two sorts of things: first that which is relatively *permanent* in it,

30   the practice, the act, the "drama," a certain strict sequence of procedures; on the other hand that which is *fluid* in it, the meaning, the purpose, the expectation tied to the execution of such procedures. It is presupposed here without further ado, per analogy, according to the main viewpoint of the historical methodology just developed, that the procedure itself will

35   be something older, earlier than its use for punishment, that the latter was first placed into, interpreted into the procedure (which had long existed, but was practiced in another sense)—in short, that things are *not*

as our naive genealogists of morality and law have thus far assumed, all of
whom thought of the procedure as *invented* for the purpose of punishing,
as one once thought of the hand as invented for the purpose of grasping.
Now as for that other element in punishment—that which is fluid, its
"meaning"—in a very late state of culture (for example in present-day   5
Europe), the concept "punishment" in fact no longer represents a single
meaning at all but rather an entire synthesis of "meanings": the previous
history of punishment in general, the history of its exploitation for the
most diverse purposes, finally crystallizes into a kind of unity that is difficult to dissolve, difficult to analyze and—one must emphasize—is com-   10
pletely and utterly *undefinable*. (Today it is impossible to say for sure why
we actually punish: all concepts in which an entire process is semiotically
summarized elude definition; only that which has no history is definable.)
In an earlier stage, by contrast, that synthesis of "meanings" still appears
more soluble, also more capable of shifts; one can still perceive in each   15
individual case how the elements of the synthesis change their valence
and rearrange themselves accordingly, so that now this, now that element
comes to the fore and dominates at the expense of the remaining ones,
indeed in some cases one element (say the purpose of deterrence) seems
to cancel out all the rest of the elements. To give at least some idea of how
uncertain, how after-the-fact, how accidental "the meaning" of punish-   20
ment is and how one and the same procedure can be used, interpreted,
arranged with respect to fundamentally different intentions: I offer here
the schema that offered itself to me on the basis of a relatively small and
random body of material. Punishment as rendering-harmless, as preven-   25
tion of further injury. Punishment as payment to the injured party for the
injury, in any form (even in that of a compensating affect). Punishment as
isolation of a disturbance of equilibrium in order to prevent a further
spreading of the disturbance. Punishment as instilling fear of those who
determine and execute the punishment. Punishment as a kind of com-   30
pensation for the benefits the criminal has enjoyed up to that point (for
example when he is made useful as a slave in the mines). Punishment as
elimination of a degenerating element (in some cases of an entire branch,
as according to Chinese law: thus as a means for preserving the purity of
the race or for maintaining a social type). Punishment as festival, namely   35
as mocking and doing violence to a finally defeated enemy. Punishment as
making a memory, whether for the one who suffers the punishment—so-
called "improvement"—or for the witnesses of the execution. Punishment as payment of an honorarium, stipulated on the part of the power
that protects the evil-doer from the excesses of revenge. Punishment as   40

compromise with the natural state of revenge, insofar as the latter is still upheld and claimed as a privilege by powerful clans. Punishment as declaration of war and war-time measure against an enemy of peace, of law, of order, of authority, whom one battles—with the means that war furnishes—as dangerous to the community, as in breach of contract with respect to its presuppositions, as a rebel, traitor, and breaker of the peace.—

14

This list is certainly not complete; obviously punishment is overladen with utilities of all kinds. All the more reason to subtract from it a *supposed* utility that admittedly counts in popular consciousness as its most essential one,—precisely the one in which belief in punishment, teetering today for several reasons, still finds its most forceful support. Punishment is supposed to have the value of awakening in the guilty one the *feeling of guilt*; one seeks in it the true *instrumentum* of that reaction of the soul called "bad conscience," "pang of conscience." But by so doing one lays a hand on reality and on psychology, even for today—and how much more for the longest part of the history of man, his prehistory! Precisely among criminals and prisoners the genuine pang of conscience is something extremely rare; the prisons, the penitentiaries are *not* the breeding places where this species of gnawing worm most loves to flourish:—on this there is agreement among all conscientious observers, who in many cases render a judgment of this sort reluctantly enough and against their most personal wishes. In general, punishment makes hard and cold; it concentrates; it sharpens the feeling of alienation; it strengthens the power of resistance. If it should happen that it breaks the vigor and brings about a pitiful prostration and self-abasement, such a result is surely even less pleasing than the average effect of punishment—which is characterized by a dry gloomy seriousness. But if we think, say, of those millennia *before* the history of man, then one may unhesitatingly judge that it is precisely through punishment that the development of the feeling of guilt has been most forcefully *held back*—at least with respect to the victims on whom the punishing force vented itself. For let us not underestimate the extent to which precisely the sight of the judicial and executive procedures prevents the criminal from feeling his deed, the nature of his action, as *in itself* reprehensible, for he sees the very same kind of actions committed in the service of justice and then approved, committed with a good conscience: thus spying, outwitting, bribery, entrapment, the whole tricky and cunning art of police and prosecutors; moreover—based on principle, without even the excuse of emotion—robbing, overpowering, slandering, taking captive, torturing, murdering as displayed in the various kinds of punishment—all of these thus actions his judges in no way reject and condemn *in themselves*, but rather only in a certain respect and practical application. The "bad conscience," this most uncanny and interesting plant of our earthly vegetation, did *not* grow on this ground,—indeed, in the consciousness of the ones judging, the ones punishing, there was for the longest time *nothing* expressed that suggested one was dealing with a "guilty one." But rather with an instigator of injury, with an irresponsible piece of fate. And the one himself upon whom the punishment afterwards fell, again like a piece of fate, had no other "inner pain" than he would have had at the sudden occurrence of something unanticipated, of a frightful natural event, of a plummeting, crushing boulder against which one can no longer fight.

15

This once entered Spinoza's consciousness in an ensnaring manner (to the vexation of his interpreters, who really *exert* themselves to misunderstand him at this point, for example Kuno Fischer) when one afternoon, bothered by who knows what kind of memory, he dwelt on the question of what actually remained for him of the famous *morsus conscientiae*—he who had sent good and evil into exile among the human illusions and had fiercely defended the honor of his "free" God against those blasphemers who claimed something to the effect that God works everything *sub ratione boni* ("that, however, would be to subject God to fate and would in truth be the greatest of all absurdities"—). For Spinoza the world had stepped back again into that innocence in which it had lain before the invention of the bad conscience: what had become of the *morsus conscientiae* in the process? "The opposite of *gaudium*," he finally said to himself,—"a sadness, accompanied by the image of a past matter that has turned out in a manner contrary to all expectation." Eth. III propos. XVIII schol. I. II. For thousands of years instigators of evil overtaken by punishment have felt *no different than Spinoza* with regard to their "transgression": "something has unexpectedly gone wrong here," *not*: "I should

morsus conscientiae] sting of conscience.
sub ratione boni] for the sake of the good.
gaudium] joy.

not have done that"—they submitted themselves to the punishment as one submits to a sickness or a misfortune or to death, with that stout-hearted fatalism without revolt by which the Russians, for example, even today have the advantage over us Westerners in dealing with life. If there was a critique of the deed back then, it was prudence that exercised this critique on the deed: without question we must seek the actual *effect* of punishment above all in a sharpening of prudence, in a lengthening of memory, in a will hereafter to proceed more cautiously, more mistrust-fully, more secretively, in the insight that one is once and for all too weak for many things, in a kind of improvement in self-assessment. Generally what can be achieved among humans and animals through punishment is an increase of fear, a sharpening of prudence, mastery of the appetites: punishment thus *tames* man, but it does not make him "better"—one might with greater justification maintain the opposite. ("Injury makes prudent," say the common folk: insofar as it makes prudent, it also makes bad. Fortunately, it often enough makes stupid.)

16

At this point I can no longer avoid helping my own hypothesis on the origin of the "bad conscience" to a first, preliminary expression: it is not easy to present and needs to be considered, guarded, and slept over for a long time. I take bad conscience to be the deep sickness into which man had to fall under the pressure of that most fundamental of all changes he ever experienced—the change of finding himself enclosed once and for all within the sway of society and peace. Just as water animals must have fared when they were forced either to become land animals or to perish, so fared these half animals who were happily adapted to wilderness, war, roaming about, adventure—all at once all of their instincts were devalued and "disconnected." From now on they were to go on foot and "carry themselves" where they had previously been carried by the water: a horri-ble heaviness lay upon them. They felt awkward doing the simplest tasks; for this new, unfamiliar world they no longer had their old leaders, the regulating drives that unconsciously guided them safely—they were reduced to thinking, inferring, calculating, connecting cause and effect, these unhappy ones, reduced to their "consciousness," to their poorest and most erring organ! I do not believe there has ever been such a feeling of misery on earth, such a leaden discomfort—and yet those old instincts had not all at once ceased to make their demands! It's just that it was diffi-cult and seldom possible to yield to them: for the most part they had to seek new and as it were subterranean gratifications. All instincts that do not discharge themselves outwardly *turn themselves inwards*—this is what I call the *internalizing* of man: thus first grows in man that which he later calls his "soul." The entire inner world, originally thin as if inserted between two skins, has spread and unfolded, has taken on depth, breadth, height to the same extent that man's outward discharging has been *obstructed*. Those terrible bulwarks with which the organization of the state protects itself against the old instincts of freedom—punishments belong above all else to these bulwarks—brought it about that all those instincts of the wild free roaming human turned themselves backwards *against man himself*. Hostility, cruelty, pleasure in persecution, in assault, in change, in destruction—all of that turning itself against the possessors of such instincts: *that* is the origin of "bad conscience." The man who, for lack of external enemies and resistance, and wedged into an oppressive narrowness and regularity of custom, impatiently tore apart, persecuted, gnawed at, stirred up, maltreated himself; this animal that one wants to "tame" and that beats itself raw on the bars of its cage; this deprived one, consumed by homesickness for the desert, who had to create out of himself an adventure, a place of torture, an uncertain and dangerous wilderness—this fool, this longing and desperate prisoner became the inventor of "bad conscience." In him, however, the greatest and most uncanny of sicknesses was introduced, one from which man has not recovered to this day, the suffering of man *from man*, from *himself*—as the consequence of a forceful separation from his animal past, of a leap and plunge, as it were, into new situations and conditions of existence, of a declaration of war against the old instincts on which his energy, desire, and terribleness had thus far rested. Let us immediately add that, on the other hand, with the appearance on earth of an animal soul turned against itself, taking sides against itself, something so new, deep, unheard of, enigmatic, contradictory, *and full of future* had come into being that the appearance of the earth was thereby essentially changed. Indeed, divine spectators were necessary to appreciate the spectacle that thus began and whose end is still by no means in sight—a spectacle too refined, too wonderful, too paradoxical to be permitted to play itself out senselessly-unnoticed on some ridiculous star! Since that time man is *included* among the most unexpected and exciting lucky throws in the game played by the "big child" of Heraclitus, whether called Zeus or chance—he awakens for himself an interest, an anticipation, a hope, almost a certainty, as if with him something were announcing itself, something preparing itself, as if man were not a goal but only a path, an incident, a bridge, a great promise ...

17

To the presupposition of this hypothesis on the origin of bad conscience belongs first, that this change was not gradual, not voluntary, and that it presented itself not as an organic growing into new conditions, but rather as a break, a leap, a compulsion, an inescapable doom, against which there was no struggle and not even any *ressentiment*. Second, however, that this fitting of a previously unrestrained and unformed population into a fixed form, given its beginning in an act of force, could be brought to its completion only by acts of force—that the oldest "state" accordingly made its appearance as a terrible tyranny, as a crushing and ruthless machinery, and continued to work until finally such a raw material of people and half-animals was not only thoroughly kneaded and pliable but also *formed*. I use the word "state": it goes without saying who is meant by this—some pack of blond beasts of prey, a race of conquerors and lords, which, organized in a warlike manner and with the power to organize, unhesitatingly lays its terrible paws on a population enormously superior in number perhaps, but still formless, still roaming about. It is in this manner, then, that the "state" begins on earth: I think the flight of fancy that had it beginning with a "contract" has been abandoned. Whoever can give orders, whoever is "lord" by nature, whoever steps forth violently, in deed and gesture—what does he have to do with contracts! With such beings one does not reckon, they come like fate, without basis, reason, consideration, pretext; they are there like lightning is there: too terrible, too sudden, too convincing, too "different" even to be so much as hated. Their work is an instinctive creating of forms, impressing of forms; they are the most involuntary, unconscious artists there are:—where they appear, in a short time something new stands there, a ruling structure that *lives*, in which parts and functions are delimited and related to one another, in which nothing at all finds a place that has not first had placed into it a "meaning" with respect to the whole. They do not know what guilt, what responsibility, what consideration is, these born organizers; in them that terrible artists' egoism rules, that has a gaze like bronze and that knows itself already justified to all eternity in its "work," like the mother in her child. *They* are not the ones among whom "bad conscience" grew, that is clear from the outset—but it would not have grown *without them*, this ugly growth, it would be missing, if an enormous quantity of freedom had not been banished from the world, at least from visibility, and made *latent* as it were, under the pressure of the blows of their hammers, of their artist's violence. This *instinct for freedom*, forcibly made latent—we have already grasped it—this instinct for freedom, driven back, suppressed, imprisoned within, and finally discharging and venting itself only on itself: this, only this, is *bad conscience* in its beginnings.

18

One should guard against forming a low opinion of this entire phe-   5
nomenon just because it is ugly and painful from the outset. After all, the active force that is at work on a grander scale in those violence-artists and organizers and that builds states, is basically the same force that here— inwardly, on a smaller, pettier scale, in a backwards direction, in the "lab- yrinth of the breast," to use Goethe's words—creates for itself the bad   10
conscience and builds negative ideals: namely that *instinct for freedom* (speaking in my language: the will to power). Only here the matter on which this force's formative and violating nature vents itself is precisely man himself, his entire animal old self—and *not*, as in that larger and more conspicuous phenomenon, the *other* human, the *other* humans.   15
This secret self-violation, this artists' cruelty, this pleasure in giving one- self—as heavy resisting suffering matter—a form, in burning into one- self a will, a critique, a contradiction, a contempt, a "no"; this uncanny and horrifying-pleasurable work of a soul compliant-conflicted with itself, that makes itself suffer out of pleasure in making-suffer, this entire   20
active "bad conscience," as the true womb of ideal and imaginative events, finally brought to light—one can guess it already—a wealth of new disconcerting beauty and affirmation and perhaps for the first time beauty *itself* ... For what would be "beautiful" if contradiction had not first come to a consciousness of itself, if the ugly had not first said to   25
itself "I am ugly"? ... After this hint, that enigma will at the least be less enigmatic, namely, to what extent an ideal, a beauty can be suggested by contradictory concepts like *selflessness, self-denial, self-sacrifice*; and we know one thing henceforth, this I do not doubt—namely what kind of *pleasure* it is that the selfless, the self-denying, the self-sacrificing feel   30
from the very start: this pleasure belongs to cruelty.—So much for the present on the origins of the "unegoistic" as a *moral* value and toward staking out the ground from which this value has grown: bad conscience, the will to self-maltreatment, first supplies the presupposition for the *value* of the unegoistic.—   35

19

It is a sickness, bad conscience—this admits of no doubt—but a sickness as pregnancy is a sickness. Let us seek out the conditions under which this sickness has come to its most terrible and most sublime pinnacle:—we shall see just what it was that thus first made its entry into the
5   world. For this we need a long breath,—and to start off we must return once again to an earlier viewpoint. The civil-law relationship of the debtor to his creditor, of which I have already spoken at length, was once again—and indeed in a manner that is historically exceedingly curious and questionable—interpreted into a relationship in which it is for us modern
10 humans perhaps at its most incomprehensible: namely the relationship of *those presently living* to their *ancestors*. Within the original clan association—we are speaking of primeval times—the living generation always acknowledges a juridical obligation to the earlier generation, and particularly to the earliest one, which founded the clan (and by no means a mere
15 sentimental obligation: one might with good reason even deny the latter altogether for the longest part of the existence of the human race). Here the conviction holds sway that it is only through the sacrifices and achievements of the ancestors that the clan *exists* at all,—and that one has to *repay* them through sacrifices and achievements: one thereby acknowl-
20 edges a *debt* that is continually growing, since these ancestors, in their continued existence as powerful spirits, do not cease to use their strength to bestow on the clan new benefits and advances. For nothing perhaps? But to those brutal and "soul-poor" ages there is no "for nothing." What can one give back to them? Sacrifices (initially only nourishment, in the
25 coarsest sense), festivals, shrines, tributes, above all obedience—for all customs, as works of the ancestors, are also their statutes and commands—: does one ever give them enough? This suspicion remains and grows: from time to time it forces a great redemption, lock, stock, and barrel, some enormity of a counter-payment to the "creditor" (the notori-
30 ous sacrifice of the firstborn, for example; blood, human blood in any case). The fear of the progenitor and his power, the consciousness of debts toward him necessarily increases, according to this kind of logic, to exactly the same degree that the power of the clan itself increases, that the clan itself stands ever more victorious, independent, honored, feared. By no
35 means the other way around! Rather every step toward the atrophying of the clan, all miserable chance occurrences, all signs of degeneration, of approaching dissolution always *diminish* the fear of the spirit of the founder and give an ever more reduced notion of his shrewdness, his fore-

sightedness, and his presence as power. If one imagines this brutal kind of logic carried through to its end: finally, through the imagination of growing fear the progenitors of the *most powerful* clans must have grown into enormous proportions and have been pushed back into the darkness of a divine uncanniness and unimaginability:—in the end the progenitor is necessarily transfigured into a *god*. This may even be the origin of the gods, an origin, that is, out of *fear*! ... And those who think it necessary to add: "but also out of piety!" would hardly be right with regard to the longest period of the human race, its primeval period. All the more, admittedly, for the *middle* period in which the noble clans take shape:— who in fact returned, with interest, to their originators, the ancestors (heroes, gods) all of the qualities that had in the meantime become apparent in them, the *noble* qualities. Later we will take another look at the aristocratizing and ennobling of the gods (which is by no means their "hallowing"): for the present let us simply bring the course of this whole development of guilt consciousness to a conclusion.

20

As history teaches, the consciousness of having debts to the deity by no means came to an end even after the decline of the "community" organized according to blood-relationships; in the same way that it inherited the concepts "good and bad" from the clan nobility (together with its basic psychological propensity for establishing orders of rank), humanity also inherited, along with the deities of the clan and tribe, the pressure of the still unpaid debts and of the longing for the redemption of the same. (The transition is made by those broad slave and serf populations who adapted themselves to the cult of the gods practiced by their lords, whether through force or through submissiveness and mimicry: starting from them, this inheritance then overflows in all directions.) For several millennia the feeling of guilt toward the deity did not stop growing and indeed grew ever onward in the same proportion as the concept of god and the feeling for god grew on earth and was borne up on high. (The whole history of ethnic fighting, triumphing, reconciling, merging—everything that precedes the final rank-ordering of all ethnic elements in every great racial synthesis—is reflected in the genealogical confusion of their gods, in the legends of their fights, triumphs, and reconciliations; development toward universal empires is also always development toward universal deities; despotism with its overpowering of the independent nobility also always prepares the way for some kind of

monotheism.) The rise of the Christian god as the maximum god that has
been attained thus far therefore also brought a maximum of feelings of
guilt into appearance on earth. Assuming that we have by now entered
into the *reverse* movement, one might with no little probability deduce
5   from the unstoppable decline of faith in the Christian god that there
would already be a considerable decline in human consciousness of guilt
as well; indeed the prospect cannot be dismissed that the perfect and
final victory of atheism might free humanity from this entire feeling of
having debts to its beginnings, its *causa prima*. Atheism and a kind of *sec-*
10   *ond innocence* belong together.—

21

So much for the present, in short and roughly speaking, on the connection of the concepts "guilt," "duty" to religious presuppositions: I
have until now intentionally left aside the actual moralization of these
concepts (their being pushed back into conscience, more precisely the
15   entanglement of *bad* conscience with the concept of god) and at the end of
the previous section even spoke as if there were no such moralization,
consequently, as if those concepts were now necessarily coming to an end
now that their presupposition, the faith in our "creditor," in God, has
fallen. The facts of the case diverge from this in a terrible manner. With
20   the moralization of the concepts guilt and duty, with their being pushed
back into *bad* conscience, we have in actual fact the attempt to *reverse* the
direction of the development just described, at least to bring its movement to a standstill: precisely the prospect of a conclusive redemption
shall now pessimistically close itself off once and for all; the gaze *shall* now
25   bleakly deflect off, deflect back from a brazen impossibility; those concepts "guilt" and "duty" *shall* now turn themselves backwards—and
against whom? There can be no doubt: first against the "debtor," in whom
bad conscience now fixes itself firmly, eats into him, spreads out, and
grows like a polyp in every breadth and depth until finally, with the
30   impossibility of discharging the debt, the impossibility of discharging
penance is also conceived of, the idea that it cannot be paid off ("*eternal*
punishment")—; finally, however, even against the "creditor," think here
of the *causa prima* of man, of the beginning of the human race, of its progenitor, who is now burdened with a curse ("Adam," "Original Sin,"
35   "unfreedom of the will") or of nature, from whose womb man arises and

causa prima] first cause.

into which the evil principle is now placed ("demonizing of nature") or of existence generally, which is left as *valueless in itself* (nihilistic turning away from it, longing into nothingness or longing into its "opposite," a being-other, Buddhism and related things)—until all at once we stand before the paradoxical and horrifying remedy in which tortured humanity 5 found temporary relief, *Christianity's* stroke of genius: God sacrificing himself for the guilt of man, God himself exacting payment of himself, God as the only one who can redeem from man what has become irre- deemable for man himself—the creditor sacrificing himself for his debtor, out of *love* (is that credible?—), out of love for his debtor! ... 10

22

One will already have guessed *what* actually happened with all of this and *under* all of this: that will to self-torment, that suppressed cruelty of the animal-human who had been made inward, scared back into himself, of the one locked up in the "state" for the purpose of taming, who invented the bad conscience in order to cause himself pain after the *more* 15 *natural* outlet for this *desire to cause pain* was blocked,—this man of bad conscience has taken over the religious presupposition in order to drive his self-torture to its most gruesome severity and sharpness. Guilt before *God*: this thought becomes an instrument of torture for him. In "God" he captures the most extreme opposites he can find to his actual and inescap- 20 able animal instincts; he reinterprets these animal instincts themselves as guilt before God (as hostility, rebellion, insurrection against the "lord," the "father," the primal ancestor and beginning of the world); he har- nesses himself into the contradiction "God" and "devil"; he takes all the "no" that he says to himself, to nature, naturalness, the facticity of his 25 being and casts it out of himself as a "yes," as existing, corporeal, real, as God, as holiness of God, as judgeship of God, as executionership of God, as beyond, as eternity, as torture without end, as hell, as immeasurability of punishment and guilt. This is a kind of madness of the will in psychic cruelty that has absolutely no equal: the *will* of man to find himself guilty 30 and reprehensible to the point that it cannot be atoned for; his *will* to imagine himself punished without the possibility of the punishment ever becoming equivalent to the guilt; his *will* to infect and make poisonous the deepest ground of things with the problem of punishment and guilt in order to cut off the way out of this labyrinth of *"idées fixes"* once and for 35 all; his *will* to erect an ideal—that of the "holy God"—in order, in the face of the same, to be tangibly certain of his absolute unworthiness. Oh,

this insane sad beast man! What ideas occur to it, what anti-nature, what
paroxysms of nonsense; what *bestiality of idea* immediately breaks forth
when it is hindered only a little from being a *beast of deed*!... All of this is
interesting to the point of excess, but also of such black gloomy unnerving
sadness that one must forcibly forbid oneself to look too long into these
abysses. Here there is *sickness*, beyond all doubt, the most terrible sickness
that has thus far raged in man:—and whoever is still capable of hearing
(but one no longer has the ears for it today!—) how in this night of torture
and absurdity the cry *love* resounded, the cry of the most longing delight,
of redemption in *love*, will turn away, seized by an invincible horror ...
There is so much in man that is horrifying! ... The earth has been a madhouse for too long! ...

23

Let this suffice once and for all concerning the origins of the "holy
God."—That *in itself* the conception of gods does not necessarily lead to
this degradation of the imagination, which we could not spare ourselves
from calling to mind for a moment, that there are *more noble* ways of making use of the fabrication of gods than for this self-crucifixion and self-
defilement of man in which Europe's last millennia have had their mastery—this can fortunately be read from every glance one casts on the
Greek gods, these reflections of noble and autocratic human beings in
whom the *animal* in man felt itself deified and *did not* tear itself apart, *did
not* rage against itself! For the longest time these Greeks used their gods
precisely to keep "bad conscience" at arm's length, to be able to remain
cheerful about their freedom of soul: that is, the reverse of the use which
Christianity made of its god. They took this to *great lengths*, these splendid and lionhearted childish ones; and no lesser authority than that of the
Homeric Zeus himself gives them to understand here and there that they
make it too easy for themselves. "A wonder!" he says once—it concerns
the case of Aegisthus, a *very* bad case—

A wonder, how much the mortals complain against the gods!
Only from us is there evil, they think; but they themselves
Create their own misery through lack of understanding,
      even counter to fate.

But one hears and sees at the same time that even this Olympian spectator and judge is far from being angry at them for this and from thinking

evil of them: "how *foolish* they are!" so he thinks in the face of the misdeeds of the mortals,—and "foolishness," "lack of understanding," a little
"disturbance in the head," this much even the Greeks of the strongest,
bravest age *allowed* themselves as the reason for much that was bad and
doom-laden:—foolishness, *not* sin! do you understand that? ... But even 5
this disturbance in the head was a problem—"indeed, how is it even possible? whence could it actually have come, given heads such as *we* have, we
men of noble descent, of happiness, of optimal form, of the best society, of
nobility, of virtue?"—thus the noble Greek wondered for centuries in the
face of every incomprehensible atrocity and wanton act with which one of 10
his equals had sullied himself. "A god must have beguiled him," he said to
himself finally, shaking his head ... This way out is *typical* of the Greeks
... In this manner the gods served in those days to justify humans to a
certain degree even in bad things, they served as causes of evil—in those
days it was not the punishment they took upon themselves but rather, as 15
is *more noble*, the guilt ...

24

—I close with three question marks, as one can of course see. "Is an
ideal actually being erected here or is one being demolished?" thus one
might ask me ... But have you ever asked yourselves enough how dearly
the erection of *every* ideal on earth has exacted its payment? How much 20
reality always had to be libeled and mistaken, how much lying sanctified,
how much conscience disturbed, how much "god" had to be sacrificed
each time? So that a sanctuary can be erected, *a sanctuary must be shattered*: that is the law—show me a case where it is not fulfilled! ... We modern humans, we are the heirs of millennia of conscience-vivisection and 25
cruelty to the animal-self: in this we have our longest practice, our artistry
perhaps, in any case our sophistication, our overrefinement of taste. For
all too long man has regarded his natural inclinations with an "evil eye,"
so that in him they have finally become wedded to "bad conscience." A
reverse attempt would *in itself* be possible—but who is strong enough for 30
it?—namely to wed to bad conscience the *unnatural* inclinations, all those
aspirations to the beyond, to that which is contrary to the senses, contrary
to the instincts, contrary to nature, contrary to the animal—in short the
previous ideals which are all ideals hostile to life, ideals of those who libel
the world. To whom to turn today with *such* hopes and demands? ... In so 35
doing one would have precisely the *good* human beings against oneself;
and, in fairness, the comfortable, the reconciled, the vain, the enraptured,

the tired ... What is there that insults more deeply, that separates off so
fundamentally, as letting others notice something of the strictness and
height with which one treats oneself? And on the other hand—how
accommodating, how full of love the whole world shows itself toward us as
soon as we do like all the world and "let ourselves go" like all the world!
... For this goal one would need a *different* kind of spirits than are probable in this of all ages: spirits strengthened by wars and victories, for whom
conquering, adventure, danger, pain have even become a need; for this
one would need acclimatization to sharp high air, to wintry journeys, to
ice and mountain ranges in every sense; for this one would need a kind of
sublime malice itself, an ultimate most self-assured mischievousness of
knowledge, which belongs to great health; one would need, in brief and
gravely enough, precisely this *great health*! ... Is this even possible today?
... But someday, in a stronger time than this decaying, self-doubting
present, he really must come to us, the *redeeming* human of the great love
and contempt, the creative spirit whose compelling strength again and
again drives him out of any apart or beyond, whose loneliness is misunderstood by the people as if it were a flight *from* reality—: whereas it is
only his submersion, burial, absorption *in* reality so that one day, when he
again comes to light, he can bring home the *redemption* of this reality: its
redemption from the curse that the previous ideal placed upon it. This
human of the future who will redeem us from the previous ideal as much
as from that *which had to grow out of it*, from the great disgust, from the
will to nothingness; this bell-stroke of noon and of the great decision, that
makes the will free again, that gives back to the earth its goal and to man
his hope; this Anti-Christ and anti-nihilist; this conqueror of God and of
nothingness—*he must one day come* ...

25

—But what am I saying? Enough! Enough! At this point there is only
one thing fitting for me, to be silent: otherwise I would be laying a hand
on that which only a younger one is free to choose, a "more future one," a
stronger one than I am—which only *Zarathustra* is free to choose, *Zarathustra the godless* ...

Third Treatise: What Do Ascetic Ideals Mean?

Carefree, mocking, violent—thus wisdom wants *us*:
she is a woman, she always loves only a warrior.

Thus Spoke Zarathustra

1

What do ascetic ideals mean?—Among artists nothing or too many different things; among philosophers and scholars something like a nose and instinct for the most favorable preconditions of higher spirituality; among women, at best, one *more* charming trait of seduction, a little *morbidezza* on beautiful flesh, the angelicalness of a pretty, fat animal; among the physiologically failed and out of sorts (among the *majority* of mortals) an attempt to appear to oneself to be "too good" for this world, a holy form of excess, their principal instrument in the battle with slow pain and with boredom; among priests the true priests' faith, their best tool of power, also the "most high" permission to power; among saints, finally, a pretext for hibernation, their *novissima gloriae cupido*, their rest in nothingness ("God"), their form of madness. *That* the ascetic ideal has meant so much to man, however, is an expression of the basic fact of the human will, its *horror vacui*: *it needs a goal*,—and it would rather will *nothingness* than *not* will.—Am I understood? Have I been understood? ... *"Absolutely not! dear Sir!"*—Then let us start at the beginning.

2

What do ascetic ideals mean?—Or, to take an individual case, about which I have often enough been asked for advice, what does it mean, for example, when, in his old age, an artist like Richard Wagner pays homage to chastity? In a certain sense, admittedly, he has always done this; but only at the very end in an ascetic sense. What does this change of "sense,"

novissima gloriae cupido] the last thing, passion for glory. Tacitus, *Histories* IV, 6.
horror vacui] horror of emptiness.

this radical reversal of sense mean?—for that is what it was, Wagner thus
suddenly somersaulted directly into his opposite. What does it mean
when an artist suddenly somersaults into his opposite? ... Here we are at
once reminded—supposing we are willing to pause a moment at this
question—of what was perhaps the best, strongest, most cheerful-
hearted, *most courageous* time in Wagner's life: it was back when the idea
of Luther's marriage occupied him inwardly and deeply. Who knows on
what chance events it actually depended that today instead of this marriage music we have the *Meistersinger?* And how much of the former still
resounds in the latter? But there is no doubt that this "Marriage of
Luther," too, would have been a praise of chastity. To be sure, also a praise
of sensuality:—and precisely so would it seem to me to be in order, precisely so would it also have been "Wagnerian." For between chastity and
sensuality there is no necessary opposition; every good marriage, every
true affair of the heart is beyond this opposition. Wagner would have
done well, it seems to me, to have brought home this *pleasant* fact to his
Germans once again with the help of a lovely and stout-hearted Luther
comedy, for there are and always have been many libelers of sensuality
among the Germans; and perhaps nowhere has Luther performed a
greater service than precisely in having had the courage to his *sensuality* (it
was called in those days, delicately enough, the "Protestant freedom" ...)
But even in the case where there really is that opposition between chastity
and sensuality, it is fortunately by no means necessary that it be a tragic
opposition. This would seem to hold at least for all better-formed, more
high-spirited mortals who are far from automatically counting their labile
balance between "animal and angel" among the arguments against existence,—the subtlest and brightest, like Goethe, like Hafiz, have even seen
in this one *more* enticement to life. Precisely such "contradictions" seduce
to existence ... On the other hand it is only too clear that when swine who
have come to ruin are once brought to the point of worshipping chastity—and there are such swine!—they will see and worship in it only their
opposite, the opposite of swine come to ruin—oh with what tragic grunt-
ing and zeal! one can imagine it—the embarrassing and superfluous
opposite that Richard Wagner indisputably still wanted to set to music
and put on stage at the end of his life. *And to what end?* as one may in fairness ask. For what were the swine to him, what are they to us?—

3

And yet admittedly that other question cannot be avoided here: just
what was that manly (alas, so unmanly) "simplicity from the country" to

him, that poor devil and lad of nature Parsifal, whom he with such ensnaring means finally made Catholic—what? was this Parsifal meant at all *seriously?* For one could be tempted to conjecture, even to wish the
opposite—that the Wagnerian Parsifal were meant lightheartedly, a clos-
ing piece and satyr-play, as it were, with which the tragedian Wagner   5
wanted to take leave of us, also of himself, above all *of tragedy* in a manner
fitting for and worthy of him, namely with an excess of highest and most
mischievous parody of the tragic itself, of the entire gruesome earthly seriousness and wretchedness of earlier times, of the *coarsest form*—now
finally overcome—found in the anti-nature of the ascetic ideal. This, as   10
noted, would have been worthy precisely of a great tragedian: who, like
every artist, only arrives at the final pinnacle of his greatness when he is
able to see himself and his art *beneath* him,—when he is able to *laugh* at
himself. Is Wagner's *Parsifal* his secret laughter of superiority at himself,
the triumph of this final highest artist's freedom, artist's otherworldliness?   15
As stated, one would like to wish it: for what would a *seriously intended
Parsifal* be? Is it really necessary to see in it (as someone put it in conversation with me) "the product of an insane hatred of knowledge, spirit, and
sensuality"? A curse on senses and spirit in a single hatred and breath? An
apostasy and return to obscurantist and Christian-diseased ideals? And   20
finally even a negating of self, a crossing-out of self on the part of an artist
who until that point had been out with all the might of his will after the
opposite, namely the *highest spiritualization and sensualization* of his art?
And not only of his art: also of his life. Recall how enthusiastically in his
day Wagner walked in the footsteps of the philosopher Feuerbach: Feuer-   25
bach's word concerning "healthy sensuality"—in the thirties and forties
this sounded to Wagner as to many Germans (—they called themselves
the "*young* Germans") like the word of redemption. Did he in the end
learn otherwise? Since it seems at least that in the end he had the will *to
teach otherwise* ... And not only from the stage, with the *Parsifal*-trom-   30
bones:—in the murky writings of his last years, just as unfree as they are
clueless, there are a hundred passages in which a secret wish and will
betrays itself, a despondent, uncertain, unacknowledged will to preach, in
essence, changing of one's way, conversion, negation, Christianity, Middle
Ages and to say to his disciples: "it is nothing! Seek your salvation else-   35
where!" Even the "blood of the Redeemer" is invoked at one point ...

4

To state my opinion in a case of this sort, in which there is much that
is embarrassing—and it is a *typical* case—: one certainly does best to

separate an artist from his work to the extent of not taking him as seriously as his work. He is in the end only the precondition of his work, the
womb, the ground, in some cases the fertilizer and manure on which, out
of which, it grows,—and thus in most cases something one must forget if
5   one wants to enjoy the work itself. Looking into the *origins* of a work is
the business of physiologists and vivisectors of the spirit: never ever of
the aesthetic human being, the artist! The poet and shaper of *Parsifal* was
no more spared a deep, thorough, even frightening acclimatization and
descent into medieval contrasts of the soul, a hostile aloofness from all
10   height, rigor, and discipline of the spirit, a kind of intellectual *perversity*
(if one will pardon the word) than a pregnant woman is spared the repulsive and strange aspects of pregnancy: which one must *forget*, as noted,
in order to enjoy the child. One should be on guard against the confusion
into which an artist himself all too easily falls, out of psychological conti-
15   guity, to put it as the English do: as if he himself *were* what he is able to
depict, think up, express. In fact, the situation is such that *if* he were precisely that, he would certainly not depict, think up, express it; a Homer
would not have written an Achilles nor Goethe a Faust if Homer had
been an Achilles or if Goethe had been a Faust. A perfect and whole artist
20   is separated to all eternity from the "real," the actual; on the other hand
one understands how he can at times become tired to the point of despair
of this eternal "irreality" and falseness of his innermost existence—and
that he makes the attempt to encroach for once upon what is most forbidden precisely to him, upon what is real—makes the attempt truly to *be*.
25   With what success? One can guess ... It is *the typical velleity* of the artist:
the same velleity into which Wagner lapsed, having grown old, and for
which he had to pay so dearly, so fatefully (—through it he lost the valuable part of his friends). Finally, however, still disregarding this velleity
entirely, who would not like to wish for Wagner's own sake that he had
30   taken leave of us and of his art *differently*, not with a *Parsifal*, but rather
in a manner that was more victorious, more self-assured, more Wagnerian—less misleading, less ambiguous about what he really wanted, less
Schopenhauerian, less nihilistic? ...

5

—What then do ascetic ideals mean? In the case of an artist, as we
35   have grasped by now: *absolutely nothing*! ... Or so many things that it is as
good as absolutely nothing! ... Let us first of all eliminate artists: they are
far from standing independently enough in the world and *against* the

world for their valuations and the changes in these to deserve interest *in themselves*! In all ages they have been valets of a morality or philosophy or religion; quite apart from the fact that, unfortunately, they have often enough been the all-too-pliant courtiers of their disciples and patrons, and flatterers with a good nose for old or newly rising powers. At the very least they always need a protective armor, a backing, a previously established authority: artists never stand by themselves, standing alone goes against their deepest instincts. Thus Richard Wagner, for example, took the philosopher Schopenhauer as his front man, as his protective armor when "the time had come":—who could consider it even thinkable that he would have had the courage for an ascetic ideal without the backing that Schopenhauer's philosophy offered him, without Schopenhauer's authority, which was gaining *predominance* in Europe in the seventies? (not yet having assessed whether an artist would have even been possible in the *new* Germany without the milk of a pious, imperially pious way of thinking).—And with this we have arrived at the more serious question: what does it mean when a real *philosopher* pays homage to the ascetic ideal, a spirit who really stands on his own, like Schopenhauer, a man and knight with a brazen glance, who has the courage to himself, who knows how to stand alone and does not first wait for front men and nods from on high?—Let us immediately consider here the strange and for many kinds of people even fascinating stance Schopenhauer took toward *art*: it was, after all, clearly for the sake of this that Richard Wagner *initially* converted to Schopenhauer (convinced to do so by a poet, as is well known, by Herwegh), and to such an extent that a complete theoretical contradiction thus opened up between his earlier and his later aesthetic beliefs— the former expressed for example in "Opera and Drama," the latter in the writings he published from 1870 on. In particular, from here on Wagner ruthlessly changed—this is perhaps the most disconcerting thing of all—his judgment concerning the value and status of *music* itself: what did it matter to him that he had previously made a means out of it, a medium, a "woman," that simply had to have a purpose, a man in order to prosper—namely drama! He grasped all at once that with Schopenhauer's theory and innovation more could be done *in majorem musicae gloriam*—namely with the *sovereignty* of music as Schopenhauer understood it: music set apart from all other arts, the independent art in itself, *not*, like these, offering representations of phenomenality, but rather speaking the language of *the* will itself, directly out of the "abyss," as its most

in majorem musicae gloriam] for the greater glory of music.

authentic, most original, least derivative revelation. With this extraordinary rise in the value of music, as it seemed to grow forth out of Schopenhauerian philosophy, *the musician* himself all at once rose in price to an unheard-of degree: he now became an oracle, a priest, indeed more than a
5   priest, a kind of mouthpiece of the "in itself" of things, a telephone of the beyond—henceforth he spoke not only music, this ventriloquist of God—he spoke metaphysics: any wonder that one day he finally spoke *ascetic ideals?* ...

6

Schopenhauer used the Kantian formulation of the aesthetic problem
10   for his own purpose—although he most certainly did not view it with Kantian eyes. Kant intended to honor art when, among the predicates of the beautiful, he privileged and placed in the foreground those that constitute the honor of knowledge: impersonality and universal validity. Whether this was not on the whole a mistake cannot be dealt with here; I
15   wish only to underscore that Kant, like all philosophers, instead of envisaging the aesthetic problem starting from the experiences of the artist (the one who creates), thought about art and the beautiful from the viewpoint of the "spectator" and thus, without it being noticed, got the "spectator" himself into the concept "beautiful." If only this "spectator" had at least
20   been sufficiently familiar to the philosophers of the beautiful, however!— namely as a great *personal* fact and experience, as a wealth of most personal intense experiences, desires, surprises, delights in the realm of the beautiful! But I fear the opposite was always the case: and thus we receive from them, right from the beginning, definitions in which, as in that
25   famous definition Kant gives of the beautiful, the lack of more refined self-experience sits in the form of a fat worm of basic error. "The beautiful," Kant said, "is what pleases *without interest*." Without interest! Compare this definition with one made by a real "spectator" and artist— Stendhal, who in one place calls the beautiful *une promesse de bonheur*.
30   What is *rejected* and crossed out here, in any case, is precisely the one thing Kant emphasizes in the aesthetic condition: *le désintéressement*. Who is right, Kant or Stendhal?—Admittedly, if our aestheticians never tire of throwing into the balance in Kant's favor that under the enchantment of beauty one can look at *even* robeless female statues "without interest,"
35   then certainly one may laugh a little at their expense:—the experiences of

une promesse de bonheur] a promise of happiness.

artists in connection with this sensitive point are "more interesting," and
Pygmalion was in any case *not* necessarily an "unaesthetic human being."
Let us think all the more highly of the innocence of our aestheticians that
is reflected in such arguments; for example, let us give Kant credit for
what he knows to teach—with the naïveté of a country priest—about the   5
characteristic nature of the sense of touch!—And here we come back to
Schopenhauer, who stood much closer to the arts than Kant and still did
not get out from under the spell of the Kantian definition: how did this
happen? The circumstance is odd enough: he interpreted the expression
"without interest" in the most personal manner, on the basis of what must   10
have been one of his most regular experiences. There are few things about
which Schopenhauer speaks so certainly as about the effect of aesthetic
contemplation: he says of it that it counteracts precisely *sexual* "interest-
edness," much like lupulin and camphor, that is; he never grew tired of
glorifying *this* breaking free from the "will" as the greatest merit and use   15
of the aesthetic condition. Indeed, one might be tempted to ask whether
his basic conception of "will and representation," the thought that there
can be a redemption from the "will" only through "representation," did
not originate from a generalization of that sexual experience. (In all questions relating to Schopenhauerian philosophy, by the way, one must never   20
ignore the fact that it is the conception of a twenty-six-year-old young
man; so that it participates not only in that which is specific to Schopenhauer but also in that which is specific to that season of life.) Let us hear,
for example, one of the most explicit of the countless passages he wrote in
honor of the aesthetic condition (World as Will and Representation I,   25
231), let us hear the tone, the suffering, the happiness, the gratitude with
which such words were spoken. "This is the painless condition that Epicurus praised as the highest good and as the condition of the gods; we are,
for that moment, freed from the base drive of the will, we celebrate the
Sabbath of the prison-house work of willing, the wheel of Ixion stands   30
still" ... What vehemence of words! What images of torture and of pro-
longed satiety! What an almost pathological temporal juxtaposition of
"that moment" and the usual "wheel of Ixion," the "prison-house work of
willing," the "base drive of the will"! But supposing that Schopenhauer
were right a hundred times over for himself, what would this have con-   35
tributed to our insight into the essence of the beautiful? Schopenhauer
described *one* effect of the beautiful, the will-calming one—is it even a
regularly occurring one? Stendhal, as noted, a no less sensual but more
happily-formed nature than Schopenhauer, emphasizes a different effect
of the beautiful: "the beautiful *promises* happiness"—to him it is precisely   40

the *excitement of the will* ("of interest") by the beautiful that seems to be
the fact of the matter. And could one not finally urge upon Schopenhauer
himself the objection that he was very wrong in thinking himself a Kantian in this, that he did not at all understand the Kantian definition of the
5   beautiful in a Kantian sense—that the beautiful is pleasing to him, too,
out of an "interest," even out of the strongest of all, the most personal of
all interests: that of the tortured one who breaks free from his torture? ...
And, to come back to our first question, "what does it *mean* when a philosopher pays homage to the ascetic ideal?," we get at least a first hint
10 here: he wants *to break free from a torture.*—

7

Let us take care not to make gloomy faces right away at the word "torture": in this case in particular there is still plenty to count on the other
side of the ledger, plenty to deduct—there is even still something to laugh
at. For let us not underestimate the fact that Schopenhauer, who in fact
15 treated sexuality as a personal enemy (including its tool, woman, this
"instrumentum diaboli"), *needed* enemies in order to remain in good spirits;
that he loved grim bilious black-green words; that he became angry for the
sake of being angry, out of passion; that he would have become sick, would
have become a *pessimist* (—for he was not one, as much as he wished it)
20 without his enemies, without Hegel, woman, sensuality, and the entire
will to being-here, remaining-here. Schopenhauer would otherwise *not*
have remained here, one can bet on that, he would have run away: his enemies, however, held him fast, his enemies seduced him again and again
into existence, just as with the ancient Cynics, his anger was his balm, his
25 recreation, his compensation, his *remedium* against disgust, his *happiness.*
So much with respect to what is most personal in Schopenhauer's case; on
the other hand there is also something typical in him—and only here do
we again come to our problem. It is indisputable that for as long as there
have been philosophers on earth and wherever there have been philoso-
30 phers (from India to England, to take the polar opposites in talent for philosophy) there has existed a characteristic philosophers' irritability and
rancor against sensuality—Schopenhauer is only its most eloquent and, if
one has the ear for it, also most rousing and most enchanting outburst;—
there has likewise existed a characteristic philosophers' prepossession and

"instrumentum" diaboli] instrument of the devil.
remedium] medicine.

cordiality regarding the whole ascetic ideal; one ought not to entertain any illusions about or against this. Both belong, as noted, to the type; if both are absent in a philosopher then he is always—of this one may be certain—only a "so-called" philosopher. What does that *mean?* For one must first interpret this set of facts: in itself it stands there, stupid to all eternity, like every "thing in itself." Every animal, thus also *la bête philosophe*, instinctively strives for an optimum of favorable conditions under which it can vent its power completely and attain its maximum in the feeling of power; just as instinctively, and with a keenness of scent that "surpasses all understanding," every animal abhors troublemakers and obstacles of every kind that do or could lay themselves across its path to the optimum (—it is *not* its path to "happiness" of which I speak, but rather its path to power, to the deed, to the most powerful doing, and in most cases in actual fact its path to unhappiness). In this manner the philosopher abhors *marriage* together with that which might persuade him to it—marriage as obstacle and doom along his path to the optimum. What great philosopher thus far has been married? Heraclitus, Plato, Descartes, Spinoza, Leibniz, Kant, Schopenhauer—they were not; still more, one cannot even *imagine* them being married. A married philosopher belongs *in comedy*, that is my proposition: and that exception Socrates, the malicious Socrates, it seems, married *ironice*, expressly to demonstrate *this* very proposition. Every philosopher would speak as Buddha once spoke when the birth of a son was announced to him: "Râhula has been born to me, a fetter has been forged for me" (here Râhula means "a small daemon"); to every "free spirit" a thoughtful hour must come, supposing he has previously had a thoughtless one, such as once came to the same Buddha—"narrowly constrained, he thought to himself, is life in the house, a place of impurity; freedom is in leaving the house": "as he was thinking thus, he left the house." The ascetic ideal points out so many bridges to *independence* that a philosopher cannot, without inner jubilation and clapping of hands, hear the story of all those determined ones who one day said "no" to all unfreedom and went into some sort of *desert*—even supposing that they were merely strong asses and completely and utterly the opposite of a strong spirit. What, accordingly, does the ascetic ideal mean for a philosopher? My answer is—one will have guessed it long ago: at its sight the philosopher smiles at an optimum of the conditions for highest and boldest spirituality—in this he does *not* negate "existence," rather he affirms *his* existence and *only* his existence, and this perhaps to the degree that the

la bête philosophe] the philosophical animal.

wanton wish is never far away: *pereat mundus, fiat philosophia, fiat philoso-phus, fiam!* ...

8

One can see these are no unbribed witnesses and judges of the *value* of the ascetic ideal, these philosophers! They are thinking of *themselves*—
5   what is "the saint" to them! They are thinking all the while of what is most indispensable precisely *to them*: freedom from compulsion, distur-bance, noise, from business, duties, cares; clarity in the head; dance, leap, and flight of ideas; good air, thin, clear, free, dry, as the air in high places is, in which all animal being becomes more spiritual and acquires wings;
10   quiet in all souterrains; all dogs neatly put on a chain; no barking of hos-tility and shaggy rancor; no gnawing worms of injured ambition; unde-manding and submissive intestines, diligent as mill-works but distant; the heart in a foreign place, in the beyond, in the future, posthumous—at the mention of the ascetic ideal they think, all in all, of the lighthearted ascet-
15   icism of an animal that has been deified and become fully fledged, that roams more than rests above life. One knows the three great pomp words of the ascetic ideal: poverty, humility, chastity: and now just look at the lives of all great fruitful inventive spirits close up—one will always find all three to a certain degree. Certainly *not*, as goes without saying, as if
20   these were their "virtues"—what does this kind of human being have to do with virtues!—but rather as the truest and most natural conditions of their *best* existence, of their *most beautiful* fruitfulness. At the same time it is entirely possible that for the present their dominant spirituality had to put reins on an unbridled and irritable pride or a willful sensuality or that
25   it perhaps had a difficult enough time keeping up its will to the "desert" against an inclination to luxury and to the most exquisite things, likewise against a wasteful liberality of heart and hand. But it did it, precisely as the *dominant* instinct that forced through all its demands against those of all other instincts—it is still doing so; if it didn't do so, it would not dom-
30   inate. In this, then, there is nothing of "virtue." Incidentally, the *desert* of which I just spoke, into which the strong, independent-natured spirits retreat and grow lonely—oh how different it looks from the desert as the learned dream it!—for in some cases they themselves are this desert, these learned ones. And it is certain that no actor of the spirit would be at

pereat mundus ... philosophus, fiam!] let the world perish, let there be philosophy, let there be the philosopher, *let there be me!*

all able to endure living in it—for them it is not nearly romantic and Syr-
ian enough, not nearly enough of a stage desert! Admittedly there is also
no lack of camels in it: but here the entire similarity ends. A voluntary
obscurity perhaps; a steering-clear of oneself; an aversion to noise, veneration, newspaper, influence; a modest position, a daily routine, something   5
that conceals more so than it brings to light; an occasional association
with harmless lighthearted beasts and fowl, the sight of which refreshes; a
mountain range for company, but not a dead one, rather one with *eyes*
(that is with lakes); perhaps even a room in a crowded run-of-the-mill
inn, where one is sure of being mistaken for someone else and can speak   10
to anyone with impunity—that is "desert" here: oh it is lonely enough,
believe me! When Heraclitus retreated into the courtyards and colon-
nades of the enormous temple of Artemis, this "desert" was more digni-
fied, I concede: why are we *lacking* such temples? (—perhaps we are not
lacking them: I was just thinking of my most beautiful study, of the Piazza   15
di San Marco, assuming it is spring, likewise forenoon, the time between
10 and 12.) That which Heraclitus was evading, however, is still the same
thing *we* steer clear of: the noise and the democratic chatter of the Ephesians, their politics, their news from the "empire" (Persia, you understand me), their market stuff of "today"—for we philosophers need rest   20
from *one* thing before all else: from all "today." We venerate what is silent,
cold, noble, distant, past, in general every kind of thing at whose sight the
soul does not have to defend itself and lace itself shut—something with
which one can talk without talking *out loud*. Just listen to the sound a
spirit has when he talks: every spirit has its sound, loves its sound. This   25
one over there, for example, must be an agitator, that is to say a hollow
head, hollow pot: whatever it is that goes into him, each thing comes back
out dull and thick, weighed down with the echo of great emptiness. That
one there seldom speaks other than hoarsely: did he perhaps *think* himself hoarse? That would be possible—ask the physiologists—but whoever   30
thinks in *words* thinks as a speaker and not as a thinker (it betrays the fact
that he basically does not think facts, not factually, but rather only with
respect to facts, that he really thinks *himself* and his listeners). This third
one talks obtrusively, he steps too close to us, his breath brushes us—we
close our mouths involuntarily although it is a book through which he   35
speaks to us: the sound of his style tells us the reason—that he has no
time, that he has little faith in himself, that he will never again get a word
in if not today. A spirit who is sure of itself, however, speaks softly; it
seeks seclusion, it makes others wait. One can recognize a philosopher by
the fact that he keeps clear of three bright and loud things: fame, princes,   40

and women—which is not to say they don't come to him. He shies away
from all-too-bright light: therefore he shies away from his time and its
"day." In this he is like a shadow: the more the sun sets for him the
greater he becomes. As for his "humility," he can also bear, as he bears the
5   dark, a certain dependence and obscurity: still more, he fears being disturbed by lightning, he shrinks back from the unprotectedness of an all-
too-isolated and exposed tree on which every bad weather vents its
moods, every mood its bad weather. His "motherly" instinct, the secret
love of that which grows in him directs him to situations where one
10   relieves him of thinking of *himself,* in the same sense in which the instinct
of the *mother* in woman has until now preserved the dependent situation
of woman generally. In the end they demand little enough, these philosophers; their motto is "whoever possesses, will be possessed"—: *not,* as I
must say again and again, out of a virtue, out of a meritorious will to con-
15   tentedness and simplicity, but rather because their supreme lord demands
it *thus* of them, demands prudently and relentlessly: he has a mind for
only one thing and gathers everything—time, energy, love, interest—
only for this, saves it only for this. This kind of human does not like to be
disturbed by enmities, also not by friendships: he forgets or holds in con-
20   tempt easily. He thinks it in bad taste to play the martyr; "to *suffer* for the
truth"—he leaves that to the ambitious and to the stage heroes of the
spirit and whoever else has time enough for it (—the philosophers themselves, they have something to *do* for the truth). They use great words
sparingly; it is said that they even find the word "truth" repellent: it
25   sounds pompous ... Finally, as for the "chastity" of philosophers, this
kind of spirit obviously has its fruitfulness somewhere other than in children; perhaps elsewhere also the continued existence of their name, their
little immortality (among philosophers in ancient India one expressed
oneself still more immodestly: "to what end progeny for one whose soul is
30   the world?"). In this there is nothing of chastity out of any ascetic scruple
and hatred of the senses, just as little as it is chastity when an athlete or
jockey abstains from women: rather it is their dominant instinct that
wants it this way, at least during times of great pregnancy. Every artist
knows how harmful the effect of intercourse is in conditions of great spir-
35   itual tension and preparation; the most powerful and sure-of-instinct
among them do not first require experience, negative experience—rather
it is their "motherly" instinct here that ruthlessly commands all other
stores and allowances of energy, of animal vigor, for the benefit of the
growing work: the greater energy then *consumes* the lesser one.—Inciden-
40   tally, piece together the above discussed case of Schopenhauer according

to this interpretation: in him the sight of the beautiful apparently acted as a triggering stimulus on the *principal force* of his nature (the force of contemplation and of the engrossed gaze); so that this then exploded and became all at once lord of his consciousness. This is in no way meant to preclude the possibility that the peculiar sweetness and fullness characteristic of the aesthetic condition might have its origins precisely in the ingredient "sensuality" (just as that "idealism" characteristic of marriageable girls stems from the same source)—that sensuality is thus not suspended at the onset of the aesthetic condition, as Schopenhauer believed, but rather only transfigures itself and no longer enters consciousness as sexual stimulus. (I will return to this viewpoint at another time in connection with still more delicate problems of the thus far so untouched, so unexplored *physiology of aesthetics*.)

9

A certain asceticism—we have seen it—a hard and lighthearted renunciation with the best of intentions, belongs to the most favorable conditions of highest spirituality, likewise also to its most natural consequences: from the outset, then, it will not astonish us if the ascetic ideal has always been treated with considerable prepossession precisely by philosophers. A serious historical reckoning proves the tie between ascetic ideal and philosophy to be even closer and stricter still. One could say that it was only on the apron strings of this ideal that philosophy ever learned to take its first steps and half-steps on earth—alas, ever so clumsily, alas, with ever so discouraged faces, alas, so ready to fall down and lie on its belly, this shy little blunderer and milquetoast with crooked legs! In the beginning philosophy fared as have all good things,—for a long time they hadn't the courage to themselves, they were always looking around to see if there weren't someone who would come to their help, still more, they were afraid of everyone who watched them. Just list the individual drives and virtues of the philosopher one after the other—his doubting drive, his negating drive, his wait-and-see ("ephectic") drive, his analytical drive, his exploring, searching, venturing drive, his comparing, balancing drive, his will to neutrality and objectivity, his will to every *"sine ira et studio"*—: have we already grasped that for the longest time they all went against the first demands of morality and of conscience? (not to mention *reason* itself, which, even in his late day, Luther loved to call

---

sine ira et studio] *without* anger and partiality. Tacitus, *Annales* I, 1.

Fraw Klüglin the shrewd whore). That a philosopher, if he _were_ to come
to a consciousness of himself, would have had to feel himself to be none
other than the _"nitimur in vetitum"_ incarnate—and accordingly was on
guard against "feeling himself," against coming to a consciousness of
5   himself? ... Things are, as stated, no different with all good things of
which we are proud today; even measured by the standard of the ancient
Greeks our entire modern being, insofar as it is not weakness but rather
power and consciousness of power, appears as nothing but hubris and
godlessness: for the longest time those very things that are the reverse of
10   what we venerate today had conscience on their side and God as their
watchman. Hubris is our entire stance toward nature today, our violation
of nature with the help of machines and the so thoughtless inventiveness
of technicians and engineers; hubris is our stance toward God, that is to
say toward some alleged spider of purpose and morality behind the great
15   snare-web of causality—we could say with Charles the Bold in battle
with Louis XI _"je combats l'universelle araignée"_—; hubris is our stance
toward _ourselves_—for we experiment with ourselves as we would not permit ourselves to do with any animal and merrily and curiously slit open
our souls while the body is still living: what do we care anymore about the
20   "salvation" of the soul! Afterwards we heal ourselves: being sick is
instructive, we have no doubt, even more instructive than being
healthy—today the _ones who make sick_ appear to us to be even more necessary than any medicine men and "saviors." We do violence to ourselves
now, there is no doubt, we nutcrackers of souls, we questioners and ques-
25   tionable ones, as if life were nothing but nutcracking; precisely in so
doing we must of necessity become, with each passing day, ever more
questionable, _worthier_ of questioning, perhaps also worthier—of living?
... All good things were once bad things; every original sin has become an
original virtue. Marriage, for example, seemed for a long time to be a sin
30   against the rights of the community; one once paid a penalty for having
been so immodest and having arrogated a wife for oneself alone (the _jus
primae noctis_ belongs here, for example—even today still the privilege of
the priests in Cambodia, these guardians of "old good customs"). For the
longest time meek, benevolent, yielding, compassionate feelings—by

Fraw Klüglin] Early New High German: "Lady Shrewd."
"nitimur in vetitum"] we strive for _what is forbidden_. Ovid, _Amores_, III, 4, 17.
"je combats l'universelle araignée"] I combat the universal spider.
jus primae noctis] right of the first night—alleged right of the feudal lord to have
sexual intercourse with his vassal's bride on the wedding night.

now so high in value that they are almost "the values in themselves"—
had precisely self-contempt against them: one was ashamed of leniency
as one is today ashamed of harshness (cf. *Beyond Good and Evil* section
260). Submission to the *law*:—oh with what resistance of conscience the
noble dynasties everywhere on earth renounced vendettas and granted   5
the law power over themselves! For a long time the "law" was a *vetitum*, a
wanton act, an innovation; it appeared with force, *as* force, to which one
could not yield without feeling ashamed of oneself. In former times every
smallest step on earth was won through spiritual and bodily torments:
this entire viewpoint "that not only marching forward, no! marching,   10
movement, change had need of their countless martyrs" sounds so for-
eign precisely today—I first brought this to light in *Daybreak* 18. "Nothing has been more dearly bought," it says there, "than that little bit of
human reason and feeling of freedom that now makes up our pride.
Because of this pride, however, it is now becoming almost impossible for   15
us to empathize with those enormous stretches of time characterized by
the 'morality of custom,' which lie before 'world history' as the real and
decisive principal history that established the character of humankind:
when suffering counted everywhere as virtue, cruelty as virtue, dissimu-
lation as virtue, revenge as virtue, denial of reason as virtue; on the other   20
hand well-being as danger, desire for knowledge as danger, peace as danger, compassion as danger, being pitied as disgrace, work as disgrace,
madness as divinity, *change* as the essence of what is immoral and pregnant with ruin!"—

10

In the same book, section 42, is set forth within what valuation, under   25
what *pressure* of valuation the earliest race of contemplative humans had
to live,—held in contempt to the same degree they were not feared! Contemplation first appeared on earth in disguised form, with an ambiguous
appearance, with an evil heart and often with a frightened head: of this
there is no doubt. The inactive, brooding, unwarriorlike elements in the   30
instincts of contemplative human beings laid a deep mistrust around
them for a long time: against this there was no other remedy than deci-
sively to awaken *fear* of themselves. And in this the ancient Brahmins, for
example, were experts! The earliest philosophers knew how to give their
existence and appearance a meaning, a support and background against   35

vetitum] something forbidden.

which one learned to *fear* them: more precisely considered, out of an even
more fundamental need, namely to win fear and reverence from themselves. For within themselves they found all value judgments turned
against them, they had to fight down every kind of suspicion and resis-
5   tance against "the philosopher in them." This they did, as human beings
of terrible ages, with terrible means: cruelty against themselves, inventive
self-castigation—that was the principal means of these power-thirsty her-
mits and innovators of ideas who first needed to lay waste to the gods and
10 tradition within themselves in order even to be able to *believe* in their
innovation. I call attention to the famous story of king Vishvamitra, who
from a thousand years of self-torments won such a feeling of power and
self-confidence that he undertook to build a *new heaven*: an uncanny symbol of the earliest and latest histories of philosophers on earth—anyone
15 who ever built a "new heaven" first found the power to do so in his *own
hell* ... Let us compress the whole state of affairs into brief formulas: at
first the philosophical spirit always had to slip into the disguise and
chrysalis of the *previously established* types of contemplative human
beings—as priest, magician, soothsayer, as religious human generally—in
20 order even to *be possible* in any degree at all: for a long time *the ascetic ideal*
served the philosopher as the form in which he could appear, as presupposition of existence—he had to *act* it in order to be able to be a philosopher, he had to *believe* it in order to be able to act it. The characteristic
aloof stance of philosophers, world-negating, hostile toward life, not
25 believing in the senses, de-sensualized, a stance which has been preserved
up to the most recent time and has thus won acceptance as the virtual
philosopher's pose in itself,—it is above all a consequence of the poverty of
conditions under which philosophy came about and survived at all: for
the longest time philosophy would *not* have been *at all possible* on earth
30 without an ascetic covering and mantle, without an ascetic self-misunder-
standing. Graphically and clearly expressed: until the most recent time
the *ascetic priest* has functioned as the repulsive and gloomy caterpillar-
form in which alone philosophy was allowed to live and in which it crept
around ... Has this really *changed*? Has the colorful and dangerous
35 winged animal, the "spirit" that this caterpillar concealed within itself,
really—thanks to a sunnier, warmer, more brightly lit world—finally
been unfrocked after all and let out into the light? Is there already enough
pride, daring, bravery, self-assuredness in existence today, enough will of
the spirit, will to responsibility, *freedom of the will* so that henceforth on
40 earth "the philosopher" is truly—*possible*? ...

11

Only now that we have gotten the *ascetic priest* in sight do we seriously begin to tackle our problem: what does the ascetic ideal mean?—only now does it become "serious": henceforth we have opposite us the true *representative of seriousness* itself. "What does all seriousness mean?"—perhaps already here this still more fundamental question comes to our lips: a question for physiologists, as is fair, but one we will still slip past for the present. The ascetic priest has not only his faith in that ideal but also his will, his power, his interest. His *right* to existence stands and falls with that ideal: no wonder we run into a terrible opponent here—supposing, that is, that we were the opponents of that ideal?—one who fights for his existence against the deniers of that ideal? ... On the other hand it is from the outset improbable that so interested a stance toward our problem will be of particular use to it; the ascetic priest will hardly even be the most successful defender of his ideal—for the same reason that a woman tends to fail when she wishes to defend "woman in herself"—much less the most objective assessor and judge in the controversy that has been stirred up here. It is hence more likely that we will yet have to help him defend himself effectively against us—this much is already clear as day—than that we should have to fear being too effectively refuted by him ... The idea we are fighting about here is the *valuation* of our life on the part of the ascetic priest: he relates our life (together with that to which it belongs: "nature," "world," the entire sphere of becoming and of transitoriness) to an entirely different kind of existence, which it opposes and excludes, *unless*, perhaps, it were to turn against itself, *to negate itself*: in this case, the case of an ascetic life, life is held to be a bridge for that other existence. The ascetic treats life as a wrong path that one must finally retrace back to the point where it begins; or as an error that one refutes through deeds—*should* refute: for he *demands* that one go along with him; where he can, he forces *his* valuation of existence. What does that mean? Such a monstrous manner of valuation is not inscribed into the history of humankind as an exception and curiosity: it is one of the broadest and longest facts there is. Read from a distant star the majuscule script of our earthly existence would perhaps tempt one to conclude that the earth is the true *ascetic star*, a nook of discontented, arrogant, and repulsive creatures who could not get rid of a deep displeasure with themselves, with the earth, with all life and who caused themselves as much pain as possible out of pleasure in causing pain:—probably their only pleasure. Let us consider after all how regularly, how universally, how in almost all ages the

ascetic priest emerges; he does not belong to any single race; he flourishes
everywhere; he grows forth from every social rank. Not that he breeds
and propagates his manner of valuation through heredity: the opposite is
the case—a deep instinct forbids him, broadly speaking, reproduction. It
must be a necessity of the first rank that makes this species that is *hostile to
life* grow and prosper again and again—it must be in the *interest of life
itself* that this type of self-contradiction not die out. For an ascetic life is a
self-contradiction: here a *ressentiment* without equal rules, that of an unsatiated instinct and power-will that would like to become lord not over
something living but rather over life itself, over its deepest, strongest,
most fundamental preconditions; an attempt is made here to use energy
to stop up the source of the energy; here the gaze is directed greenly and
maliciously against physiological flourishing itself, in particular against its
expression, beauty, joy; whereas pleasure is felt and *sought* in deforma-
tion, atrophy, in pain, in accident, in the ugly, in voluntary forfeit, in un-
selfing, self-flagellation, self-sacrifice. This is all paradoxical in the highest degree: we stand here before a conflict that *wants* itself to be conflicted, that *enjoys* itself in this suffering and even becomes ever more self-
assured and triumphant to the extent that its own presupposition, physiological viability, *decreases.* "Triumph precisely in the final agony": under
this hyperbolic sign the ascetic ideal has fought from time immemorial; in
this enigma of seduction, in this image of delight and torment it recognized its brightest light, its salvation, its ultimate victory. *Crux, nux,
lux*—in the ascetic ideal they all belong together.—

12

Supposing that such an incarnate will to contradiction and anti-nature
is prevailed upon to *philosophize*: on what will he vent his innermost capri-
cious will? On what is most certainly felt to be true, real: he will seek *error*
precisely where the true life instinct most unconditionally posits truth.
For example, he will—as the ascetics of the Vedânta philosophy did—
demote physicality to an illusion, likewise pain, multiplicity, the whole
conceptual opposition "subject" and "object"—errors, nothing but
errors! To refuse to believe in the self, to deny one's own "reality"—what a
triumph!—already no longer merely over the senses, over appearance, but
a much higher kind of triumph, a violence and cruelty to *reason*: this lust
reaches its peak when the ascetic self-contempt, self-derision of reason

Crux, nux, lux] Cross, nut, light.

decrees: "there *is* a realm of truth and being, but precisely reason is *excluded* from it!" ... (Incidentally: even in the Kantian concept of the "intelligible character of things" there remains something of this lascivious ascetic conflict, which loves to turn reason against reason: for in Kant "intelligible character" means a kind of constitution of things, of which the intellect comprehends just this much: that for the intellect it is—*completely and utterly incomprehensible.*)—Finally let us, particularly as knowers, not be ungrateful toward such resolute reversals of the familiar perspectives and valuations with which the spirit has raged against itself all too long now, apparently wantonly and futilely: to see differently in this way for once, *to want* to see differently, is no small discipline and preparation of the intellect for its future "objectivity"—the latter understood not as "disinterested contemplation" (which is a non-concept and absurdity), but rather as the capacity to have one's pro and contra *in one's power*, and to shift them in and out: so that one knows how to make precisely the *difference* in perspectives and affective interpretations useful for knowledge. For let us guard ourselves better from now on, gentlemen philosophers, against the dangerous old conceptual fabrication that posited a "pure, will-less, painless, timeless subject of knowledge"; let us guard ourselves against the tentacles of such contradictory concepts as "pure reason," "absolute spirituality," "knowledge in itself": here it is always demanded that we think an eye that cannot possibly be thought, an eye that must not have any direction, in which the active and interpretive forces through which seeing first becomes seeing-something are to be shut off, are to be absent; thus, what is demanded here is always an absurdity and non-concept of an eye. There is *only* a perspectival seeing, *only* a perspectival "knowing"; and *the more* affects we allow to speak about a matter, *the more* eyes, different eyes, we know how to bring to bear on one and the same matter, that much more complete will our "concept" of this matter, our "objectivity" be. But to eliminate the will altogether, to disconnect the affects one and all, supposing that we were capable of this: what? would that not be to *castrate* the intellect? ...

13

But let us return to our problem. In an accounting that is physiological and no longer psychological, a contradiction such as the ascetic seems to represent, "life *against* life," is—this much is immediately clear as day— simply nonsense. It can only be *apparent*; it must be a kind of provisional expression, an interpretation, formula, arrangement, a psychological

misunderstanding of something whose actual nature could not be understood for a long time, could not be designated *in itself*—a mere word,
jammed into an old *gap* in human knowledge. And to oppose this with a
brief statement of the facts of the matter: *the ascetic ideal springs from the*
protective and healing instincts of a degenerating life that seeks with every
means to hold its ground and is fighting for its existence; it points to a
partial physiological hindrance and tiredness against which the deepest
instincts of life, which have remained intact, fight incessantly with new
means and inventions. The ascetic ideal is such a means: it is exactly the
opposite of what its venerators suppose—in it and through it life is wres-
tling with death and *against* death; the ascetic ideal is an artifice for the
preservation of life. That this ideal has been able to rule and achieve power
over humans to the extent that history teaches us it has, in particular
wherever the civilization and taming of man has been successfully carried
out, expresses a great fact: the *diseasedness* of the previous type of human,
at least of the human made tame, the physiological struggle of man with
death (more precisely: with satiety with life, with tiredness, with the wish
for the "end"). The ascetic priest is the incarnate wish for a different
existence, an existence somewhere else, and in fact the highest degree of
this wish, its true fervor and passion: but the very *power* of his wishing is
the shackle that binds him here; in this very process he becomes a tool
that must work at creating more favorable conditions for being-here and
being-human—with this very *power* he ties to existence the entire herd of
the deformed, out of sorts, short-changed, failed, those of every kind who
suffer from themselves, by instinctively going before them as shepherd.
One understands me already: this ascetic priest, this seeming enemy of
life, this *negating one*—precisely he belongs to the very great *conserving*
and yes-*creating* forces of life ... Whence it stems, this diseasedness? For
man is sicker, more unsure, more changing, more undetermined than any
other animal, of this there is no doubt—he is *the* sick animal: how does
this come about? Certainly he has also dared more, innovated more,
defied more, challenged fate more than all the other animals taken
together: he, the great experimenter with himself, the unsatisfied, unsatiated one who wrestles with animal, nature, and gods for final dominion—
he, the one yet unconquered, the eternally future one who no longer finds
any rest from his own pressing energy, so that his future digs inexorably
like a spur into the flesh of every present:—how could such a courageous
and rich animal not also be the most endangered, the most prolongedly
and most deeply sick among all sick animals? ... Man is fed up with it,
often enough, there are entire epidemics of this being-fed-up (—around

1348, at the time of the Dance of Death): but even this loathing, this tiredness, this vexation with himself—everything emerges so powerfully in him that it immediately becomes a new shackle. As if by magic, the "no" that he says to life brings to light an abundance of tender "yes's"; even when he *wounds* himself, this master of destruction, self-destruc- 5 tion—afterwards it is the wound itself that compels him *to live* ...

14

The more normal the diseasedness in man is—and we cannot deny this normality—the higher one should honor the rare cases of powerfulness in soul and body, the *strokes of luck* among humans; the more strictly one should guard the well-formed against the worst air, against the air of the 10 sick. Do we do this? ... The sick are the greatest danger to the healthy; it is *not* from the strongest that harm comes to the strong, but rather from the weakest. Do we know this? ... Broadly speaking, it is by no means the fear of man one might wish lessened: for this fear compels the strong to be strong, in some cases to be terrible—it keeps the well-formed type of 15 human *upright*. What is to be feared, what has a doomful effect such as no other doom, would not be the great fear but rather the great *disgust* at man; likewise the great *compassion* for man. Supposing that these two should mate one day, then immediately something of the most uncanny nature would unavoidably come into the world, the "last will" of man, his 20 will to nothingness, nihilism. And indeed: much is prepared for this. Whoever has not only a nose for smelling but also eyes and ears will sense something like madhouse air, like hospital air almost everywhere he might go today—I am speaking, in fairness, of the man's cultural regions, of every kind of "Europe" there is on earth by now. The *diseased* are man's 25 great danger: *not* the evil, *not* the "beasts of prey." Those who from the outset are failed, downcast, broken—they are the ones, the *weakest* are the ones who most undermine life among humans, who most dangerously poison and call into question our confidence in life, in man, in ourselves. Where might one escape it, that veiled look from which one carries away a 30 deep sadness, that backward-turned look of one deformed from the begin- ning, a look that betrays how such a human speaks to himself—that look that is a sigh. "If only I might be someone else!" thus sighs this look: but there is no hope. "I am who I am: how could I get free from myself. And yet—*I am fed up with myself*!" ... On such ground of self-contempt, a true 35 swamp-ground, every weed grows, every poisonous plant, and all of it so small, so hidden, so dishonest, so cloying. Here the worms of vengeful and

grudging feelings teem; here the air stinks of things that are secret and
cannot be acknowledged; here the web of the most vicious conspiracy
spins itself constantly—the conspiracy of the sufferers against the well-
formed and victorious; here the appearance of the victorious one is *hated*.
5 And what mendacity not to acknowledge this hate as hate! What expenditure of great words and poses, what art of "righteous" defamation! These
deformed ones: what noble eloquence streams forth from their lips! How
much sugary, slimy, humble submission swims in their eyes! What do they
actually want? At least to *represent* justice, love, wisdom, superiority—that
10 is the ambition of these "undermost ones," of these sick ones! And how
skillful such an ambition makes one! One should particularly admire the
counterfeiter's skill with which the stamp of virtue, even the cling-clang,
the golden tone of virtue, is copied. They have now taken virtue in lease
completely and utterly for themselves, these weak and incurably diseased
15 ones, of this there is no doubt: "we alone are the good, the just," so they
speak, "we alone are the *homines bonae voluntatis*." They walk about
among us as bodily reproaches, as warnings to us—as if health, being
well-formed, strength, pride, a feeling of power were depraved things in
themselves, for which one will someday have to atone, bitterly atone: oh
20 how ready they themselves basically are to *make* others atone, how they
thirst to be *hangmen*! Among them there are plenty of vengeful ones disguised as judges, who constantly carry the word "justice" in their mouths
like poisonous saliva, forever with pursed lips, forever ready to spit on
everything that does not look dissatisfied and that goes its way in good
25 spirits. Among them there is no lack of that most disgusting species of the
vain—the mendacious misbirths who are out to play the role of "beautiful
souls" and who for instance bring their mangled sensuality, wrapped in
verses and other diapers, onto the market as "purity of heart": the species
of the moral onanist and "self-gratifier." The will of the sick to represent
30 *any* form of superiority, their instinct for secret paths that lead to a tyranny over the healthy—where might this not be found, this will of precisely the weakest to power! The sick woman in particular: no one excels
her in refinements for ruling, oppressing, tyrannizing. Furthermore the
sick woman does not spare anything living, anything dead; she digs the
35 most buried of things up again (the Bogos say: "woman is a hyena"). Look
into the background of every family, every corporation, every community:
everywhere the battle of the sick against the healthy—a silent battle for the
most part with little poisonous powders, with needle pricks, with insidi-

homines bonae voluntatis] men of good will. Luke 2: 14.

ous plays of martyr expressions, at times, however, even with the *loud* gestures of an invalid's pharisaism, which loves most of all to play "noble indignation." It would like to make itself heard all the way into the hallowed halls of science, this hoarse indignant bark of the diseased dogs, the biting mendacity and rage of such "noble" Pharisees (—once again I remind readers who have ears of that Berliner apostle of revenge, Eugen Dühring, who is making the most indecent and repulsive use of moral boom-boom in present-day Germany: Dühring, the foremost moral bigmouth there now is, even among his own kind, the anti-Semites). They are all human beings of *ressentiment*, these physiologically failed and worm-eaten ones, a whole trembling earth of subterranean revenge, inexhaustible, insatiable in outbursts against the happy, and likewise in masquerades of revenge, in pretexts for revenge: when would they actually arrive at their last, finest, most sublime triumph of revenge? Undoubtedly, if they should succeed in *shoving* their own misery, all misery generally *into the conscience* of the happy: so that the happy would one day begin to be ashamed of their happiness and perhaps say among themselves: "it is a disgrace to be happy! *there is too much misery!*" ... But there could not be any greater and more doomful misunderstanding than when the happy, the well-formed, the powerful of body and soul begin to doubt their *right to happiness*. Away with this "inverted world"! Away with this disgraceful softening of the feelings! That the sick *not* make the healthy sick—and this would be such a softening—that should certainly be the highest viewpoint on earth:—but this would require above all else that the healthy remain *separated* from the sick, guarded even against the sight of the sick, that they not confuse themselves with the sick. Or would it perhaps be their task to be nurses or physicians? ... But they could in no way more gravely mistake and deny *their* task—the higher *must* not degrade itself to a tool of the lower, the pathos of distance *must* also keep their tasks separated to all eternity! Their right to exist, the privilege of the bell with full sound over the dissonant, cracked one is of course a thousandfold greater one: they alone are the *guarantors* of the future, they alone have been *given responsibility* for the human future. What *they* can do, what *they* should do, a sick person can never and should never do: but *in order for* them to be able to do what only *they* should do, how could they be free to choose to be physician, comforter, "savior" for the sick? ... And therefore good air! good air! And in any case away from the proximity of all madhouses and hospitals of culture! And therefore good company, *our* company! Or solitude if it must be! But in any case away from the foul vapors of inward corruption and the secret wormfodder of invalids! ... So that we may defend ourselves, my friends, at least for a while yet, against what may be the two gravest epidemics that have been reserved just for us—against the *great disgust at the sight of man*! against the *great compassion for man*! ...

15

     If one has grasped in all its depth—and I demand that precisely here
5   one *reach* deeply, grasp deeply—why it positively can *not* be the task of
the healthy to nurse the sick, to make the sick well, then a further necessity has also been grasped—the necessity of physicians and nurses *who are themselves sick*: and now we have and hold with both hands the meaning of the ascetic priest. The ascetic priest must be counted as the foreordained
10 savior, shepherd, and advocate of the sick herd: only then do we understand his historic mission. *Dominion over ones who suffer* is his realm, it is to this that his instinct directs him, in this he has his most characteristic art, his mastery, his kind of happiness. He must be sick himself, he must be related to the sick and short-changed from the ground up in order to
15 understand them—in order to get along with them; but he must also be strong, lord over himself more than over others, with his will to power intact, so that he has the confidence and the fear of the sick, so that for them he can be a foothold, resistance, support, compulsion, disciplinarian, tyrant, god. He is to defend them, his herd—against whom? Against
20 the healthy, no doubt, also against envying the healthy; he must by nature oppose *and hold in contempt* all coarse, tempestuous, unbridled, hard, violent-predatory health and powerfulness. The priest is the first form of the *more delicate* animal that holds in contempt even more readily than it hates. He will not be spared waging war with the beasts of prey, a war of
25 cunning (of the "spirit") more than of force, as goes without saying—to this end he will perhaps need almost to develop in himself, at least *to signify*, a new type of beast of prey—a new animal terribleness in which the polar bear, the lithe cold wait-and-see tiger cat, and not least of all the fox appear to be bound into a unity just as attractive as it is fear-inspiring.
30 Supposing that necessity compels him, he then steps into the very midst of the other kind of beast of prey with bearish seriousness, venerable, cold, shrewd, deceptively superior, as herald and mouthpiece of mysterious forces, determined to sow sorrow, conflict, self-contradiction on this ground wherever he can and, only too sure of his art, to become lord over
35 *sufferers* at all times. He brings along ointments and balm, no doubt; but he first needs to wound in order to be a physician; as he then stills the pain that the wound causes, *he poisons the wound at the same time*—for in this

above all he is an expert, this magician and tamer of beasts of prey, in whose vicinity everything healthy necessarily becomes sick and everything sick, tame. He defends his sick herd well enough indeed, this strange shepherd—he defends it against itself as well, against what smolders within the herd itself: badness, deceitfulness, maliciousness and whatever else is characteristic of all the sick and invalids when among themselves; he fights shrewdly, hard, and secretively against the anarchy and ever-incipient self-dissolution within the herd, where that most dangerous blasting and explosive material, *ressentiment*, is constantly mounting and mounting. To discharge this explosive in such a way that it does not blow up either the herd or the shepherd, that is his true feat, also his supreme usefulness; if one wanted to sum up the value of the priestly mode of existence in the shortest formula one would have to say straight away: the priest *changes the direction* of *ressentiment*. For every sufferer instinctively seeks a cause for his suffering; still more precisely, a perpetrator, still more specifically, a *guilty* perpetrator who is receptive to suffering—in short, some living thing on which, in response to some pretext or other, he can discharge his affects in deed or in effigy: for the discharge of affect is the sufferer's greatest attempt at relief, namely at *anesthetization*—his involuntarily craved narcotic against torment of any kind. It is here alone, according to my surmise, that one finds the true physiological causality of *ressentiment*, of revenge, and of their relatives—that is, in a longing for *anesthetization of pain through affect*:—this causality has been commonly sought, very mistakenly it seems to me, in the defensive counterblow, a mere reactive protective measure, a "reflex movement" in the case of some sudden harm and endangerment, of the kind that a frog without a head still carries out in order to get rid of a corrosive acid. But the difference is fundamental: in the one case, one wishes to prevent further damage; in the other case, one wishes, by means of a more vehement emotion of any kind, to *anesthetize* a tormenting, secret pain that is becoming unbearable and, at least for the moment, to put it out of consciousness—for this one needs an affect, as wild an affect as possible and, for its excitation, the first best pretext. "Someone must be to blame for the fact that I feel bad"—this kind of reasoning is characteristic of all those who are diseased, indeed the more the true cause of their feeling bad, the physiological one, remains concealed from them (—it can lie for instance in a sickening of the *nervus sympathicus* or in an excessive secretion of bile, or in a deficiency of potassium sulfate or phosphate in the

nervus sympathicus] sympathetic nerve (nervous system).

blood or in pressure conditions in the abdomen that stop the circulation of the blood, or in degeneration of the ovaries and the like). Those who suffer are one and all possessed of a horrifying readiness and inventiveness in pretexts for painful affects; they savor even their suspicion, their brooding over bad deeds and apparent curtailments; they dig around after dark questionable stories in the viscera of their past and present, where they are free to wallow in a tormenting suspicion and to intoxicate themselves on their own poison of malice—they tear open the oldest wounds, they bleed to death from scars long healed, they make malefactors out of friend, wife, child and whatever else stands closest to them. "I am suffering: for this someone must be to blame"—thus every diseased sheep thinks. But his shepherd, the ascetic priest, says to him: "That's right, my sheep! someone must be to blame for it: but you yourself are this someone, you alone are to blame for it—*you alone are to blame for yourself!*" ... That is bold enough, false enough: but one thing at least has been achieved by it, in this way, as noted, the direction of the *ressentiment* has been—*changed*.

16

One can guess by now what I think life's healing-artist instinct has at least *attempted* through the ascetic priest and to what end a temporary tyranny of such paradoxical and paralogical concepts as "guilt," "sin," "sinfulness," "corruption," "damnation" has had to serve him: to make the sick to a certain degree *harmless*, to destroy the incurable through themselves, to strictly direct the more mildly sick toward themselves, to give a backwards direction to their *ressentiment* ("one thing is needful") and in this manner to *exploit* the bad instincts of all sufferers for the purpose of self-discipline, self-supervision, self-overcoming. As goes without saying, with a "medication" of this kind, a mere affect-medication, it absolutely cannot be a matter of a true *healing* of the sick in the physiological sense; one could not even claim that the instinct of life in any way has healing in mind or in intention. A kind of crowding together and organizing of the sick, on the one hand (—the word "church" is the most popular name for this), a kind of provisional securing of the more healthily formed, the more fully cast, on the other, thus the tearing open of a chasm between healthy and sick—for a long time that was all! And it was a great deal! it was a *very great deal*! ... [In this treatise I am proceeding, as one can see, on the presupposition, which I do not first have to justify as far as readers of the type I need are concerned: that "sinfulness" in

humans is not a factual state but rather only the interpretation of a factual state, namely of being physiologically out of sorts—the latter seen from a moral-religious perspective that is no longer binding on us.—
That someone *feels* "guilty," "sinful" does not at all prove he is right in feeling so; just as little as someone is healthy merely because he feels healthy. Just recall the famous witch trials: back then the most sharp-sighted and philanthropic judges did not doubt that there was guilt; the "witches" *themselves did not doubt it*—and still there was no guilt.—To express that presupposition in expanded form: "pain of the soul" itself does not at all count as a factual state but rather only as an interpretation (causal interpretation) of factual states that could not yet be exactly formulated: thus something that is still entirely up in the air and is not scientifically binding—actually only a fat word in the place of a very thin question mark. If someone cannot cope with his "pain of the soul" it is *not*, crudely put, due to his "soul"; more likely to his belly (crudely put, as stated: which in no way expresses a wish also to be heard crudely, understood crudely …) A strong and well-formed human digests his experiences (deeds, misdeeds included) as he digests his meals, even when he has hard bites to swallow. If he "cannot cope" with an experience, this kind of indigestion is just as physiological as that other one—and in many cases in fact only one of the consequences of that other.—
With such a conception one can, speaking among ourselves, still be the strictest opponent of all materialism …]

17

But is he actually a *physician*, this ascetic priest?—We have already grasped why it is hardly permissible to call him a physician, as much as he likes to feel himself to be a "savior," to allow himself to be venerated as a "savior." He combats only suffering itself, the listlessness of the one suffering, *not* its cause, *not* the actual state of sickness—this must form our most fundamental objection to priestly medication. If, however, one adopts for once that perspective as only the priest knows and has it, one will not easily come to the end of one's amazement at all he has seen, sought, and found from within it. The *alleviation* of suffering, "comforting" of every kind—this turns out to be his very genius: how inventively he has understood his task as comforter, how unhesitatingly and boldly he has chosen the means for it! One might call Christianity in particular a great treasury of the most ingenious means for comforting, so much that is invigorating, alleviating, narcotizing has been heaped up in it; so much

that is most dangerous and most audacious has been ventured for this
purpose; so subtle, so sophisticated, so Mediterraneanly sophisticated
has Christianity been in intuiting what kind of stimulant-affects can conquer, at least for a time, the deep depression, the leaden tiredness, the
5   black sadness of the physiologically inhibited. For stated generally: with
all great religions the main concern is to combat a certain tiredness and
heaviness that have become epidemic. From the outset one can posit as
probable that from time to time at certain places on earth a *feeling of*
physiological inhibition must almost necessarily become lord over broad
10   masses of people; from a lack of physiological knowledge, however, this
feeling does not enter into consciousness as such, so that its "cause," its
remedy can only be sought and attempted in the psychological-moral
realm (—indeed this is my most general formula for that which is commonly called a "*religion*"). Such a feeling of inhibition can be of the most
15   varied extraction: for instance as consequence of the crossbreeding of
races that are too different from each other (or of social ranks—social
ranks always express differences of extraction and race as well: the European "*Weltschmerz*," the "pessimism" of the nineteenth century is essentially the consequence of a nonsensically sudden mixing of the social
20   ranks); or conditioned by a flawed emigration—a race that has ended up
in a climate for which its power of adaptation is not sufficient (the case of
the Indians in India); or the after-effect of age and exhaustion of the race
(Parisian pessimism from 1850 on); or of a wrong diet (alcoholism of the
Middle Ages; the nonsense of vegetarians, who admittedly have the
25   authority of Sir Andrew in Shakespeare on their side); or of corruption
of the blood, malaria, syphilis, and the like (German depression after the
Thirty-Years' War, which infected half of Germany with bad diseases
and thereby prepared the soil for German servility, German timidity). In
such cases a *battle with the feeling of listlessness* is always attempted on the
30   grandest scale; let us instruct ourselves briefly in its most important
practices and forms. (I ignore here entirely, as is fair, the actual *philoso-*
phers' battle against the feeling of listlessness, which always tends to go
on simultaneously—it is interesting enough, but too absurd, too inconse-
quential in practical terms, too much in the manner of cobweb-spinners
35   and idlers, as, say, when pain is to be proven an error under the naive presupposition that the pain *would have to* disappear once the error in it has
been recognized—but behold! it guarded itself against disappearing ...)

"*Weltschmerz*"] "world-pain," an emotional state in which the predominant tone is
a feeling of pain or sadness because of the inadequacy of the world.

This dominant feeling of listlessness is combatted, *first*, by means that reduce the general feeling of life to its lowest point. If possible no willing at all, not another wish; avoiding whatever stirs up affect, whatever stirs up "blood" (no eating salt: hygiene of the fakir); no loving; no hating; apathy; no avenging oneself; no making oneself rich; no working; beg- 5
ging; if possible no woman, or as little woman as possible: in respect to the spiritual the principle of Pascal *"il faut s'abêtir."* The result, expressed in psychological-moral terms: "un-selfing," "hallowing"; expressed physiologically: hypnotization—the attempt to achieve something for man that approximates what *hibernation* is for some species of animals, 10
what *aestivation* is for many plants in hot climates, a minimum of consumption and metabolism whereby life just barely continues without actually entering into our consciousness anymore. An astounding amount of human energy has been expended on this goal—perhaps in vain? ...
There is certainly no doubt that such sportsmen of "holiness," who 15
abound in all ages, among almost all peoples, have in fact found a real redemption from that which they combatted with such rigorous training—in countless cases they really got *free* of that deep physiological depression with the help of their system of hypnotics: for which reason their methodology counts as one of the most universal ethnological facts. 20
There is likewise nothing that would permit us to count such an intention to starve physicality and desire as in itself among the symptoms of madness (as it pleases a clumsy kind of roastbeef-eating "free spirit" and Sir Andrew to do). It is all the more certain that it forms, can form, the *path* to all kinds of mental disturbances, to "inner lights," for example, as 25
with the Hesychasts of Mount Athos, to hallucinations of sounds and figures, to lustful effusions and ecstasies of sensuality (story of Saint Theresa). The interpretation given to conditions of this kind by those who are afflicted with them has always been as fanatically false as possible, this goes without saying: but do not fail to hear the tone of the most 30
convinced gratitude that resounds already in the *will* to such a manner of interpretation. The highest condition, *redemption* itself, that final achievement of total hypnotization and stillness, always counts for them as the mystery in itself, for the expression of which even the highest symbols are insufficient, as a turning in and returning home into the ground 35
of things, as becoming free from all illusion, as "knowledge," as "truth," as "being," as escaping from every goal, every wish, every doing, as a state beyond good and evil as well. "Good and evil," the Buddhist

"il faut s'abêtir"] one must make oneself stupid.

says,—"both are shackles: over both the perfect one became lord"; "that which has been done and that which has been left undone," says the believer of the Vedânta, "cause him no pain; good and evil he shakes from himself, as a wise man; his realm no longer suffers through any deed; over good and evil, over both he passed beyond": a pan-Indian conception then, just as brahmanistic as buddhistic. (Neither in the Indian nor in the Christian manner of thinking is this "redemption" considered to be *attainable* through virtue, through moral improvement, however high they may fix the value of virtue as a hypnotic: make note of this,—it corresponds, moreover, to the facts of the matter. To have remained *true* in this may perhaps be considered the best piece of realism in the three greatest, otherwise so fundamentally moralized religions. "For the knowing one there is no duty" ... "Redemption is not brought about by the *addition* of virtues—for it consists in being one with brahma, which is not capable of any addition of perfection—and just as little by the *discarding* of faults: for brahma, to be one with which constitutes redemption, is eternally pure"—these passages from the commentary of Shankara, quoted from Europe's first real *expert* on Indian philosophy, my friend Paul Deussen.) Let us then honor "redemption" in the great religions; but it is a bit difficult to remain serious when faced with the esteem in which *deep sleep* is held by these people, who are tired of life, too tired even for dreaming—deep sleep, that is, as already an entering into brahma, as *achieved unio mystica* with God. "When he has then fallen asleep completely and utterly"—it says concerning this in the oldest most venerable "Scripture"—"and has completely come to rest so that he no longer sees any dream images, then he is, oh dear one, united with That Which Is, he has entered into himself—embraced by the knowledge-like self, he no longer has any consciousness of that which is outside or inside. Day and night do not cross over this bridge, age does not, death does not, suffering does not, good works do not, evil works do not." "In deep sleep," the faithful of this deepest of the three great religions likewise say, "the soul raises itself out of this body, enters into the highest light, and thereby appears in its own form: there it is the highest spirit itself, which walks about while joking and playing and delighting itself, be it with women or with carriages or with friends; there it no longer thinks back on this appendage of a body to which the *prâna* (the breath of life) is harnessed like a draught animal to the cart." Nevertheless let us bear in mind here, too, as in the case of "redemption," that what is expressed in the preceding, however much in the splendor of oriental exaggeration, is simply the same esteem as that of the clear, cool,

Greek-cool, but suffering Epicurus: the hypnotic feeling of nothingness, the rest of the deepest sleep, in short, *absence of suffering*—this may count already as the highest good, as value of values for those who suffer and are thoroughly out of sorts, this *must* be appraised by them as positive, felt to be *the* positive itself. (According to the same logic of feelings, in all   5
pessimistic religions nothingness is called *God*.)

18

Much more frequent than this sort of hypnotic general suppression of sensitivity, of susceptibility to pain—which presupposes even rarer forces, above all courage, contempt of opinion, "intellectual stoicism,"—is the attempt at a different kind of training against conditions of depres-   10
sion, one that is in any case easier: *mechanical activity.* That this relieves a suffering existence to a not inconsiderable degree is beyond all doubt: today this fact is called, somewhat dishonestly, "the blessing of work." The relief consists in this: that the interest of the sufferer is thoroughly diverted from the suffering—that it is continually doing and yet again   15
only doing that enters into consciousness and, consequently, that little room remains in it for suffering: for it is *narrow*, this chamber of human consciousness! Mechanical activity and that which belongs to it—like absolute regularity, punctual unreflected obedience, one's way of life set once and for all, the filling up of time, a certain permission for, indeed   20
discipline in "impersonality," in self-forgetfulness, in *"incuria sui"*—: how thoroughly, how subtly the ascetic priest knew how to use these in the battle with pain! Precisely when he had to deal with sufferers of the lower social ranks, with work slaves or prisoners (or with women: who are of course usually both at the same time, work slaves and prisoners), it   25
required little more than a small art of name-changing and rebaptizing to make them henceforth see in hated things a boon, a relative bit of good fortune:—in any case the dissatisfaction of the slave with his lot was *not* invented by priests.—A still more valued means in the battle with depres-sion is the prescription of a *small joy* that is easily accessible and can be   30
made a regular practice; this medication is frequently made use of in con-nection with the one just discussed. The most frequent form in which joy is thus prescribed as a means to a cure is the joy of *giving* joy (as doing good, giving gifts, relieving, helping, encouraging, comforting, praising, honoring); by prescribing "love of one's neighbor" the ascetic priest is   35

"incuria sui"] neglect of oneself.

basically prescribing an arousal of the strongest, most life-affirming drive, even if in the most cautious of doses—the *will to power*. The happiness of the "smallest superiority," such as accompanies all doing good, being useful, helping, honoring, is the most plentiful means of consolation that the physiologically inhibited tend to make use of, assuming they are well advised: otherwise they cause each other pain, in obedience to the same basic instinct, naturally. When one looks for the beginnings of Christianity in the Roman world, one finds associations for mutual support, pauper-, invalid-, burial-associations, which sprung up on the undermost soil of the society of that time, and in which that principal medicine against depression, the small joy, that of mutual good deeds was consciously cultivated—perhaps this was something new back then, a true discovery? In a "will to mutuality," to herd-formation, to "community," to "cenacle" elicited in this manner, the will to power thus aroused in the process—even if it is on the smallest scale—must now in turn come to a new and much fuller outburst: *herd-formation* is an essential step and victory in the battle with depression. With the growth of the community a new interest also grows strong in the individual, one that often enough lifts him above and beyond that which is most personal in his ill-humor, his aversion to *himself* (the *"despectio sui"* of Geulincx). Out of a longing to shake off the dull listlessness and the feeling of weakness, all the sick, the diseased strive instinctively for a herd organization: the ascetic priest intuits this instinct and fosters it; wherever there are herds it is the instinct of weakness that willed the herds and the shrewdness of priests that organized them. For do not overlook this: the strong strive just as naturally and necessarily *away* from each other as the weak strive *toward* each other; when the former band together it occurs only with a view to an aggressive joint action and joint satisfaction of their will to power, with a great deal of resistance from the individual conscience; the latter, on the other hand, arrange themselves into groups with *pleasure* precisely in the arrangement into groups—their instinct is satisfied in the process just as much as the instinct of the born "lords" (that is of the solitary beast-of-prey species of human) is at bottom irritated and disquieted by organization. Beneath every oligarchy—all of history teaches this—*tyrannical* craving always lies hidden; every oligarchy trembles constantly from the tension that every individual in it needs in order to remain lord over this craving. (Thus it was for example with the *Greeks*: Plato attests it in a hundred passages, Plato who knew his own kind—*and* himself ...)

despectio sui] contempt of oneself.

19

The means employed by the ascetic priest with which we have thus far become acquainted—the general muffling of the feeling of life, mechanical activity, the small joy, above all that of "love of one's neighbor," the herd organization, the awakening of the communal feeling of power, whereby the individual's vexation with himself is drowned out by his pleasure in the prospering of the community—these are, measured according to a modern standard, his *innocent* means in the battle with listlessness: let us now turn to the more interesting ones, the "guilty" ones. They are all concerned with one thing: some kind of *excess of the emotions*—used as the most effective means of anesthetizing the dull paralyzing long painfulness; for which reason priestly inventiveness has been virtually inexhaustible in thinking through this single question: "*by what means* does one achieve an emotional excess?" ... That sounds harsh: it is clear as day that it would sound more pleasant and perhaps suit the ears better if I said, for instance, "the ascetic priest has always taken advantage of the *enthusiasm* that lies in all strong affects." But why stroke the tender ears of our modern milquetoasts? Why should *we* give in even one step to their Tartuffery of words? For us psychologists there would already be a Tartuffery *of deed* in this; not to mention that it would disgust us. For in this, if in anything, a psychologist today has his *good taste* (—others may say: his righteousness), that he resists the disgracefully *moralized* manner of speaking that clings like slime to virtually all modern judging of humans and things. For do not deceive yourself in this: what constitutes the most characteristic feature of modern souls, modern books is not the lie, but rather the ingrained *innocence* in their moralistic mendacity. To have to discover this "innocence" everywhere again and again—this constitutes perhaps the most repulsive piece of work in all the questionable work a psychologist must take upon himself today; it is a piece of *our* great danger—it is a path that perhaps leads precisely *us* to the great disgust ... I do not doubt *what purpose* alone modern books (supposing that they have any permanence, which is admittedly not to be feared, and likewise supposing that there will one day be a posterity with stricter, harsher, *healthier* taste)—what purpose absolutely *everything* modern would serve, could serve for this posterity: as emetics—and this by virtue of its moral cloyingness and falseness, of its innermost feminism that likes to call itself "idealism" and in any case believes itself to be idealism. Our educated ones of today, our "good ones" do not lie—this is true; but it is *not* to their credit! The true lie, the authentic resolute "honest" lie (concerning whose

value one should listen to Plato) would be something far too rigorous, too
strong for them; it would demand what one is not *permitted* to demand of
them, that they open their eyes toward themselves, that they know how to
distinguish between "true" and "false" in their own case. The *dishonest lie*
5   alone befits them; whatever feels itself to be a "good human being" today
is completely incapable of relating to any issue except in a manner that is
dishonestly mendacious, abysmally mendacious, but innocently mendacious, trustingly mendacious, blue-eyedly mendacious, virtuously mendacious. These "good human beings"—they are all moralized down to the
10 roots now and with respect to honesty spoiled and ruined to all eternity:
which of them could still endure a *truth* "about humankind"! ... Or, more
concretely asked: which of them could bear a *true* biography! ... A few
signs of this: Lord Byron wrote down a considerable number of most personal things about himself but Thomas Moore was "too good" for it: he
15 burned the papers of his friend. Dr. Gwinner, the executor of Schopenhauer's will, is supposed to have done the same thing: for Schopenhauer
as well had written down a considerable amount about himself and perhaps even against himself (*"eis heauton"*). The able American Thayer, the
biographer of Beethoven, stopped all at once in his work: having arrived
20 at some point or other in this venerable and naive life he could no longer
endure it ... Moral: what prudent man would write an honest word about
himself anymore today?—for he would have to belong to the Order of
Holy Foolhardiness. We are promised an autobiography of Richard Wagner: who doubts that it will be a *prudent* autobiography? ... Let us also call
25 to mind the comical horror that the Catholic priest Janssen aroused in
Germany with his inconceivably simplistic and innocuous picture of the
German Reformation movement; what would one do if someone were to
narrate this movement *differently* some day, if a real psychologist were to
narrate a real Luther some day, no longer with the moralistic simplicity of
30 a country cleric, no longer with the cloying and discreet prudishness of
Protestant historians, but rather, say, with a *Taine*-like dauntlessness, out
of *strength of the soul* and not out of a prudent indulgence toward strength?
... (The Germans, incidentally, have in the end brought forth the classical
type of the latter nicely enough—they may indeed count him as one of
35 their own, count him to their credit: namely their Leopold Ranke, this
born classical *advocatus* of every *causa fortior*, this most prudent of all prudent "factual ones.")

"eis heauton"] about himself *or* against himself.
causa fortior] stronger cause.

20

But you will have understood me already:—all in all reason enough, isn't there, that we psychologists nowadays cannot get rid of considerable mistrust *of ourselves?* ... We, too, are probably still "too good" for our trade; we, too, are probably still the victims, the booty, the invalids of this moralized taste of the times, as much as we may feel ourselves to be ones who hold it in contempt—it probably infects *us* too. What was it of which that diplomat warned when speaking to his peers? "Let us mistrust above all, gentlemen, our first impulses!" he said, *"they are almost always good"* ... Thus, too, every psychologist today should speak to his peers ... And with that we come back to our problem, which indeed demands considerable strictness of us, considerable mistrust, in particular of "first impulses." *The ascetic ideal serving an intent to produce emotional excess:*— whoever recalls the previous treatise will already anticipate the essential content of what remains to be presented—pressed into these ten words. To free the human soul from all its moorings for once, to immerse it in terrors, frosts, blazes, and ecstasies in such a way that it is freed from everything that is small and small-minded in listlessness, dullness, being out of sorts as if by a bolt of lightning: which paths lead to *this* goal? And which of them most surely? ... Basically all great affects have the capacity to do so, assuming that they discharge themselves suddenly: anger, fear, lust, revenge, hope, triumph, despair, cruelty; and indeed the ascetic priest has unhesitatingly taken into his service the *whole* pack of wild dogs in man and unleashed first this one, then that one, always for the same purpose, to waken man out of slow sadness, to put to flight, at least for a time, his dull pain, his lingering misery, always under a religious inter- pretation and "justification." Every such emotional excess *exacts payment* afterwards, that goes without saying—it makes the sick sicker—and therefore this kind of remedy for pain is, measured by a modern standard, a "guilty" kind. Since fairness demands it, however, one must insist all the more that it has been applied *with a good conscience*, that the ascetic priest has prescribed it with the deepest faith in its usefulness, indeed indispensability—and often enough almost breaking down in the face of the wretchedness he has created; likewise, that the vehement physiologi- cal avengings of such excesses, perhaps even mental disturbances, do not actually contradict the overall sense of this kind of medication: which, as has previously been shown, is *not* out to heal sicknesses, but rather to combat the listlessness of depression, to alleviate it, to anesthetize it. And it was *thus* that this goal was achieved. The principal bow stroke the

5

10

15

20

25

30

35

ascetic priest allowed himself in order to cause the human soul to resound
with wrenching and ecstatic music of every kind was executed—everyone
knows this—by exploiting the *feeling of guilt*. The previous treatise briefly
suggested its origins—as a piece of animal psychology, no more: there the
5   feeling of guilt first confronted us in its raw state as it were. Only in the
hands of the priest, this true artist of the feeling of guilt, did it take on
form—oh what a form! "Sin"—for thus reads the priestly reinterpretation of the animal's "bad conscience" (cruelty turned backwards)—has so
far been the greatest event in the history of the sick soul: in it we have the
10   most dangerous and doom-laden feat of religious interpretation. Man,
suffering from himself in some way or other, physiologically in any case,
somewhat like an animal locked in a cage, uncertain why, to what end?
desirous of reasons—reasons alleviate—desirous also of cures and nar-
cotics, finally holds counsel with one who also knows concealed things—
15   and behold! he receives a hint; from his magician, the ascetic priest, he
receives the *first* hint concerning the "cause" of his suffering: he is to seek
it in *himself*, in a *guilt*, in a piece of the past, he is to understand his suffering itself as a *state of punishment* ... He has heard, he has understood, the
unhappy one: now things stand with him as with the hen around whom a
20   line has been drawn. He can no longer get out of this circle of lines: out of
the invalid "the sinner" has been made ... And now one will not be rid of
the sight of this invalid, of "the sinner," for a couple of millennia—will
one ever be rid of him again?—wherever one looks, everywhere the hypnotic gaze of the sinner forever moving in the same direction (in the
25   direction of "guilt" as the *only* causality of suffering); everywhere bad
conscience, this "hideous animal," to use Luther's words; everywhere the
past regurgitated, the deed twisted around, the "green eye" for all activity; everywhere that *wanting*-to-misunderstand-suffering made into life's
meaning, the reinterpretation of suffering into feelings of guilt, fear, and
30   punishment; everywhere the whip, the hair shirt, the starving body, con-
trition; everywhere the sinner breaking himself on the cruel wheels of a
restless, diseased-lascivious conscience; everywhere mute torment,
extreme fear, the agony of a tortured heart, the cramps of an unknown
happiness, the cry for "redemption." Indeed, through this system of pro-
35   cedures the old depression, heaviness, and tiredness was thoroughly *overcome*, life became *very* interesting again: awake, eternally awake, in need of
sleep, glowing, charred, exhausted and still not tired—this is what the
human being looked like, "the sinner" who was initiated into *these* mys-
teries. This old great magician in the battle with listlessness, the ascetic
40   priest—he had obviously been victorious, *his* kingdom had come: people

no longer protested *against* pain, they *thirsted* after pain; "*more* pain! *more* pain!" thus cried the longing of his disciples and initiates for centuries. Every emotional excess that caused pain, everything that shattered, toppled, crushed, entranced, enraptured, the secret of places of torture, the inventiveness of hell itself—everything had now been discovered, guessed, exploited, everything stood at the disposal of the magician, everything served henceforth to the victory of his ideal, of the ascetic ideal ... "My kingdom is not of *this* world"—he spoke now as before: did he really still have the right to speak so? ... Goethe claimed that there were only thirty-six tragic situations: one can guess from this, if one didn't already know it, that Goethe was no ascetic priest. He—knows more ...

21

With respect to *this* entire kind of priestly medication, the "guilty" kind, any word of criticism is too much. That an emotional excess such as the ascetic priest tends to prescribe for his sick ones in this case (under the holiest name, as goes without saying, likewise imbued with the holiness of his purpose) has really *been of use* to any sick person, who would have any desire to uphold a claim of this kind? One should at least be clear about the expression "be of use." If by this one intends to express that such a system of treatment has *improved* man, then I will not contradict: I only add what "improve" means for me—the same as "tamed," "weakened," "discouraged," "sophisticated," "pampered," "emasculated" (hence almost the same as *injured* ...) If, however, we are dealing chiefly with those who are sick, out of sorts, depressed, then such a system makes the sick, even supposing that it makes him "better," at all events *sicker*; just ask doctors who work with the insane what a methodical application of penitential torments, contritions, and cramps of redemption always brings on. Likewise interrogate history: wherever the ascetic priest has succeeded in establishing this treatment of the sick, diseasedness has always grown in depth and breadth with uncanny speed. What was the "success" in every case? A shattered nervous system, added to that which was already sick anyway; and this on the largest as on the smallest scale, with individuals as with masses. In the wake of penitence and redemption training we find enormous epileptic epidemics, the greatest known to history, like those of the St. Vitus' and St. John's dancers of the Middle Ages; as another form of its postlude we find terrible paralyses and chronic depressions with which in some cases the temperament of a people or city

(Geneva, Basel) changes once and for all into its opposite;—witch hysteria belongs here as well, something related to somnambulism (eight great
epidemic outbursts between 1564 and 1605 alone)—; in its wake we likewise find those death-seeking mass deliria whose horrifying cry *"evviva la*
5   *morte"* was heard across all of Europe, interrupted now by lustful, now by
destructive idiosyncrasies: even today the same alternation of affects, with
the same intermittences and sudden leaps, is still to be observed everywhere, in every case in which the ascetic doctrine of sin once again
achieves a great success (religious neurosis *appears* as a form of "evil
10 spirit": there is no doubt about this. What it is? *Quaeritur.*) To put it
bluntly, the ascetic ideal and its sublime-moral cult, this most ingenious,
most unsuspected and most dangerous systematizing of all the instruments of emotional excess under the aegis of holy intentions, has
inscribed itself in a terrible and unforgettable way into the entire history
15 of man; and unfortunately *not only* into his history ... There is hardly anything else I could point out that has pressed so destructively upon *health*
and racial robustness, particularly of Europeans, as this ideal; without any
exaggeration one may call it *the true doom* in the history of European
health. At best, that the specifically Germanic influence might be compa
20 rable to its influence: I mean the alcohol poisoning of Europe that has
thus far kept strict pace with the political and racial predominance of the
Germanic peoples (—wherever they injected their blood, they injected
their vice as well).—Third in line one ought to mention syphilis—*magno
sed proxima intervallo.*

22

25   The ascetic priest has ruined the health of the soul wherever he has
come to power, he has consequently ruined *taste* in *artibus et litteris* as
well—he is still ruining it. "Consequently"?—I hope one will simply concede me this consequently; at any rate, I do not wish to prove it first. A
single pointer: it is directed at the basic book of Christian literature, its
30 true model, its "book in itself." Even in the midst of Greco-Roman glory,
which was also a glory of books, in the face of a classical scripture-world
that was not yet atrophied and decimated, at a time when one could still

"evviva la morte"] long live death!
Quaeritur] one asks—i.e., "that is the question."
magno sed proxima intervallo] next, but by a great distance. Cf. Virgil, *Aeneid*, Book
5, line 320.

read a few books for whose possession one would now give half of a
nation's literature, the simplicity and vanity of Christian agitators—one
calls them Church Fathers—already dared to decree: "*we* too have our
classical literature, *we do not need that of the Greeks*"—and at the same
time one pointed proudly to books of legends, apostolic epistles, and little   5
apologetic tracts, in roughly the same way as the English "Salvation
Army" today fights its battle against Shakespeare and other "heathens"
with a related literature. I have no love for the "New Testament," one can
guess that already; it almost makes me uneasy to stand so alone in my taste
regarding this most esteemed, most overestimated scriptural work (the   10
taste of two millennia is *against* me): but what good does it do! "Here I
stand, I can do no other"—I have the courage of my bad taste. The *Old*
Testament—now that is something entirely different: I take my hat off to
the Old Testament! In it I find great human beings, a heroic landscape,
and something most rare on earth, the incomparable naïveté of the *strong*   15
heart; still more, I find a people. In the New, on the other hand, nothing
but petty sectarian economy, nothing but rococo of the soul, nothing but
embellishment, crookedness, oddness, nothing but conventicle air, not to
forget an occasional breath of bucolic cloyingness that belongs to that
epoch (*and* to the Roman province) and is not so much Jewish as Hellenis-   20
tic. Humility and pomposity side by side; a garrulousness of feeling that
almost numbs; passionateness, no passion; embarrassing play of gestures;
it is obvious that all good breeding was lacking here. How can one be
allowed to make such a fuss about one's little bad habits as these pious little men do! No cock will crow about this, much less God. Finally they   25
even want to have "the crown of eternal life," all these little people from
the province: and to what end? and for what? one cannot push immodesty
further than this. An "immortal" Peter: who could endure *that*! They have
an ambition that makes one laugh: *this one* openly chews what is most personal to him, his foolishnesses, sadnesses, and idler's worries, as if the in-   30
itself-of-things were obliged to take care of it all; *that one* never tires of
drawing God himself into the pettiest distress in which they are stuck.
And this constant familiarity with God, in the worst taste! This Jewish,
not merely Jewish impertinence toward God with muzzle and paw! ...
There are minor despised "heathen peoples" in the east of Asia from   35
whom these first Christians could have learned something substantial,
some *tact* of reverence; as Christian missionaries attest, the former do not
permit themselves to give voice to the name of their god at all. This seems
delicate enough to me; what is certain is that it is not only "first" Christians who find it too delicate: to feel the contrast just recall Luther, for   40

instance, this "most eloquent" and immodest peasant that Germany has had, and the Lutheran tone that precisely he liked best in his conversations with God. In the final analysis, Luther's resistance to the mediator saints of the Church (particularly to "the devil's sow, the pope") was, there is no doubt, the resistance of a boor annoyed by the *good etiquette* of the Church, that reverential etiquette of hieratic taste, which admits only the more devoted and more silent into the Holy of Holies and locks it against the boors. Precisely here these boors are absolutely not to be allowed to speak—but Luther, the peasant, wanted it otherwise, it wasn't *German* enough for him as it was: above all he wanted to speak directly, to speak himself, to speak "uninhibitedly" with his God ... Well, he did it.—The ascetic ideal, one will likely guess it, was never and nowhere a school of good taste, still less of good manners—in the best case it was a school of hieratic manners—: that is because it has something in its very flesh that is the mortal enemy of all good manners—lack of measure, aversion to measure, it is itself a *"non plus ultra."*

23

The ascetic ideal has not only ruined health and taste, it has also ruined a third, fourth, fifth, sixth something—I will restrain myself from saying *what* all (when would I come to an end!). It is not what this ideal has *done* that I propose to bring to light here; rather solely what it *means*, what it hints at, what lies hidden behind it, beneath it, in it, for which it is the provisional, indistinct expression, overladen with question marks and misunderstandings. And it is only with respect to *this* purpose that I am not permitted to spare my readers a look at the enormity of its effects, of its doomful effects as well: namely in order to prepare them for the last and most terrible aspect that the question of the meaning of this ideal has for me. What does the very *power* of this ideal mean, the *enormity* of its power? Why has it been given room to this extent? why has there not been better resistance? The ascetic ideal expresses a will: *where* is the opposing will in which an *opposing ideal* expresses itself? The ascetic ideal has a *goal*—it is general enough that all other interests of human existence appear small-minded and narrow measured against it; it relentlessly interprets ages, peoples, human beings according to this one goal, it refuses to tolerate any other interpretation, any other goal, it rejects, negates, affirms, confirms solely in accordance with *its* interpretation (—and was

non plus ultra] the highest or ultimate of its kind; literally: not more beyond.

there ever a system of interpretation more thoroughly thought to the end?); it submits itself to no power, rather it believes in its privilege over every other power, in its unconditional *distance of rank* with respect to every power—it believes that there is no instance of power on earth that does not first have to receive from it a meaning, a right to existence, a value, as a tool in *its* work, as a way and means to *its* goal, to *one* goal ... Where is the *counterpart* to this closed system of will, goal, and interpretation? Why is the counterpart *lacking*? ... Where is the *other* "*one* goal"? ... But I am told it is *not* lacking, it has not only fought a long successful battle with this ideal but rather has already become lord over that ideal in all essential matters: our entire modern *science* is said to be witness to this—this modern science, which, as a true philosophy of reality, clearly believes in itself alone, clearly possesses the courage to itself, the will to itself and has so far got along well enough without God, the beyond, and virtues that negate. Nevertheless, in my case one accomplishes nothing with such noise and agitator-babble: these trumpeters of reality are bad musicians, it is easy enough to hear that their voices do *not* come from the depths, it is *not* the abyss of the scientific conscience that speaks through them—for the scientific conscience is an abyss today—in such trumpeter-mouths the word "science" is simply an obscenity, a misuse, a shameless act. Precisely the opposite of what is claimed here is the truth: science has utterly *no* faith in itself today, to say nothing of an ideal *above* itself—and where it is at all still passion, love, ardor, *suffering*, it is not the opposite of that ascetic ideal but rather *its most recent and noblest form*. Does that sound strange to you? ... Of course even among the scholars of today there are enough steady and modest working folk who like their little corner and therefore, because they like it there, from time to time speak up rather immodestly with the demand that one *should* be satisfied in general today, above all in the sciences—there is so much that is useful that needs doing precisely there. I won't contradict; least of all do I want to ruin the pleasure these honest workers take in their craft: for I enjoy their work. But the fact that one now works rigorously in the sciences and that there are contented workers does *not* by any means prove that as a whole science today has a goal, a will, an ideal, the passion of a great faith. As stated, the opposite is the case: where it is not the most recent manifestation of the ascetic ideal—there it is a matter of cases too rare, noble, select to over-turn the general judgment—science today is a *hiding place* for every kind of ill-humor, unbelief, gnawing worm, *despectio sui*, bad conscience—it is the very *unrest* of being without an ideal, the suffering from the *lack* of a great love, the discontent in an *involuntary* contentedness. Oh what does

science today not conceal! how much it is at least *supposed* to conceal! The
competence of our best scholars, their mindless diligence, their heads
smoking day and night, their very mastery of their craft—how often all
this has its true sense in preventing something from becoming visible to
oneself! Science as a means of self-anesthetization: *are you acquainted with*
that? ... By means of a harmless word one sometimes cuts them to the
quick—everyone who keeps company with scholars experiences this—
one embitters one's scholarly friends toward oneself at the very moment
one means to honor them, one drives them beside themselves merely
because one was too coarse to guess with whom one was actually dealing—with *sufferers* who do not want to admit to themselves what they are,
with anesthetized and unconscious ones who fear only one thing: *coming*
to consciousness ...

24

—And now take a look, by comparison, at those rarer cases of which I
spoke, the last idealists there are among philosophers and scholars today:
do we perhaps have in them the sought-after *opponents* of the ascetic ideal,
its *counter-idealists?* Indeed they *believe* themselves to be such, these
"unbelieving ones" (for that they all are); they are so serious on this point,
here in particular becoming so passionate in word, in gesture, that precisely this seems to be their last bit of belief, that they are opponents of
this ideal:—need it therefore be *true*, what they believe? ... We "knowers"
are mistrustful of every kind of believer by now; our mistrust has gradually trained us to infer the opposite of what one formerly inferred: namely,
wherever the strength of a belief comes strikingly to the fore to infer a certain weakness of demonstrability, even the *improbability* of what is
believed. We too do not deny that faith "makes blessed": it is *precisely for*
this reason that we deny that faith *proves* anything—a strong faith that
makes blessed raises suspicion against that in which it believes, it does not
establish "truth," it establishes a certain probability—of *deception*. And
how do things stand in this case?—These negating and aloof ones of
today, these who are unconditional on one point—the claim to intellectual
cleanliness—these hard, strict, abstinent, heroic spirits who constitute
the honor of our age, all these pale atheists, anti-Christians, immoralists,
nihilists, these skeptics, ephectics, *hectics* of the spirit (all of them are the
latter in some sense or other), these last idealists of knowledge in whom
alone the intellectual conscience today dwells and has become flesh—in
fact they believe themselves to be as detached as possible from the ascetic

ideal, these "free, *very* free spirits": and yet, to divulge to them what they themselves cannot see—for they stand too close to themselves—this ideal is precisely *their* ideal as well, they themselves represent it today, and perhaps they alone; they themselves are its most spiritualized outgrowth, the troop of warriors and scouts it deploys on the front line, its most entrapping, most tender, most incomprehensible form of seduction:—if I am a guesser of riddles in anything then let it be with *this* proposition! ... These are by no means *free* spirits: *for they still believe in truth* ... When the Christian crusaders in the Orient came across that invincible order of Assassins, that order of free spirits *par excellence* whose lowest degree lived in an obedience the like of which no order of monks has attained, they also received, through some channel or other, a hint about that symbol and tally-word reserved for the uppermost degrees alone, as their *secretum*: "nothing is true, everything is permitted" ... Now *that* was *freedom* of the spirit, *with that*, belief in truth itself was *renounced* ... Has any European, any Christian free spirit ever lost his way in this proposition and its labyrinthine *consequences*? does he know the Minotaur of this cave *from experience*? ... I doubt it, still more, I know otherwise:—nothing is more foreign to these who are unconditional on one point, these *so-called* "free spirits," than precisely freedom and breaking one's fetters in this sense, in no respect are they more firmly bound; precisely in their belief in truth they are more firm and unconditional than anyone else. I know all of this from too close a proximity perhaps: that commendable philosophers' abstinence to which such a belief obligates; that stoicism of the intellect that finally forbids itself a "no" just as strictly as a "yes"; that *wanting* to halt before the factual, the *factum brutum*; that fatalism of *"petits faits"* (*ce petit faitalisme*, as I call it), in which French science now seeks a kind of moral superiority over German science, that renunciation of all interpretation (of doing violence, pressing into orderly form, abridging, omitting, padding, fabricating, falsifying and whatever else belongs to the *essence* of all interpreting)—broadly speaking, this expresses asceticism of virtue as forcefully as does any negation of sensuality (it is basically only a *modus* of this negation). What *compels* one to this, however, this unconditional will to truth, is the *belief in the ascetic*

secretum] medieval Latin, elliptical for: *sigillum secretum*, "privy seal"—a personal or private seal.
"petits faits"] little facts. The parenthesis that follows puns on the word *fait* (fact) by replacing the first three letters of the French *fatalism* (fatalism) with this similar-sounding word, a pun that doesn't quite work in English: "that little *factal*-ism."

ideal itself, even if as its unconscious imperative—do not deceive yourself about this,—it is the belief in a *metaphysical* value, a value *in itself of truth* as it is established and guaranteed by that ideal alone (it stands and falls with that ideal). There is, strictly speaking, absolutely no science "without presuppositions," the thought of such a science is unthinkable, paralogical: a philosophy, a "belief" must always be there first so that science can derive a direction from it, a meaning, a boundary, a method, a *right* to existence. (Whoever understands it the other way around—for example, whoever sets out to place philosophy "on a strictly scientific foundation"—first needs to turn not only philosophy but also truth itself *on its head*: the grossest violation of propriety there can be with regard to two such venerable ladies!) Why, there is no doubt—and with this I will give my *Gay Science* a chance to speak, cf. its fifth book (section 344)—"the truthful one, in that audacious and ultimate sense presupposed by the belief in science, *thus affirms another world* than that of life, nature, and history; and insofar as he affirms this "other world," what? must he not, precisely in so doing, negate its counterpart, this world, *our* world? ... It is still a *metaphysical* belief on which our belief in science rests—we knowers today, we godless ones and anti-metaphysicians, we too still take *our* fire from that great fire that was ignited by a thousand-year old belief, that belief of Christians, which was also Plato's belief, that God is truth, that truth is *divine* ... But what if precisely this is becoming ever more implausible, if nothing proves to be divine any longer, unless perhaps error, blindness, lie—if God himself proves to be our *longest lie?*"——At this point it is necessary to pause and to reflect for a long time. Science itself now is *in need of* a justification (which is not to say that there is one). On this question, just look at the earliest and the most recent philosophies: all of them lack a consciousness of the extent to which the will to truth itself first needs a justification, here there is a gap in every philosophy—why is that? Because the ascetic ideal has until now been *lord* over all philosophy, because truth was posited as being, as God, as highest authority; because truth was simply not *permitted* to be a problem. Do you understand this "permitted"?—From the moment belief in the god of the ascetic ideal is negated, *there is also a new problem*: that of the *value* of truth.—The will to truth is in need of a critique—let us thus define our own task—the value of truth is for once to be experimentally *called into question* ... (Anyone who finds this stated too briefly is advised to read the section of the *Gay Science* that bears the title: "To What Extent We Too Are Still Pious" (section 344), or, best of all, the entire fifth book of said work, likewise the preface to *Daybreak*.)

25

No! Don't give me science as an answer when I look for the natural antagonist of the ascetic ideal, when I ask: "*where* is the opposing will in which its *opposing ideal* expresses itself?" Science is far from standing enough on its own for this, in every respect it first needs a value-ideal, a value-creating power in whose *service* it *may believe* in itself—it is itself never value-creating. Its relationship to the ascetic ideal is still by no means inherently antagonistic; on the whole it is even more likely that science represents the forward-driving force in the inner shaping of this ideal. On closer scrutiny its protest and battle are not in the least directed at the ideal itself, but rather only at its outworks, sheathing, play of masks, at its temporary solidification, lignification, dogmatization—by negating what is exoteric about this ideal, it sets the life in it free again. These two, science and ascetic ideal, they do, after all, stand on one and the same ground—I have already suggested that this is so—: namely on the same overestimation of truth (more correctly: on the same belief in the *in*assessability, the *un*criticizability of truth), precisely in this they are *necessarily* confederates—so that, supposing one combats them, they can only be combatted and called into question together. An assessment of the value of the ascetic ideal unavoidably entails an assessment of the value of science as well: open your eyes and prick up your ears to this while the time is right! (*Art*, to state it beforehand, for I will come back to it sometime in greater length—art, in which precisely the *lie* hallows itself, in which the *will to deception* has good conscience on its side, is much more fundamentally opposed to the ascetic ideal than is science: this was sensed instinctively by Plato, this greatest enemy of art that Europe has yet produced. Plato *contra* Homer: that is the complete, the genuine antagonism—there the "otherworldly one" with the best of wills, the great slanderer of life; here its involuntary deifier, *golden* nature. An artist's subservience in the service of the ascetic ideal is therefore the truest *corruption* of the artist there can be, unfortunately one of the most common: for nothing is more corruptible than an artist.) Science also rests on the same ground as the ascetic ideal when calculated physiologically: a certain *impoverishment of life* is a presupposition here as well as there—the affects become cool, the tempo slowed, dialectic in place of instinct, *seriousness* impressed on faces and gestures (seriousness, this most unmistakable mark of a more laborious metabolism, of a struggling, harder-working life). Look at those ages in the history of a people when the scholar comes to the fore: they are ages of tiredness, often of evening, of decline—overflowing energy, certainty of

life, certainty of the *future* are lost. The predominance of the mandarin is
never a sign of anything good: any more than the rise of democracy, of
peace-arbitration courts in place of wars, of equal rights for women, of the
religion of compassion, and whatever other symptoms of declining life
there are. (Science understood as problem; what does science mean?—on
this cf. the preface to "The Birth of Tragedy.")—No! this "modern science"—just keep your eyes open for this!—is for the present the *best* con-
federate of the ascetic ideal, and this precisely because it is the most
unconscious, the most involuntary, the most secret and subterranean one!
They have until now played one game, the "poor of the spirit" and the scientific adversaries of that ideal (beware, by the way, of thinking that they
are the antithesis of the former, say, as the *rich* of the spirit:—this they are
not; I called them hectics of the spirit). These famous *victories* of the latter: undoubtedly they are victories—but over what? The ascetic ideal was
in no way conquered in them, rather it was made stronger, which is to say
more incomprehensible, more spiritual, more ensnaring by the fact that
again and again a wall, an outwork that had attached itself to this ideal and
was coarsening its appearance was ruthlessly removed, demolished by science. Does anyone really think that, for instance, the defeat of theological
astronomy meant the defeat of that ideal? ... Has man perhaps become
less in need of an otherworldly solution to his riddle of existence now that
this existence looks even more arbitrary, more loiterer-like, more dispens-
able in the *visible* order of things? Hasn't precisely the self-belittlement of
man, his *will* to self-belittlement been marching relentlessly forward since
Copernicus? Alas, the belief in his dignity, uniqueness, irreplaceability in
the hierarchy of beings is lost—he has become an *animal*, without simile,
qualification, or reservation an animal, he who in his earlier belief was
almost god ("child of God," "God-man") ... Since Copernicus man
seems to have stumbled onto an inclined plane—he is now rolling faster
and faster away from the center—whither? into nothingness? into the
"*penetrating* feeling of his nothingness?" ... So be it! exactly this would be
the straight path—into the *old* ideal? ... *All* science (and by no means only
astronomy, concerning whose humiliating and debasing effect Kant made
a noteworthy confession, "it annihilates my importance" ...), all science,
the natural as well as the *unnatural*—which is what I call the self-critique
of knowledge—today aims to talk man out of his previous respect for
himself, as if this were nothing but a bizarre self-conceit; one could even
say that science's own pride, its own austere form of stoical ataraxy consists in upholding this hard-won *self-contempt* of man as his last, most
serious claim to respect from himself (with good reason in fact: for the

one who holds in contempt is still one who "has not forgotten how to
respect" …) Does this actually *work against* the ascetic ideal? Does anyone in all seriousness still think (as the theologians for a time imagined)
that, say, Kant's *victory* over the conceptual dogmatism of theology
("God," "soul," "freedom," "immortality") did damage to that ideal?—it   5
is of no concern for the present whether Kant himself even remotely
intended anything of the kind. What is certain is that since Kant all kinds
of transcendentalists are again playing a winning game—they are emanci-
pated from the theologians: what good fortune!—he betrayed to them that
secret path on which they may now pursue their "heart's desires" on their   10
own initiative and with the best scientific decorum. Likewise: who could
henceforth hold it against the agnostics, as the venerators of the unknown
and mysterious in itself, if they now worship *the question mark itself* as
God? (Xaver Doudan speaks at one point of the ravages caused by *"l'habitude d'admirer l'inintelligible au lieu de rester tout simplement dans*   15
l'inconnu"; it is his opinion that the ancients were free of this. Supposing
that everything man "knows" fails to satisfy his desires, moreover, that it
contradicts them and makes one shudder—what divine escape, to be permitted to seek the blame for this not in "desiring" but rather in "knowing"! … "There is no knowing: *consequently*—there is a God": what a   20
novel *elegantia syllogismi*! what a *triumph* of the ascetic ideal!—

26

—Or did the whole of modern historiography perhaps show a stance
more sure of life, more sure of its ideal? Its most noble claim now runs in
the direction of being a *mirror*; it rejects all teleology; it no longer wants
to "prove" anything; it scorns playing the judge and has its good taste in   25
this—it affirms as little as it negates, it ascertains, it "describes" … All of
this is to a high degree ascetic; at the same time, however, it is to a still
higher degree *nihilistic*, do not deceive yourselves about this! One sees a
sad, hard, but determined look—an eye that *looks outward* as an isolated
arctic traveller looks outward (perhaps in order not to look inward? in   30
order not to look back? …) Here there is snow, here life has become
silent; the last crowings heard here are "To what end?," "In vain!,"
"*Nada!*"—here nothing more prospers or grows, at best St. Petersburg

"l'habitude … dans l'inconnu"] "the habit *of admiring* the unintelligible instead of
staying quite simply in the unknown."
elegantia syllogismi] elegance of the syllogism.

metapolitics and Tolstoyian "compassion." As for that other kind of historian, however, an even more "modern" kind perhaps, a hedonistic, lascivious kind, who makes eyes at life just as much as at the ascetic ideal, who uses the word "artist" as a glove and has leased the praise of con-

5   templation completely and utterly for himself these days: oh what thirst these sweet ingenious ones arouse, even for ascetics and winter landscapes! No! the devil take this "contemplative" folk! How much more would I prefer to journey with those historical nihilists through the most dismal gray cold fogs!—indeed, supposing I must choose, I wouldn't be

10   against lending an ear even to one who is truly unhistorical, anti-historical (like Dühring, whose tones have intoxicated a previously still shy, still unacknowledgeable species of "beautiful souls" in present-day Germany, the species *anarchistica* within the educated proletariat). A hundred times worse are the "contemplatives"—: I know of nothing as disgusting

15   as this sort of "objective" armchair, this sort of sweet-smelling hedonist facing history, half priest, half satyr, perfume Renan, who betrays already with the high falsetto of his cheers what he is lacking, *where* he is lacking, *where* in this case the Fate has oh! all-too-surgically wielded her cruel scissors! This goes against my taste, also against my patience: let those

20   who have nothing to lose by it keep their patience at such sights—such a sight enrages me, such "spectators" embitter me toward the "spectacle" still more than the spectacle itself (history itself, you understand me), in the process Anacreontic moods come over me unawares. This nature that gave to the bull its horns, to the lion *chasm' odonton*, why did nature give

25   me a foot? … To kick with, by holy Anacreon! and not just for running away: for kicking apart the rotted armchairs, the cowardly contemplativeness, the lecherous eunuchry in the face of history, the making-eyes at ascetic ideals, the justice-Tartuffery of impotence! All my reverence to the ascetic ideal, *as long as it is honest*! as long as it believes in itself and

30   does not present us with a facade of clownery! But I do not like all these coquettish bugs who have an insatiable ambition for smelling out the infinite, until finally the infinite smells of bugs; I do not like the whited sepulchers that play-act life; I do not like the tired and used-up who wrap themselves in wisdom and look about "objectively"; I do not like the agi-

35   tators spruced up into heroes, who wear a magic concealing-cap of an ideal on their straw-whisk of a head; I do not like the ambitious artists who would like to act the role of ascetics and priests and are basically only tragic buffoons; I do not like them either, these newest speculators

chasm' odonton] "chasm of teeth," from *Anacreonta*, Poem 24.

in idealism, the anti-Semites, who roll their eyes nowadays in a Christian-Aryan-Philistine manner and try to stir up all the horned-cattle elements among the people through a misuse of the cheapest tool of agitation, moral posturing—a misuse that exhausts all patience (—that *no* kind of swindle-spiritism goes without success in present-day Germany is linked to the positively undeniable and already tangible desolation of the German spirit, whose cause I seek in an all-too-exclusive diet of newspapers, politics, beer, and Wagnerian music, including that which supplies the presupposition for this diet: first, the national constriction and vanity, the strong but narrow principle *"Deutschland, Deutschland über alles,"* second, however, the *paralysis agitans* of "modern ideas"). Europe today is rich and inventive above all in excitants, it seems there is nothing it needs more than stimulants and fire-waters: hence also the enormous counterfeiting of ideals, these fieriest waters of the spirit; hence also the repulsive, foul-smelling, mendacious, pseudo-alcoholic air everywhere. I would like to know how many shiploads of imitation idealism, of hero-costumes and grand-word-noisemakers, how many barrels of sugared spirituous sympathy (firm of: *la religion de la souffrance*), how many wooden legs of "noble indignation" for the assistance of the spiritually flat-footed, how many *comedians* of the Christian-moral ideal would have to be exported out of Europe today in order for its air to smell cleaner again ... Obviously a new *trade* opportunity has opened up with respect to this overproduction; obviously there is a new "business" to transact in little ideal-idols and accompanying "idealists"—don't overlook this none-too-subtle hint! Who has enough courage for it?—we have the means in *hand* to "idealize" the entire earth! ... But why am I talking about courage: here only one thing is needed, precisely the hand, an uninhibited, a very uninhibited hand ...

27

—Enough! Enough! let's leave these curiosities and complexities of the modern spirit, where there is as much to laugh about as to be vexed at: precisely *our* problem can do without them, the problem of the *mean-*

"*Deutschland, Deutschland über alles*"] "Germany, Germany above all else." Fallersleben, *Das Lied der Deutschen*, 1841.
paralysis agitans] shaking disability, i.e., "shaking palsy" or Parkinson's disease.
la religion de la souffrance] the religion of suffering.

ing of the ascetic ideal—what does it have to do with yesterday and today!
I will tackle those things more rigorously and more thoroughly in
another context (under the title "On the History of European Nihilism";
with regard to this I refer to a work that I am preparing: *The Will to*
5   *Power, Attempt at a Re-valuation of All Values*). All I care to have pointed
out here is this: in the spiritual sphere as well, the ascetic ideal has in the
meantime only one kind of real enemy and *injurer*: the comedians of this
ideal—for they arouse mistrust. Everywhere else that the spirit is strictly
and powerfully at work today without any counterfeiting, it now does
10   without ideals entirely—the popular expression for this abstinence is
"atheism"—*except for its will to truth*. This will, however, this *remnant* of
an ideal is, if one is willing to believe me, that ideal itself in its strictest,
most spiritual formulation, completely and utterly esoteric, stripped of
all outworks, thus not so much its remnant as its *core*. Unconditional
15   honest atheism (—and *its* is the only air we breathe, we more spiritual
human beings of this age!) is accordingly *not* in opposition to that ideal,
as appearance would have it; it is rather only one of its last stages of
development, one of its final forms and inner logical consequences—it is
the awe-inspiring *catastrophe* of a two-thousand-year discipline in truth,
20   which in the end forbids itself the *lie involved in belief in God*. (The same
course of development in India, completely independent of the former
and therefore proving something; the same ideal compelling to the same
conclusion; the decisive point reached five centuries before the point
from which Europeans reckon time, with Buddha, more precisely:
25   already with the Samkhya philosophy, this then popularized and made
into a religion by Buddha.) Asking in all strictness, *what* actually *triumphed* over the Christian god? The answer is found in my *Gay Science*
(section 357); "Christian morality itself, the ever more strictly understood concept of truthfulness, the father-confessor subtlety of the Chris-
30   tian conscience, translated and sublimated into the scientific conscience,
into intellectual cleanliness at any price. Looking at nature as if it were a
proof of the goodness and guardianship of a god; interpreting history to
the honor of divine reason, as constant witness of a moral world order
and moral final intentions; interpreting one's own experiences as pious
35   human beings have long enough interpreted them, as if everything were
an act of providence, everything a sign, everything thought up and sent
for the sake of the soul's salvation: this is henceforth *past*, it has conscience *against* it, it is regarded by all subtler consciences as indecent,
dishonest, as mendacity, feminism, weakness, cowardice—it is precisely
40   in this strictness, if in anything, that we are *good Europeans* and heirs of

Europe's longest and bravest self-overcoming" ... All great things perish through themselves, through an act of self-cancellation: thus the law of life wills it, the law of the *necessary* "self-overcoming" in the essence of life—in the end the call always goes forth to the lawgiver himself: *"patere legem, quam ipse tulisti."* In this manner Christianity *as dogma* perished of   5 its own morality; in this manner Christianity *as morality* must now also perish—we stand at the threshold of *this* event. Now that Christian truthfulness has drawn one conclusion after the other, in the end it draws its *strongest conclusion*, its conclusion *against* itself; this occurs, however, when it poses the question, *"what does all will to truth mean?"* ... And   10 here I again touch on my problem, on our problem, my *unknown* friends (—for I as yet *know* of no friends): what meaning would *our* entire being have if not this, that in us this will to truth has come to a consciousness of itself *as a problem?* ... It is from the will to truth's becoming conscious of itself that from now on—there is no doubt about it—morality will grad-   15 ually *perish*: that great spectacle in a hundred acts that is reserved for Europe's next two centuries, the most terrible, most questionable, and perhaps also most hopeful of all spectacles ...

28

If one disregards the ascetic ideal: man, the *animal* man, has until now had no meaning. His existence on earth contained no goal; "to what end   20 man at all?"—was a question without answer; the *will* for man and earth was lacking; behind every great human destiny a still greater "for noth-ing!" resounded as refrain. Precisely *this* is what the ascetic ideal means: that something *was lacking*, that an enormous *void* surrounded man—he did not know how to justify, to explain, to affirm himself; he *suffered* from   25 the problem of his meaning. He suffered otherwise as well, he was for the most part a *diseased* animal: but the suffering itself was *not* his problem, rather that the answer was missing to the scream of his question: *"to what end* suffering?" Man, the bravest animal and the one most accustomed to suffering, does *not* negate suffering in itself: he *wants* it, he even seeks it   30 out, provided one shows him a *meaning* for it, a *to-this-end* of suffering. The meaninglessness of suffering, not the suffering itself, was the curse that thus far lay stretched out over humanity—*and the ascetic ideal offered it a meaning!* Thus far it has been the only meaning; any meaning is better than no meaning at all; in every respect the ascetic ideal has been the   35

"patere ... quam ipse tulisti"] submit to the law you yourself proposed.

"faute de mieux" par excellence there has been thus far. In it suffering was *interpreted*; the enormous emptiness seemed filled; the door fell shut to all suicidal nihilism. The interpretation—there is no doubt—brought new suffering with it, deeper, more inward, more poisonous, gnawing more at
5   life: it brought all suffering under the perspective of *guilt* ... But in spite of all this—man was *rescued* by it, he had a *meaning*, he was henceforth no longer like a leaf in the wind, a plaything of nonsense, "without-sense," now he could *will* something—no matter for the moment in what direction, to what end, with what he willed: *the will itself was saved*. One simply
10   cannot conceal from oneself *what* all the willing that has received its direction from the ascetic ideal actually expresses: this hatred of the human, still more of the animal, still more of the material, this abhorrence of the senses, of reason itself, this fear of happiness and of beauty, this longing away from all appearance, change, becoming, death, wish, longing
15   itself—all of this means—let us dare to grasp this—a *will to nothingness*, an aversion to life, a rebellion against the most fundamental presuppositions of life; but it is and remains a *will*! ... And, to say again at the end what I said at the beginning: man would much rather will *nothingness* than *not* will ...

"*faute de mieux*"] for lack of anything better.

End Notes

Preface

Title   *On the Genealogy of Morality*] This work, *Zur Genealogie der Moral* (GM), is usually referred to in English as "On the Genealogy of Morals" (Kaufmann's well-known translation) or "Towards the Genealogy of Morals." Some recent scholars seem to prefer the latter title on the grounds that it avoids giving the impression that Nietzsche here proposes to give the last word on the genealogy in question. The view of the present translators is that the "zur" (=to) in Nietzsche's title indicates that he sees the three treatises of GM as *contributions* to the genealogy of morality, and that this point is adequately conveyed by "On." We do, however, disagree with Kaufmann's translation of *Moral* as "morals." *Moral* is used in German to designate either the entirety of moral norms, principles, values, or the quality of being moral, moral behavior. The English word "morality" seems closer to this in scope than "morals" does—and Kaufmann himself translates *Moral* as "morality" in nearly all other passages where Nietzsche uses it, including several passages in GM itself. Nietzsche identifies himself elsewhere (e.g., *Daybreak:* Preface 4) as one who is committed to overcoming morality (*Moral*), indeed as the first who is so committed (*Ecce Homo:* IV, 2–6), though it is often unclear, and scholars are quite divided, as to exactly what it is that he seeks to overcome. It therefore seems especially important to retain the translation of *Moral* as "morality" in the title of GM, to make clear that this book claims to examine the genealogy of whatever it is that Nietzsche seeks to overcome.

1:1   *we knowers*] The German in this passage is *wir Erkennenden*, which might be rendered: we who have or are in the process of acquiring knowledge (*Erkenntnis*). German has two words for "knowledge," *Erkenntnis* and *Wissen*, and N uses two corresponding words in GM that can be translated as "knower": *Erkennende* and *Wissende*. The term *Wissende* is used only once in GM—at 96:13ff—and it occurs in a quotation. Wherever N himself speaks of the "knower," he uses the word *Erkennende*. The importance of preserving a distinction between the two terms is suggested by the fact that Kant uses *Wissen* when he states that he had to deny the possibility of knowledge (rational knowledge of things in themselves) to make room for faith (*Critique of Pure Reason B xxx*), but uses *Erkenntnis* when he refers to the kind of knowledge we can actually have. N's usage is in line with Kant's. In BT, for instance, he uses *Wissen* when he claims that Socrates identifies virtue and knowledge (rational knowledge of the ideal), but uses *Erkenntnis* when he refers to the kind of knowledge he thinks we can have. (None of this is to make a claim about the meaning of these terms. See Rolf George, "Kant's Sensationism," *Synthese 47* [1981], pp. 229–55, for discussion of the meaning of *Erkenntnis* in Kant). English does not make it easy to distinguish between the two terms for the "knower"—Kaufmann uses "man of knowledge" and Smith "seeker of knowledge" for both. Recent translators of Kant have used "cognition" for *Erkenntnis*. But the style of GM makes "we cognizers" completely impossible. We have tried to preserve the distinction instead by using "knower" only for *der Erkennende* and "knowing one" for *der Wissende*. To trace the development of N's use of "knower," see HA 34 (which gives his first portrait of what becomes "the knower" without using the word), GS 54 (which does use the word and clearly repudiates HA's portrait; cf. GS 301, 110, 335), Z II:15 ("On Immaculate Knowledge," another repudiation of HA 34), and BGE 229 and 230. When we consider GM's use of "we knowers" in the context of such passages, it is difficult to avoid the conclusion that N uses this phrase to refer to those who are committed to a naturalistic or scientific view of the universe, thus that GM is designed to offer these "knowers" the self-knowledge the preface claims they lack.

1:3–4   *"where your ... be also"*] Matthew 6: 21.

1:20   *"each is furthest from himself,"*] The original, *"jeder ist sich selbst der Fernste,"* is Nietzsche's reversal of the German saying: *"jeder ist sich selbst der Nächste"* (each is for himself the nearest one) or in other words, everyone has his own interests closest to his heart. The German saying may derive from Terence, *Andria* IV, 1, line 12: *"Proxumus sum egomet mihi,"* (I am the one nearest myself), although it seems equally probable that it was influenced by the New Testament account of the Good Samaritan—Jesus' response to the question: *Wer ist denn mein Nächster?* (And who is my neighbor?, Luke 10: 29), which translates literally as: "And who is my nearest one?"

1:22   *origins*] The word translated here and throughout as "origins" is *Herkunft*. The singular "origin" translates *Ursprung*. Some recent scholars insist that "descent" or "lineage" be used to render *Herkunft*. Although this is often the meaning N intends, the word is also used in a more general sense to indicate the origins of something, where it came from. Our translation allows readers to decide from context between the more general and the specifically genealogical sense of the term.

2:24   *"half child's play, half God in one's heart,"*] Lines 3781–82 of Goethe's *Faust, Part One:*

Halb Kinderspiele,
Halb Gott im Herzen!

In the context of the play the lines would have to be translated: "half child's play, half God in *your* heart"—the line is addressed to Gretchen. Since German does not use a personal possessive pronoun here (*"im"* = in the), N can easily use it with reference to a third person.

2:25   *first philosophic writing exercise*] this essay has not been preserved. Cf. KSA 8, 28 [7].

2:28   *immoral, at least immoralistic*] The translation of the terms rendered here as "immoral" and "immoralistic" is somewhat problematic. The original German terms, *unmoralisch* and *immoralistisch*, are not identical in meaning with the English words of similar spelling. The German *unmoralisch* is similar to the English "immoral": in conflict with accepted moral principles. The German *immoralisch* is similar to the English "unmoral": not influenced by moral principles, not concerned with morality; N's *immoralistisch* is a later formation from this word. Accordingly *unmoralische, mindestens immoralistische* should probably be translated as "immoral, at least unmoralistic." However, this obscures the connection to N's claim to be an *Immoralist*, a term that must be rendered as "immoralist" in English as well—the term means either one who promotes the violation of accepted morality or one who opposes morality. In order to preserve this connection we have decided to translate "immoralistisch" as "immoralistic," trusting that the added "-istic" is enough to make it clear that what is meant is not "in conflict with accepted morality" (i.e., "immoral") but rather "in opposition to morality." See the Introduction for more on N's immoralism.

2:29 *"categorical imperative"*] In Kant's philosophy, a categorical imperative is a demand of reason that applies categorically, i.e., regardless of one's desires or personal ends, and this is the form of all *moral* demands. The intended contrast is with imperatives of prudence, which are also demands of reason, but ones that apply only hypothetically, on the assumption that one has certain desires or purposes. We learn from experience what we want, hence which hypothetical imperatives apply to us, and we can always escape their demands by giving up the relevant desires. Neither point is true of moral imperatives: Our knowledge of the demands of morality is *a priori*, not empirical, and we can never escape its demands by abandoning a desire or purpose. Yet what can reason demand of us beyond taking the necessary means to the satisfaction of our desires? Only one thing: "Act only on that maxim such that you can will it to be a universal law." This is, according to Kant's famous formulation in *Grounding of the Metaphysics of Morals, the* categorical imperative, the only imperative that could apply to us categorically, regardless of our desires, and it is therefore the fundamental principle of morality. We can understand how we can be bound by this principle, he claims, only if we assume something we can never prove: that we are much more than we appear to be from the viewpoint of natural science, namely, free or autonomous beings who give themselves this law and are subject to it only thereby. Nietzsche's reference to the categorical imperative so early in GM is indicative of the importance of his involvement with Kant's account of morality. In *Human, All Too Human* (1878) he attempted to explain all so-called "higher" human activities in naturalistic terms (in terms of what humans are like from a purely scientific point of view), and followed Schopenhauer in denying that there are any categorical imperatives. Our recognition that we ought to obey certain rules, N claimed, is always conditioned by a desire to gain pleasure or to avoid pain (HA 34). Section 9 of *Daybreak* (1881) records a change in his views on this matter. Although he does not use the phrase, he now suggests that erroneous beliefs in supernatural powers led primitive human beings to experience the demands of customs as, in effect, categorical imperatives, as applying to them regardless of their own desires. The GM passage under consideration suggests a further development: N abandons

Daybreak's idea that only erroneous beliefs can lead one to recognize demands as categorical. He now sees himself and his own work as responsive to a categorical imperative: Demands are made on him that he cannot get out of. (Cf. *Beyond Good and Evil* 226: "*We immoralists* ... have been spun into a severe yarn and shirt of duties, and *cannot* get out of it.") If he thus sides with Kant against all "English psychologists" (see note 9:1) who would reduce imperatives to a combination of reason and desire, N insists that his categorical imperative is "anti-Kantian," for he denies both that it comes from pure reason and that it applies to all human beings.

3:12   *smart, even overly smart*] "clever, even precocious" might be more literal, but we have tried to preserve some of the word play of the original (*klug, auch altklug*). This is the first occurrence in GM of *klug*, a very important word in this book, one it would be ideal for readers to be able to track throughout the text. Unfortunately, we were not able to find one word that suits all occurrences. We translate it as "prudent" when the contrast with morality is important (see note 2:29 for the Kantian background) and as "shrewd" when it is used to refer to a clever, calculating use of intelligence. See also note 10:37.

3:17   *Dr. Paul Rée*] (1849–1901), doctor of law, philosopher, physician. N met Rée in 1873 and the two developed a close friendship and intellectual companionship, which led them to spend the winter of 1876–1877 together in Sorrento where they each pursued their mutual interest in the history of morality. They shared a commitment to providing an explanation of morality in completely naturalistic terms, without reference to religious or metaphysical sources and taking account only of what can be known of human beings from a scientific point of view. Their relationship ended badly in the winter of 1882–83 due to complications within the "trinity" the two men had formed with a young Russian woman, Lou Andreas-Salomé. See R. Binion, *Frau Lou: Nietzsche's Wayward Disciple* (Princeton: Princeton UP, 1968), for an impressive and fascinating psychoanalytical study of their "unholy trinity" (Lou's term) and its demise, which cost N what was probably the only true intellectual companionship of his adult life. He was left devastated and feeling completely alone. Rée, who received a doctorate from Halle with a dissertation on Aristotle's ethics in 1875, published an anonymous collection of psychological observations (*Psychologische Beobachtungen*) that same year. According to HA 37, he thereby became the first German to join the ranks of "Larochefoucauld and the other French masters of the examination of the psyche." HA proceeds to award even more extravagant praise to Rée's second book, *Vom Ursprung der moralischen Empfindungen* (On the Origin of Moral Sensations, 1877), whose author N calls "one of the boldest and coldest of thinkers, and whose proposition that moral man "stands no closer to the intelligible (metaphysical) world than does physical man," arrived at by "incisive and penetrating analysis of human action," is said to be one with "the weightiest consequences." Indeed, "this proposition, hardened and sharpened beneath the hammer-blow of historical knowledge, may perhaps at some future time serve as the ax which is laid to the root of the human "metaphysical need" (HA 38). This is undoubtedly one of HA's "inopportune" references to Rée. In the passage under consideration, N is clearly attempting to distance himself from its extravagant praise and to minimize Rée's importance to his own intellectual development. After the publication of two other works, *Die Entstehung des Gewissens* (The Genesis of Conscience, 1885), and *Die Illusion der Willensfreiheit* (The Illusion of Freedom of the Will, 1885), Rée returned to the university in Munich, studied medicine, and became a physician. He spent the last ten years of his life working as a doctor in rural farming communities in eastern Switzerland. Some consider his death a suicide. His final work, *Philosophie* (Philosophy, 1903), was published posthumously.

3:31   *45*] For the passages referred to here and elsewhere throughout the text, Nietzsche gives the page number from the first edition of each work. We have supplied instead the section numbers, which are the same in all editions and languages.

3:34   *"morality of custom"*] See note 36:18 in GM II.

4:15   *Schopenhauer*] Arthur Schopenhauer (1788–1860), sometimes described as the "philosopher of pessimism." Largely ignored until very late in his life, he became the most widely read German philosopher in the English-speaking world during the second half of the nineteenth century, but is now largely known for the influence he had on Nietzsche. He also significantly influenced Freud and Wittgenstein. He called Kant, Plato, and Buddha the greatest influences on his own philosophy. Schopenhauer accepted Kant's claim that the empirical world, which we know through perception and natural science, is the world only as it appears to the knower, not as it is in itself. But he rejected Kant's further claim that the thing in itself is completely unknowable. He claimed that in itself the world is will—a blind, striving impulse similar to what Freud would later call the "id." Plurality and difference belong not to the will as it is in itself, but only to its phenomena, to how it appears to the subject of knowledge. The same identical will is thus found in everything, including rocks and plants. In the latter cases, however, willing is not connected to knowing. Knowledge comes into existence only to guide the will in achieving its ends, which is possible only in those animals that can seek and select their food. Knowledge and reason only discover means to satisfy the will; they cannot discover what is good, what we should will. (This is why Schopenhauer denies that imperatives can apply to us categorically, regardless of our desires. See note 2:29.) Schopenhauer's pessimism follows from his view that there is nothing that could ultimately satisfy the will, for it actually wants nothing—except its own satisfaction. He sees pleasure or satisfaction as a purely negative state, the negation of pain, which always has its source in willing. Life is thus a "pendulum" swinging between suffering and boredom; we suffer when we want something we do not have; we are bored if we have everything we want. A "happy" life differs from an unhappy life only in that the pendulum swings more quickly in the former. One who faces up to this truth realizes that life's only point is to realize that it has no point. Salvation is to be found,

Schopenhauer argues, only through the practice of asceticism—by denying the will the particular satisfactions it seeks, beginning with sexual satisfaction. He believes that the great ascetics have been able to overcome willing completely, and have thereby entered into a state of bliss (nirvana). N, who responds critically to Schopenhauer's view of asceticism in GM III (especially 5–8), first encountered his philosophy while at the University of Leipzig. In 1865 he discovered Schopenhauer's principal work, *The World as Will and Representation*, in a book-shop, and could hardly put it down until he had finished it. In *Schopenhauer as Educator* (UO III:2), he wrote: "I belong to those readers of Schopenhauer who know for certain after they have read the first page of his work that they will read every page and listen to every word that he ever said. My confidence in him was immediately present ... I understood him as if he had written for me ..." N's development as a philosopher can be understood as a series of attempts to come to terms with the truth he recognized in Schopenhauer's view of the world without accepting the conclusions to which it had led Schopenhauer: that life is not worth living and that the ascetic life is the highest life. The "truth" in Schopen-hauer's view, as N makes plain in *Gay Science* 357, is not that the world is will, but that human existence has no given end or purpose. For Schopenhauer, the first admitted atheist among German philosophers, N writes, the "ungodliness of existence was for him something given, tangible"; his pessimism was "his horri-fied look into a de-deified ... world," but also "a way of remaining—remaining caught—in precisely the Christian ascetic perspective of morality, faith in which is renounced with faith in God." N's early devotion to Schopenhauer was some-thing he shared with Wagner (see note 67:19). In a section of *Gay Science* entitled "Schopenhauer's Followers," N implies that there was, however, a major differ-ence. Wagner was attracted by, and never moved beyond, the "barbaric" elements in Schopenhauer's philosophy, the "mystical embarrassments and subterfuges in those places where the factual thinker allowed himself to be seduced and cor-rupted by the vain urge to be the unriddler of the world," including his doctrines of "the one will" and the "nonsense about compassion" (see notes 4:18 and 4:19). N implies that he himself was also attracted by such elements, but that they even-tually drew him into "what really has value": Schopenhauer's "higher culture," his "sense for hard facts, his good will to clarity and reason, which so often makes him appear so English and un-German." He thus suggests that Schopenhauer's philosophy ultimately led him to the naturalistic standpoint he began developing in HA, and to a rejection of what had initially attracted him and remained attrac-tive to Wagner (GS 99).

4:18   *compassion*] Here and throughout the text the German *Mitleid* has been translated as "compassion." Previous translators have usually rendered it as "pity." The latter seems strange given that *Mitleid* is not only identical with "compassion" in its root meaning—they both mean "suffering with"—but is also the word rendered as "compassion" in English translations of Schopenhauer, whose connection of moral behavior with "compassion" originally provoked Nietzsche's thinking about morality. Finally, Nietzsche's claim about modern "preferential treatment" of *Mitleid* makes more sense if he means "compassion" rather than "pity." The one exception we were forced to make was the rendition of *"tragisches Mitleid"* as the idiomatic "tragic pity."

4:19–21 *Schopenhauer … in themselves,"*] Schopenhauer posits compassion as the basis of morality in both *The World as Will and Representation* and *On the Basis of Morality.* Strongly critical of Kant's claim that the motive of duty gives moral worth to actions, he insists that moral worth belongs only to actions done from compassion, from the "immediate participation" in the suffering of another person. He explains that such compassion is possible only because we can see through the illusory character of individuality and recognize the truth: the "one will" underlying all appearance (see note 4:15). This recognition is immediate or intuitive rather than rational or philosophical, however, precisely because reason can only serve the will, whereas compassion begins to turn one away from willing. This is the "nonsense about compassion" N refers to in GS 99 (see note 4:15). N accepted much of Schopenhauer's view of the importance of compassion in his early works (see especially UO III:3), but he began to "struggle" with it in HA by trying to show that all the apparent instances of compassion could be understood in terms of self-love or other egoistic motives. N's later criticism of Schopenhauer on compassion is very different. Consider especially the passage entitled "Schopenhauer" in TI (IX: 21), which claims that Schopenhauer maliciously attempted "to adduce in favor of a nihilistic total depreciation of life precisely the counter-instances, the great self-affirmations of the will to life, life's forms of exuberance." Here N explicitly includes great sympathy (*grosse Mitgefuhl*) among these "counter-instances," and as "one of the great cultural facts of humanity" (i.e., one of the great facts due to human culture). The implication is that Schopenhauer's understanding and valuation of compassion, of "suffering-with," involve a nihilistic misintepretation and incorrect valuation of sympathy, of "feeling with." N's character, Zarathustra, makes a similar point in "On the Compassionate" (Z II: 3): "Truly, I may have done this and that for sufferers; but always I seem to have done better when I learned better to feel joy. As long as there have been human beings, they have felt too little joy: that alone, my brothers, is our original sin! And learning better to feel joy, we unlearn best hurting others and thinking up hurts for them."

4:31 *Buddhism for Europeans*] i.e., Schopenhauer's teachings concerning the denial of the will as the path to salvation.

4:35 *Plato*] Greek philosopher (427–347 BC), student of Socrates and teacher of Aristotle, the philosopher to whom all other philosophy is said to be a footnote. His most well-known critique of compassion or pity is found in Book X of *Republic* (606 a-b) as part of his argument against the poets, who appeal to the emotions rather than to reason.

4:35 *Spinoza*] Baruch (Benedict) Spinoza (1632–1677), Dutch-Jewish philosopher, usually grouped with Descartes and Leibniz as one of the three most important modern rationalists; known especially for his attempt to overcome the

dualism between mind and matter and for his "geometrical" method of presenting philosophy. Spinoza's major work, *Ethica*, was published by his friends
shortly after his death. In the definitions of the affects at the end of *Ethics* III—
definition XVIII, Exp.—Spinoza observes that there "seems to be no difference
between Pity (commiseratio) and Compassion (misericordia), except perhaps that
Pity concerns the singular affect, whereas Compassion concerns the habitual dis-
position of this affect." In *Ethics* II, P 49, Schol. IV/C and *Ethics* IV, P 37, Schol.
1 he describes compassion as "unmanly." In *Ethics* III, P 32, Schol., Spinoza
writes: "for the most part human nature is so constituted that men pity the unfortunate and envy the fortunate, and [...] with greater hate the more they love the
thing they imagine the other to possess. We see, then, that from the same property
of human nature from which it follows that men are compassionate, it also follows
that the same men are envious and ambitious." The translations of passages from
Spinoza, here and elsewhere, are from the Edwin Curley translation, *The Collected
Works of Spinoza*, Princeton: Princeton UP, 1985.

4:35   *La Rochefoucauld*] François VI, duc de La Rochefoucauld (1613–
1680), French aristocrat and classical author. La Rochefoucauld's only major
work, the *Maximes*, is a collection of maxims or aphorisms—a literary form that
aims at expressing a truth in a brief and pointed and sometimes paradoxical form.
La Rochefoucauld's maxims, which usually aim to expose the self-love or self-
interest behind apparently noble or altruistic behavior, were of great interest to
Nietzsche during the period of HA, in which he attempted to explain all of
"higher" human activities in similarly egoistic terms. By the time he wrote *Daybreak* 103, N had already moved beyond what he saw as La Rochefoucauld's
"denial of morality" (though he continued to grant it importance) to a second way
of denying morality (see the Introduction to this translation and note 2:29). La
Rochefoucauld writes of compassion: "I am little receptive to pity and would like
it if I were not at all. Nevertheless there is nothing I would not do for the relief of
an afflicted person, and I believe in fact that one ought to do everything up to the
point of evincing even a great deal of compassion for his pain, for the miserable
are so foolish that this constitutes the greatest good in the world for them; but I
also hold that it is necessary to content oneself with evincing it and to guard oneself carefully against having it. It is an emotion that is not good for anything in a
soul well constituted, that only serves to weaken the heart and must be left to the
common folk who, never doing anything by reason, need emotion to move them to
do things." From *"Portrait de La Rochefoucauld par lui-même,"* in *Maximes* (Paris:
Éditions Garnier, 1967) 256–57. See also maxims 264, 463, 475, and 503.

4:35   *Kant*] Immanuel Kant (1724–1804), German philosopher, usually recognized as the most important modern philosopher, and one of the central figures
of the Enlightenment. Especially influential for N were Kant's critique of the
claim of rationalist metaphysics that the ultimate nature of reality can be known *a
priori*, through pure reason, and his denial that we can know things in themselves.
N knew Kant through his study of Schopenhauer (see note 4:15) and of Friedrich

Albert Lange's *History of Materialism*, a neo-Kantian work and important source for much of N's knowledge of contemporary science, including Darwin's theory. N read Lange's book immediately after its publication in the summer of 1866 and, according to N's biographer, Paul Curt Janz, also read Kuno Fischer's two-volume work on Kant as well as Kant's *Critique of Judgment* during the following two years (Janz, I: 199). Kant's relevant and well-known claim about compassion (*Mitleid*) is that it has no moral worth (e.g., in Section 1 of *Grounding of the Metaphysics of Morals*). It may lead people to do what morality requires, but it may also lead to the violation of duty. It is on the same level as other inclinations, such as the inclination for honor, which, if "fortunately directed to what is in fact beneficial and accords with duty," may deserve "praise and encouragement, but not esteem." Moral or intrinsic worth is to be found only in acting from the motive of duty, from respect for the moral law. Schopenhauer vehemently rejected this aspect of Kant's philosophy.

6:5 *into the blue*] The German idiom has been translated literally here in order to preserve the play on colors in this passage. The sense of the idiom should be readily apparent, given the fact that English has a similar idiom: "out of the blue." The English idiom—drawing on the meaning of "blue" the *New Shorter OED* gives as "the clear sky; the sea; the desert; the indefinite distance, the unknown"—means "without warning," "unexpectedly." The German "into the blue"—*ins Blaue*—draws on the same connotations of blue and means "without aim" or "randomly."

6:10 *Darwin*] Charles Robert Darwin (1809–1882), English naturalist, author of *On the Origin of Species by Means of Natural Selection* (1859). This book's detailed presentation of the evidence that species have evolved and its account of the mechanism of evolution (natural selection) led to an almost immediate acceptance of evolutionary theory in scholarly circles and initiated a major revolution in our understanding of human beings that is still going on. It is commonly assumed that N was basically "anti-Darwin" (the title of *Twilight of the Idols* IX: 14) and it is sometimes said that he favored Lamarck's theory over Darwin's. Although his comments about Darwin generally have a hostile tone, his actual objection to Darwin is not so obvious. It is certainly far from evident that he denies the truth of Darwin's basic theory. N's derogatory comments and grouping of Darwin with John Stuart Mill and Herbert Spencer as "respectable but mediocre Englishmen" in *Beyond Good and Evil* 253 may obscure the passage's clear implication that Darwin's theory is true. It claims that "there are some truths that are recognized best by mediocre minds," by those who do not "soar on their own paths," and that such a "mediocre" mind may be best "for scientific discoveries of Darwin's kind." In effect N concedes the realm of knowledge to Darwin in this passage. But he insists that the philosopher's task, as opposed to the scholar's or scientist's, is more "than merely to gain knowledge," that it concerns values, the presentation and representation of new values. "Anti-Darwin" in *Twilight* can also be understood in these terms: N's rejection of the "struggle for existence" and the survival of the "strong"

can be interpreted as a rejection *not* of Darwin's scientific claims, but of the
assumption that the "survival of the fittest" (Herbert Spencer's phrase) is the survival of the best or most perfect (the "strong" in N's terminology). Its point is that
Darwin's theory does not by itself provide a basis for value judgments. This passage can thus be seen as a rejection of the use social Darwinists, such as Spencer,
made of Darwin's theory—of the attempt to derive a normative ethical theory
directly from Darwinian premises—rather than as a rejection of anything Darwin
himself claimed. If Darwin is thus insufficient for N's philosophical or normative
task, he may nonetheless be seen as the major source for N's main scholarly task:
the development of a naturalistic understanding of human beings. BGE 230 offers
a powerful formulation of that "task," which it presents as bestowed upon N precisely by his commitment to knowledge: "To translate man back into nature; to
become master over the many vain and overly enthusiastic interpretations and connotations that have so far been scrawled and painted over the basic eternal text of
homo natura; to see to it that man henceforth stands before man as even today,
hardened in the discipline of science, he stands before the *rest* of nature," deaf to
old metaphysics calls ("you are more, you are higher, you are of different origins").
N's (scholarly) "task" might be seen as the further extension of the Darwinian revolution into the human realm. This was already Paul Rée's aim, as N suggests in
this passage; N's criticism is that Rée's attempt to apply Darwin to human beings
was too mechanical and *a priori*, i.e., insufficiently respectful of the details of actual
human history. For the views of a contemporary Darwinian and philosopher who
sees GM as a major contribution to the Darwinian revolution, see Daniel Dennett,
Darwin's Dangerous Idea (New York: Simon and Schuster, 1996).

6:27ff   *8*] In a letter from Venice, dated October 5, 1887, N wrote to his publisher:

To be inserted as eighth section of the preface, so that the last section of the
same henceforth bears the number 9.

8.

Finally, to point with at least a word to an enormous and still entirely undiscovered set of facts that has made itself clear to me slowly, slowly: there have
been no *more fundamental* problems thus far than the moral ones; it was their
driving energy from which all great conceptions in the realm of the previous
values originated (—everything, that is, which is commonly called "philosophy"; and this down to its final epistemological presuppositions). *But there are
still more fundamental problems than the moral ones*: these first come into view
when one has the moral prejudice behind oneself, when one knows how to look
into the world, into life, into oneself as an *immoralist*.

A postcard N sent the same day rescinded this request, however: "Most
esteemed Sir, the section of manuscript sent this morning (addendum to the preface) is *not* to be adopted; the original ordering thus remains, according to which
the preface has 8 sections."

7:5–6   *an aphorism*] See note 67:0.

First Treatise

9:1   *These English psychologists*] It has been suggested that this phrase refers to the British philosophers of the utilitarian-associationist school, perhaps especially Hume, Hartley, Hutcheson, Bentham, and Mill (David S. Thatcher "Zur Genealogie der Moral: Some Textual Annotations," in *Nietzsche-Studien* 18 [1989] 588). N had gathered considerable information about these thinkers from Lecky's *History of European Morals* (1869), a book he mentions in a postcard to his publisher (March 19, 1881), on what seems to be a list of books ordered, and for which he later had considerable praise. "English psychologists" is something of a misnomer, however, and not simply, as Thatcher points out, because Hume was Scottish rather than English. That N explicitly classifies Hume as "English" in BGE 252 already suggests that he was not using this term in the most literal sense. The only thinker specifically associated with an "English" account of morality in GM is actually not even British, but German: Paul Rée, Nietzsche's friend and intellectual companion while he was writing *Human, All Too Human* (1878). This book, sometimes called the beginning of N's "positivistic" period, was his first, and often very crude, attempt to understand human beings and their activities in completely naturalistic terms (see the Introduction to this translation). The specific "English" proposal regarding morality that Nietzsche criticizes in GM I: 3 is actually closer to the view he himself offered in *HA* (especially in HA 39 and 92) than it is to any offered by a British philosopher discussed by Lecky. On the other hand, *Daybreak* (1881) does suggest an account of the origin of morality that is very close to the summary Lecky gives of the view of the utilitarianian-associationists (D 104). It differs from the one N criticizes in GM because it is missing the element of 'forgetting.' These considerations suggest that Nietzsche uses the phrase "English psychologists" largely to call to mind earlier attempts, including his own, to explain morality in naturalistic terms. He begins his genealogy of morality by referring to his own "ancestors." Since Hume is probably the greatest of these, his naturalistic account of morality is the obvious standard against which to judge Nietzsche's claim to have made a significant advance over his predecessors.

10:20   *"usefulness,"*] Although Nietzsche is discussing utilitarianism here, he does not use the term *Utilität*—here or elsewhere—though it had been introduced into German by this time. Both the Germanic *Nützlichkeit* (usefulness) and the Latinate *Utilität* are used in translations of the works of the utilitarians; the former is used in the translation of Mill's *Utilitarianism* found in N's personal library, *Das Nützlichkeitsprincip* (Leipzig, 1869). Because *Nützlichkeit* is an everyday word, we have often translated it as "usefulness." We have translated the same word as "utility" where doing so seemed important to bring out the connection between N's argument and utilitarianism.

10:31–32   *pathos of distance*] The feeling of distance N refers to here is discussed further in BGE 257. The latter passage suggests that the ultimate importance of this *pathos* to N lies in what he thinks it made possible: "that other, more mysterious pathos ... the craving for an ever new widening of distances within the soul itself, the development of ever higher, rarer, further, wider-spanning, more comprehensive states—in brief, the enhancement of the type 'man,' the continual 'self-overcoming of man,' to take a moral formula in a sense that goes beyond morality (*in einem übermoralischen Sinne*)." Cf. BGE 213.

10:37   *every calculating prudence*] *jede berechnende Klugheit.* This is the first occurrence in GM of *Klugheit* (prudence), the noun form of *klug (*prudent or shrewd; see note 3:12). N's use of it here with the adjective "calculating" helps to bring out the intended meaning of "prudence" throughout this translation: a calculating rationality, the use of reason merely to find means to ends that are already given, rather than to reflect on the ends themselves. See note 80:1.

11:34   *Herbert Spencer*] (1820–1903), English sociologist and philosopher. An early advocate of evolutionary theory, he is the father of Social Darwinism: Spencer (and not Darwin) was the one who coined the phrase "survival of the fittest" and claimed that the fittest survive; he also defended an extreme form of economic and social *laissez-faire*. Spencer had already developed a somewhat Lamarckian theory of evolution before Darwin published the *Origin of Species;* after its publication, Spencer accepted Darwin's theory of natural selection but continued to insist that Lamarckian modifications play a role in evolution. His originality lies in his attempt to develop a systematic philosophy based on evolutionary theory. Using theories and results from the various branches of science, he tried to show that everything in the universe exemplifies the same evolutionary development from a simple state where only elementary functions are present to a more complex state characterized by more complicated functions. His major work, *The Synthetic Philosophy*, completed in 1896, traced the operation of this evolutionary principle through the various sciences; it included volumes on biology, psychology, sociology, and ethics. This work makes him a good example of those N criticizes in GM III:24 for supposing that philosophy can be placed "on a strictly scientific foundation" (110:9ff). Spencer's ethics is, however, the focus of N's interest in him. N first mentions Spencer in correspondence from 1879, and in the spring of 1880 he read the German translation of Spencer's *Data of Ethics* (now Part I of Vol. 1 of *The Principles of Ethics*; the quotations below are all taken from chapter three of this work). Unlike the "English psychologists," Spencer understands morality as a product of evolution, but, like them, his orientation is utilitarian. In *Data of Ethics*, he discusses "what good and bad mean," arguing that we obviously call inanimate things "good" or "bad" not on the basis of "intrinsic characters," but "according as they are well or ill suited to serve prescribed ends," ends prescribed, that is, by human desires, for "apart from human wants, such things have neither merits nor demerits." Likewise, when we pass from inanimate things to living ones; we still find that "these words in their current application refer to efficient subservience." The goodness or badness of other animals, Spencer assumes, is determined completely by their "fitness" for serving "the ends men use them for." Human conduct is really no different: actions are good or bad, right or wrong, depending on whether they "do or do not further the general end of self-preservation." This is not to deny that "goodness, standing by itself, suggests above all other things, the conduct of one who aids the sick in reacquiring normal functioning, assists the unfortunate to recover the means of maintaining themselves, defends those who are threatened with harm in person, property, or reputation, and aids in whatever promises to improve the living of all his fellows." But this shows only that "acts are called good or bad, according as they are well or ill adjusted to ends." Any apparent inconsistency with previous claims arises from an inconsistency in the ends. But here evolutionary theory comes in to resolve the problem, for, as Spencer claims to show in the remainder of this book, "the conduct to which we apply the name good, is the relatively more evolved conduct, and ... bad is the name we apply to conduct that is relatively less evolved." That is, since evolution "tending ever towards self-preservation, reaches its limits where individual life is greatest, both in length and breadth ... evolution becomes the highest possible when the conduct simultaneously achieves the greatest totality of life in self, in offspring, and in fellow men; so here we see that the conduct called good rises to the conduct called best when it fulfills all three classes of ends at the same time." The only assumption in "these judgments on conduct," claims Spencer, is that life is worth living, and those who argue either side of this question—optimists and pessimists alike—assume that "life is good or bad, depending on whether it does, or does not, bring a surplus of agreeable feeling." Thus, " no school can avoid taking for the ultimate moral aim a desirable state of feeling by whatever name—gratification, enjoyment, happiness." GS 4 and 12 are two of the many passages that show how fundamentally N's views differ from Spencer's.

12:13   *in the sense related to the estates*] The German here is the adverb *ständisch*, that is, "relating to the estates" (*Stände*) that existed in various forms at least up until the French Revolution: these were the basic divisions—usually three—of society; the first two were the aristocracy and the clergy, the third was once the peasant or farmer, later the burgher or bourgeois, with the peasantry now outside any estate. The term "fourth estate" could refer to any group other than these three that exercised significant power within the state—in recent times it has come to refer exclusively to the press. One could translate this as "in the class sense," but we have chosen here to use this less familiar but more literal translation to preserve the "genealogy" of N's position—he is not discussing groups of society with reference to classes in the sense popularized by Marx—that of dialectically opposed, competing interest groups—but rather with reference to earlier notions of classes or "estates" as the naturally existing component parts of a whole.

12:31   *Buckle's notorious case*] Henry Thomas Buckle (1821–1862), English historian, the first one versed in the British empiricist tradition to offer a comprehensive and detailed theory of historical development. He became famous—and, indeed, notorious—through his one and only work, *History of Civilization in England*. Holding in contempt the history of his day, which emphasized politics, war, and heroes, he aimed to make history scientific by discovering the fixed laws that govern the actions of men and therefore of societies. On the basis of large-scale surveys concerning the number of marriages, murders and suicides in particular towns and countries during successive years, he argued that human actions are subject to regularities as strict and mathematically exact as those discovered in other branches of scientific inquiry. The relative uniformity of the results of such surveys would be unintelligible, he argued, unless there are social laws capable of keeping the level constant. Because he did not always recognize the difference between causal laws and statistical frequencies, however, he seemed to be claiming something that certainly did not follow from his premises: that the mere existence of a proportional average holding over a period of time necessitated with an irresistible force the commission of a certain number of crimes in a particular year. The resulting picture of human beings as helpless victims of laws over which they have no control is what N takes to reflect the *"plebeianism* of the modern spirit"; the only possibly attractive feature of this picture is that at least everyone is equal before these laws, for no one has power (cf. BGE 22). The willingness to accept this picture of human beings is also a good example of what N refers to (at 52:6) as learning to live with the "mechanistic senselessness of all happening." When Buckle came to the details of the development of civilization, he actually said little about precise numerical regularities. The "laws" he spoke of turned out to be broad and sometimes very doubtful generalizations concerning the factors that determine the development of societies. Buckle believed that the degree of civilization attained by a society depended on the amount and distribution of its wealth, which depended on the size of its population, which was determined in turn by its food source. The ideal conditions for the development of civilization, he claimed, were found in Europe: the food supply was not so abundant as to lead to overpopulation and its problems, nor so scanty as to make leisure or the intellectual development dependent on it impossible. A number of other factors about the physical conditions ensured that Europeans were less likely to treat nature as an object of awe and veneration, hence to see it instead as something that obeyed regular laws and was therefore capable of being tamed and utilized for human purposes. Although he claimed that the development of civilization in Europe was therefore determined by "the laws of the human mind," he never said what these laws were, but claimed only that the advance and diffusion of knowledge, in particular, of science, was the main factor that gave the development of Europe its overall direction. Morality, in contrast, had little to do with this development, since it had changed little over thousands of years and therefore could not be responsible for the far-reaching transformations of European society. This is undoubtedly the "nonsense inflicted on history and morality" that N refers to in this passage. In a letter of May 20, 1887, N writes that he has just seen Buckle's "much renowned book" and discovered that he is "one of [his] strongest antagonists," adding that "it is hardly believable, how much E. Dühring has made himself dependent on the crude value judgments of this democrat in historical things." See 48:26 and related notes on Dühring.

12:34–35 *volcanoes*] In a letter of May 5, 1873, N applies this metaphor for heated and vehement writing to his own book on David Strauss (UO I), which was a polemic against the idealistic historians of his day. His critique of volcanoes in the present passage presumably applies to his own earlier self, therefore, but it also leaves open the possibility of a polemical style, say that of GM itself, that is not "oversalted, overloud, [or] common."

13:13 *Megarian poet Theognis*] (late 6th–early 5th century BC), Greek elegiac poet from Megara. At the close of his education at Pforta, N wrote a valedictorian essay on Theognis. In a connected piece, he gives the following description of him: "Theognis appears as a finely formed nobleman who has fallen on bad times, with the passions of a nobleman such as his time loved, full of fatal hatred toward the upward-striving masses, tossed about by a sad fate that wore him down and made him milder in many respects. He is a characteristic image of that old, ingenious, somewhat spoiled and no longer firmly rooted blood nobility, placed at the boundary between an old and a new era, a distorted Janus-head, since what is past seems so beautiful and enviable, that which is coming—something that basically has an equal entitlement—seems disgusting and repulsive, a typical head for all of those noble figures who represent the aristocracy prior to a popular revolution that forever threatens their privileges and that moves them to fight and struggle for the existence of the class of nobles with the same passion as for their individual existence" (translated from a quotation given in the biography of Nietzsche by Curt Paul Janz, vol. I, page 124). N's first publication—while still a student at Leipzig—was an article on the textual transmission of Theognis' maxims: "Zur Geschichte der Theognideischen Spruchsammlung" ("On the History of the Collection of the Theognideian Anthology," 1867).

13:26 *hic niger est*] he is black. The quotation is from Horace's *Satires*, I. 4, line 85: "He that backbites an absent friend, ... and cannot keep secrets, is black, O Roman, beware!"

14:7 *Virchow*] Rudolf Virchow (1821–1902), physician, professor of medicine, and liberal politician. Virchow was one of the most prominent physicians of the 19th century and did pioneering work in the field of cellular pathology—establishing the position that disease arises on the cellular level of the organism and not in the organs or tissues per se. Through his work in the analysis of skull formation he also became involved in the field of anthropology and in 1869 founded the Berlin Society for Anthropology, Ethnology, and Prehistory, of which he was president until his death. He was also editor of the society's journal, *Zeitschrift für Ethnologie*. Alongside his scientific activities Virchow was also politically active and was involved in numerous public health projects in Berlin. He was co-founder of the German Progressive Party, a member of the *Reichstag* (parliament), and one of Bismarck's most outspoken opponents.

As Thatcher has pointed out, as early as 1867–1868 N had works by Virchow on his list of books to read. Thatcher's suggestion that N's reference in GM is to an article that appeared in Virchow's *Zeitschrift für Ethnologie*—"Der Spreewald

und die Lausitz," XII (1880), p. 228—is unfounded; the article does refer to
Celtic and Germanic traces, but it is simply a discussion of artifacts found in
graves and makes no mention of hair or skin color. Virchow's article "Die Urbe-
völkerung Europas" (No. 193 in Series IX of the *Sammlung gemeinverständlicher
wissenschaftlicher Vorträge*, Berlin: Lüderitz, 1874, 1–48) does contain a discussion
such as the one N refers to, but it does not support N's claim. Virchow here
clearly groups the Celts among the Aryan peoples characterized by "white skin
color, light color of hair and eyes, namely blond or reddish (and at the same time
straight or curly) hair and blue eyes, long and narrow (dolicephale) skulls with
receding jaw structure, tall and robust bodies" in opposition to the pre-Aryan
populations, whom Virchow calls "Turanians," and who are characterized by "a
darker, more brownish or yellowish skin color, brown or black (frizzly) hair, and
dark eyes, short and broad (brachycephale) skulls with protruding jaw, delicate,
short, and weaker body build." "The depictions that have been handed down to
us from antiquity of the Celtic, Germanic, and in part of the Slavic peoples fit the
first case, the depictions of the Iberians, the Lapps, and the Estonians fit the second case" (29–30).

14:13   *"commune,"*] Although N is criticizing a general tendency here, he is
also alluding to a particular example. In March of 1871, after the French capitula-
tion to Germany in the Franco-Prussian War, nationalist resistance to the prema-
ture peace with Germany and republican resistance to monarchist tendencies in
the National Assembly led to a revolt of the National Guard against the regular
government troops. Elections organized by the central committee of the Parisian
National Guard led to the formation of the "Commune," a city parliament con-
sisting of 85 members. The Commune's activities (worker protection, cancellation
of rent debts, free schooling) tended in the direction of a socialist republic. The
Commune was unable to organize an effective political and military leadership,
however, and was soon defeated in the brutal fighting that ensued when regular
government troops reentered the city in late May.

14:18–19   *duonus*] An earlier form of *bonus*, related to *bellum* (war), and *duellum*, an earlier, poetic form of the word *bellum*. The standard work on Latin etymology, Alois Walde's *Lateinisches etymologisches Wörterbuch*, indicates that the
particular etymology N proposed here is untenable. The sense of "division"
found in the word "duel" did not develop until the late Middle Ages.

15:26   *Weir-Mitchellian isolation*] Silas Weir Mitchell (1829–1914), was a
socially prominent Philadelphian physician and novelist who specialized in treating "nervous" disorders. He became widely known in America and Europe for his
"rest cure" for such illnesses: patients were first isolated from the influence of hov-
ering, over-careful family members and restricted to bed for four to six weeks, during which they were not allowed to have visitors or to read or write. They were fed
by a nurse and given massages to keep up strength and muscle tone. When they
began to show improvement, patients were ordered to get up and take exercise.
Mitchell first made his rest cure public in the *American Journal of Medical Science*

in July of 1873. The treatment quickly gained popularity—both at home and abroad: while Mitchell was visiting the spas at Baden-Baden in 1888, the Grand Duchess of Baden invited him to an audience and told him that two of her cousins had taken the cure. Freud also mentions the cure in *Studies in Hysteria* (1895). Mitchell was also well known for his novels and stories, which often dealt with characters suffering from nervous disorders.

15:31   *brahma*] "The basic idea of the Vedanta—most briefly expressed in the Vedic words: *tat tvam asi*, 'this is what you are' ... and *aham brahma asmi*, 'I am brahma'—is *the identity of brahma and the soul*, which is to say that *brahma*, i.c. the eternal principle of all being, the force that creates all worlds, sustains them, and then takes them back into itself, is identical with *âtman*, the self or the soul, i.e., that in us which, if we truly know, we recognize as our actual self, as our inner and true being. This soul of each one of us is not a part, an effluence of brahma, but rather completely and entirely the eternal, indivisible brahma itself." From: "Brief Overview of the Teaching of the Vedanta" at the end of Paul Deussen's *System des Vedânta* (see note 78:29–30 in the third treatise).

15:31   *glass pendant*] The German here is *gläserner Knopf* (glass or glassy knob or button); what is intended is presumably the sort of bright, shiny object used to hypnotize. Kaufmann's "glass knob" might fit that description, but Diethe's and Smith's "crystal ball" (likewise the French translation of Heim, Hildenbrand, and Gratien—*boule de cristal*—and the Italian of Masini—*sfera di cristallo*) is misleading; this is not something that enables one to see the future but rather something that makes one oblivious to all else. Cf. the third section of the second treatise in GM on hypnotizing and "idées fixes." Cf. also *Gay Science* 364.

18:1   *"all the world,"*] cf. Luke 2: 1.

18:8   *sub hoc signo*] under this sign. This is a reference to the famous motto that Emperor Constantine is supposed to have seen written on a cross that he saw in a vision. In Greek the motto read simply: "by this, conquer"; in Latin it was rendered as *"in hoc signo vinces,"* "under this sign I conquer." According to the legend, Constantine carried a cross into battle against Maxentius in the year 312 and saw his victory as a fulfillment of the vision. He consequently converted to Christianity.

19:3   *ressentiment*] This French term has stronger associations with revenge than the corresponding English term "resentment." In earlier books, N had used the German term *Rache* (revenge) for the same concept. See, for instance, "On the Tarantulas" in Z II:7: *"that man be delivered from revenge*, that is for me the bridge to the highest hope." He evidently started using *ressentiment* for the same idea due to his reading of Dühring (see esp. note 49:18–19). Compare what N says in this passage about the role of *ressentiment* to BGE 219, in which moral judgments and condemnations are said to offer opportunities for revenge, but also for "acquiring spirit and becoming refined:—malice spiritualized."

21:15   *Mirabeau*] Honoré Gabriel Riqueti, Comte de Mirabeau (1749–1791), French politician, orator, and writer. A moderate and an advocate of constitutional monarchy, Mirabeau was an important figure in the National Assembly that governed France in the early phases of the French Revolution. He was gifted at Machiavellian manipulations of the various parties.

21:20   *"love of one's enemies."*] cf. Matthew 5: 43.

22:9   *inter pares*] among equals; here: 'among themselves.'

22:14   *foreign, the foreign world*] The German here is "das Fremde, *die* Fremde," literally: "that which is foreign, *the* foreign." According to its form, the second term would normally designate the quality of "foreignness," but in actual usage it means all of the world outside of the place one comes from, something like the place English-speaking persons go when they go "abroad."

22:32–33   *"to every land ... good and bad"*] Thucydides 2. 41. The meaning of this passage from Thucydides is not undisputed. In a note in the French edition of GM, Maurice de Gandillac gives a sampling of interpretations from various translations of the text: "unperishing monuments of our chastisements and our kindnesses," (his own suggestion); "to all we have done that is beautiful and good," Herwerden (1877); "remembrances of evils and of goods," (Mme de Romilly): "of defeats inflicted on our enemies and of our victories," (Jean Voilquin); "of our enterprises, of our failures as well as our successes." (Denis Roussel, Pléiade edition).

23:11   *gold, silver, bronze*] Hesiod's account of the five ages is found in *Works and Days*, lines 107–201. For the account of the Bronze age and the unnamed age that followed it see lines 144–173. N also cites this passage in *Daybreak* 189.

24: 4   *"higher man"*] Of BGE's many references to "higher men," the most important is probably BGE 256's discussion of the artists (including Richard Wagner) who taught the nineteenth century, "and it is the century of the *crowd!*— the concept 'higher man.'"The fourth part of *Thus Spoke Zarathustra* is the story of dealings between N's character Zarathustra and the "higher men."

27:8   *for they know not what they do*] cf. Luke 23: 34.

27:9   *'love of one's enemies'*] cf. Matthew 5: 44, Luke 6: 27ff.

27:13–14   *nook-and-cranny ... crouching together warmly*] The wording of this passage suggests that N has drawn on early Christian or pagan sources for this critique—or at any rate that he was familiar with them. In *Contra Celsum*, the Christian apologist Origen (ca. 185–254 AD) quotes a passage from Celsus' critique (ca. 185 AD) of the Christian sect, which R. Joseph Hoffmann translates as follows: "The cult of Christ is a secret society whose members huddle together in corners for fear of being brought to trial and punishment." This is quoted from a reconstruction and translation of Celsus' work, *On the True Doctrine* (New York/Oxford: Oxford UP, 1987).

27:23   *honor all authority*] cf. Romans 13: 1–2.

28:1   *'sweeter than honey'*] *Iliad* 18: 109–10.

28:3   *'brothers in love,'*] cf. 1 Thessalonians 3: 12.

28:10   *'in faith,' 'in love,' 'in hope.'*] cf. 1 Thessalonians 1: 3; also 1 Corinthians 13: 13.

28:21   *ingenuousness*] the German here is *Ingenuität*, which at first glance would seem to be "ingenuity" (as Kaufmann and Smith have translated it). It actually means "ingenuousness," "innocence," or "naturalness."

28:22   *"I, too, was created by eternal love"*] *Divine Comedy, Inferno* III, 5–6. The passage actually reads: *"Fecemi la divina potestate / La somma sapienza e il primo amore."* (I was created by divine power, the highest wisdom, and the first love.)

28:28   *Thomas Aquinas*] (1225–1274), Christian theologian and philosopher, canonized by Pope John XXII in 1323 and declared a Doctor of the Church by Pope Pius V in 1567. He was born at Roccasecca in southern Italy. An early branch of his noble family held the county of Aquino until 1137, and it is from there that he got his name. In 1239, Thomas likely entered the house of general studies established by Frederick II in Naples, and there first encountered the works of Aristotle, which were then being rediscovered and translated from Arabic and Greek. Prior to this time, Neoplatonism, especially under the influence of St. Augustine, had had the greatest philosophical influence on Christian theology. After joining the Dominican Order, Thomas was sent to Paris, where he studied under Albertus Magnus from 1245 to 1252. During his more that twenty years as an active teacher, Thomas was a major force in the introduction of Aristotelian themes into Christian theology. Despite strong resistance to Aristotle's natural philosophy, manifested through early prohibitions against the public readings of his works and condemnations in 1277 of certain usages (including Aquinas's) of his philosophy, he had gained a strong position in the courses of university theology. Aquinas's synthesis of the traditional Christian teachings and Aristotle's philosophy was once again given prominence by Pope Leo XIII in 1882 and remained a dominant guide for Catholic thought until recently. Among his most important works are the *Summa Theologica* and the *Summa Contra Gentiles*. (Stephen F. Brown contributed to this note.)

28:32   *church father*] Tertullian (ca. 155– after 220), important early Christian theologian, polemicist, and moralist from Carthage in North Africa. In Carthage he received an education in literature, philosophy, and law and then went to Rome to complete his education. He became interested in the Christian movement while in Rome but did not convert to Christianity until he returned to Carthage near the end of the century. He produced a large number of works on a variety of topics and was instrumental in developing ecclesiastical Latin. Late in life he became dissatisfied with the laxity of contemporary Christians and left the orthodox church to join the Montanist movement. Even they were not rigorous enough for him and he eventually broke with them and founded his own sect.

28:33–29:4   *Faith offers us … of his triumph!"*] This first part of the passage from Tertullian's *De Spectaculis* is a paraphrase, at times bordering on quotation, from chapter 29 and the first sentence of chapter 30. Nietzsche then quotes the

entirety of chapter 30—minus the first four sentences—in Latin. N wrote to
Overbeck July 17, 1887 asking him for the passage "in which this beautiful soul
depicts in advance the joys that he will enjoy in the "beyond" at the sight of the
suffering of his enemies and the anti-Christian minded: the sufferings are specialized in a very ironic and malicious manner, alluding to the former occupations of
these enemies. Can you remember the passage? and perhaps send it to me? (*origi-
naliter* or translated: I need it in German)."

29:17   *in better voice ... screamers*] N's gloss of the phrase "*magis scilicet
vocales*" simply offers two possible interpretations of "in great voice, no doubt":
either "with better voices" or "screaming more horribly than ever."

29:19   *vivos*] Nietzsche mistakenly has *vivos* (alive) where the text should read
visos (seen). The passage as N has it thus reads "not even then would I wish them
alive ..." instead of the original "not even then would I wish to see them ... ."

29:22   *designation from the Talmud*] the passage N refers to here is from the
Babylonian Talmud, Sanhedrin 106a, commentary on Joshua 13: 22 (Balaam also
the son of Beor, the soothsayer): "A soothsayer? But he was a prophet!—R. Joha-
nan said: At first he was a prophet, but subsequently a soothsayer. R. Papa
observed: This is what men say, 'She who was the descendant of princes and gov-
ernors, played the harlot with carpenters.'" In the annotations to this passage the
editors note "that Balaam is frequently used in the Talmud as a type for Jesus ... .
Though no name is mentioned to show which woman is meant, the mother of
Jesus may be alluded to, which theory is strengthened by the statement that she
mated with a carpenter." *The Babylonian Talmud*, Seder Nezikin in Four Volumes.
III: Sanhedrin. Translated by Jacob Shachter and H. Freedman. London: Son-
cino Press, 1935. Page 725.

29:34   *Per fidem*] by faith (as bold-faced in the preceding quotation); here:
'by [my] faith.' A pun on "perfidy" is also possible here.

31:8   "*convicted ... human race*"] Tacitus, *Annales*, XV, 44. The phrase
quoted here actually refers to Christians rather than Jews—Tacitus writes that
Nero blamed cases of arson on Christians as scapegoats, but that they "were convicted, not so much on the count of arson as for hatred of the human race." One
editor notes that "Jewish 'misanthropy'—which was proverbial—may have suggested the charge" (Tacitus, *The Annals*, ed. John Jackson. Cambridge: Harvard
UP, 1937: 284–85.) In *Histories* V, 5, Tacitus writes that "the Jews are extremely
loyal toward one another and always ready to show compassion, but towards every
other people they feel only hate and enmity." (*Histories*, Books IV–V, Transl. by
Clifford H. Moore. Cambridge: Harvard UP, 1931.)

32:19   *inhuman and a superhuman*] The German here is "Unmensch"
(inhuman one, monster) and "Übermensch" (superhuman one).

32:29   *perfectly tailored to*] The German expression here is "auf den Leib
geschrieben," literally, "written to the body" or "onto the body." The idiom
presumably comes from theater language, where it meant to write something

specifically for a particular actor, and has come to mean "be tailored to," "fit perfectly." Nietzsche plays here with the literal meaning as well, however, since the title is also "written onto the body" of his book.

32:32   *Note*] This note was not included in the manuscript as N sent it to the publisher. N mentions it to Heinrich Köselitz (Peter Gast) in a letter dated August 30, 1887: "I hope nothing disruptive has occurred at Naumann [N's publisher]: we still aren't any further since sheet 3. I did however insert a note (for scholars) on the blank page at the end of the first treatise."

33:32   *English biologists*] e.g., Herbert Spencer. See note 11:34.

Second Treatise

35:1]   *that is permitted to promise*] *der versprechen darf.* We have translated this phrase as literally as possible here to underscore its *normative* character while at the same time avoiding connotations that are absent from N's German. "That *may promise*" might be more literal still, but too ambiguous and confusing, given that the "permission" sense of "may" is far from its most common sense and that this is not true of the German verb. The only problem with "is permitted" is that the "is" makes it seem more passive than the German and it may suggest that some person or group is granting permission, which is clearly not what N means. Diethe's translation ("who *is able to make promises*") obscures the fact that N is using a normative or value-laden term ("may" or "is permitted") to describe the task of breeding a normative animal, an animal that accepts and lives up to norms. The "ability" involved here is not simply the ability to *make* promises (to understand the commitment involved) but the ability to *keep* them, to live up to commitments. Kaufmann and Smith do use normative terms ("with *a right to*" or "which *is entitled to make promises*") but ones that involve more specific and complicated normative ideas (rights and titles) than what is conveyed by N's more general and basic normative term. By using such a basic term from the realm of right (the realm of right and wrong, duties and obligations, fairness and justice) in this context, N suggests that nature's task in the case of man, i.e., the task of cultivating a *human* animal, centrally involves cultivating a commitment to the realm of right. If our translation raises the question as to who does the permitting, that may even be an advantage, since N's own wording here raises not merely the descriptive question about the source of norms (which GM attempts to answer directly), but also the normative question about the value or justification of these norms. Although N does not address the latter question directly in GM, section 5 of the preface suggests that such normative questions are his ultimate concern in pursuing the genealogy of morality.

35:10–11   *"inanimation" ... "incorporation,"*] N's play on words here, creating a word meaning "to take into the soul/psyche," after the pattern of the existing word "Einverleibung" (=incorporation, "to take into the body") is only possible in English when Latin roots ("corpus" and "animus") are used and is hence not as immediately intelligible as the original, which uses everyday German roots. The German word "Einverleibung" is also actually used in the specific and literal sense of "to take into the human body," whereas the English "incorporation" is not. Nevertheless, since both "corpus" and "animus" are widely familiar, it seemed worth preserving N's construction here rather than paraphrasing it.

35:24 *"process"*] The German expression used here is *fertig werden mit*, which means "to cope with," "to deal with" (literally: to get finished with). Elsewhere we have rendered this expression as "cope with." We have made an exception here, however, in order to preserve N's pun connecting mentally processing ideas with physically "processing" (digesting) food.

36:18 *"morality of custom,"*] The German here is *Sittlichkeit der Sitte*, which has no precise equivalent in English. "Morality of mores" preserves the etymological connection that exists between the German terms, but does not solve the real problem, which is that no standard English term for "morality" has as its root a standard English word for "custom." ("Mos," the singular of "mores," is not even recognizable as such by most readers of English.) In some contexts, one might preserve the root "Sitte" ("custom," socially prescribed or expected behavior) by translating "Sittlichkeit" as "customariness," the quality of being in accord with custom. This would work as an acceptable translation in these contexts, however, only if the word had developed in English as a synonym for "morality," which is of course not the case. Because "customary" tends to underscore the connotation of "conventional," it cannot suggest the binding character associated with "morality." The German term "Sittlichkeit," in contrast, does suggest this binding character, and has come to mean much the same as the Latinate "morality," but its root allows Nietzsche to use it to refer to an earlier type of morality based on social or "customary" norms—earlier, that is, than the type of morality whose genealogy he offers in GM. N's usual word for "morality," and the one used in the title of GM, is not "Sittlichkeit," but "Moral," and it is only the latter that he claims to oppose, and which he claims will "gradually perish" (GM III: 27). It would therefore be very helpful to have two English words for the two German terms we have translated as "morality." "Ethic" or "ethical life" could be used to render "Sittlichkeit," as is usually done in translations of Hegel, and this would help to make clearer that Nietzsche does not oppose all forms of ethical life (social life that imposes obligations on members) but only the moralized form analyzed in GM. Because it would make it easier to recognize the "ethic of custom" as an ancestor, rather than an actual part, of the form of ethical life N calls "morality" (*Moral*), this formulation would also encourage us to understand N's opposition to morality as a rejection not of the imposition of community standards of right and wrong, but only of the moralized version of such standards. The clear recognition that a form of ethical life existed prior to morality would also suggest that a new form of ethical life might be developed after morality perishes. Despite these advantages, we could not translate *Sittlichkeit* as "ethical life" in the present context because that would force us to render *sittlich* as "ethical," thus to translate Nietzsche as saying that "'autonomous' and 'ethical' are mutually exclusive." But that is not the view he presents here. His "sovereign" or "autonomous" individual has a "conscience," one that requires him to keep promises, including the promise to obey society's laws in exchange for the advantages of social life (cf. GM II: 9). In thus recognizing obligations, he clearly belongs to a form of ethical life. N's point is rather that autonomy is incompatible with the morality of custom—or with morality itself (the moralized form of ethical life analyzed in GM). Or both. The context suggests only the former, whereas the normal connotation of the German word (*sittlich*) suggests he means that true autonomy is incompatible with morality, an extreme reversal of Kant's claim that autonomy is possible for human beings only through morality. To avoid ruling out the latter interpretation, *sittlich* must be translated as "moral," which makes "morality" rather than "ethical life" the best translation for *Sittlichkeit* in this context, and we have used the same translation throughout.

38:16   *"at memory"*] The German phrase N uses here, "bei Gedächtnis," (literally "at memory") is his own coinage, presumably a parallel construction to the German "bei Verstand" or "bei Sinnen" (roughly: "in one's right mind"; literally: "at reason" or "at senses"). This may be intended to underscore the importance of memory as part of what we call reason, or simply to underscore the "presence" of mind required in order to remember. N also underscores the spatial sense of "presence" in intellectual activities in the first section of the preface— "we were never 'with it': we just don't have our heart there."

38:24   *"people of thinkers"*] Although the description of the Germans as the "people of thinkers [and poets]" is generally attributed to J. K. A. Musäus—in *Popular Fairy Tales of the Germans* (1782)—and Jean Paul—in *A Sermon on Peace, to Germany* (1808), neither uses this precise phrase, and in neither of these instances is it used strictly in reference to the German people. The general idea certainly gained widespread exposure in Madame de Stäel's *De l'Allemagne* (On Germany, 1810/1813) where she describes Germany as "that country in which, of all Europe, study and meditation have been carried so far, that it may be considered as the native land of thought." *Germany. Translated from the French. In Three Volumes.* London: John Murray, 1813, I: 5.

38:31–32   *millstone ... guilty one*] N's source here is Albert Hermann Post, *Bausteine für eine allgemeine Rechtswissenschaft auf vergleichend-ethnologischer Basis* (Building Blocks For a Universal Science of Law on a Comparative-Ethnological Basis) 2 vols. Oldenburg: Schulz, 1880. I: 191. "There is an analogy here in the mythical punishment in Germanic antiquity, letting a millstone fall on the head of the condemned one." N's copy of this work has pencil markings throughout the first volume. N draws on it in a number of places in GM (cf. notes 40:30, 47:14, 53:34, 55:7, 80:30, and 88:35).

38:32–33   *breaking on the wheel ... punishment!*] N's source: "In contrast, the punishment of the *wheel*, although presumably of Aryan origin, appears to be a specialty of the Germanic tribes." Post, *Bausteine*. I: 197.

38:33–34   *casting stakes*] The original here is not the German expression for
"impaling".—as Kaufmann and others have translated it. N's source here sheds
some light on the odd expression and its relation to impaling: "Is it not likely that
the spear is the origin of the punishment of impaling? After all the stake was still
thrown in Germanic antiquity." Post, *Bausteine.* I: 201. In N's personal copy of
this book the words "stake" (*"Pfahl"*) and "thrown" (*"geworfen"*) are underlined
and the entire passage marked by a line in the margin.

38:34   *having torn or trampled by horses ("quartering")*] N's source: "To
this corresponds the tying of individual members of the malefactor to the tail of a
wild horse or the tearing apart by several horses (quartering), as it occurs in Germanic antiquity and also in Rome." Post, *Bausteine.* I: 192.

38:34–35   *boiling the criminal ... centuries)*] N's source: "likewise one finds
in Germany in the 14th and 15th centuries that malefactors are boiled in oil or
wine." Post, *Bausteine.* I: 196.

38:36   *Riemenschneiden*] literally, "strap-cutting," was a medieval trade—
roughly saddle or harness-making. The designation comes from the activity of cutting the leather. In N's source: "Furthermore the punishment of flaying might also
have a more general importance. It is mentioned in Abyssinia, in the Assyrian penal
laws. One can compare with this the Germanic "strap-cutting" from the skin and
the *decalvare*, the punishment involving skin and hair, which is found similarly in
the Avesta. In China this same strap-cutting appears as a kind of torture." Post,
Bausteine, I: 197.

38:36   *flesh from the breast*] N's source: "Finally one might mention being
eaten among the Battak on Sumatra, with which one can compare the cutting of
flesh from the breast in Germanic antiquity." Post, *Bausteine.* I: 198.

38:37–39:1   *the evil-doer ... burning sun*] N's source: "Whatever other kinds
of capital punishment occur are unlikely to have any universal historical importance. When the last emperor of the second Zhou dynasty has the prince of Xu salt
cured, it is a matter of an arbitrary act, as they likewise occur in the history of
Tongking, of the Central Asian empires, and of Marocco. I would also tend to
count it here when the Kandyans on Ceylon mention as a punishment crushing in
a mortar, and also perhaps a punishment, which is reported from Bornu, according to which the thief in repeated relapse is buried up to his head, rubbed with
butter and honey, and exposed thus for twelve or eighteen hours to the burning
sun and countless flies and mosquitoes, a punishment, by the way, that is also
found in Germanic antiquity, where the criminal is likewise smeared with honey
and, under a burning sun, exposed to the bites of flies." Post, *Bausteine.* I: 198.

40:15–23   *In order to instill ... even in the grave*] cf. Josef Kohler, *Das Recht
als Kulturerscheinung* (Law as a Cultural Phenomenon, 1885) 18–19: "when legal
consequences are no longer automatic, one attempts to secure them through contractual clauses: if the debtor does not fall forfeit to the creditor automatically,
then he must *pledge himself to the creditor*: he pledges his *body*, his *freedom*, his
honor; he pledges his *bodily members*, he pledges his position in society, he pledges

even the *salvation of his soul ...*" (emphasis N's). Also on page 18: "If the debtor was *dead*, then *one laid a hand on his corpse*: the custom of denying the debtor the rest of the grave was found among the *Egyptians* ..." (emphasis N's). Finally, on page 20: "*Body, freedom, honor, salvation of the soul*, everything was put in jeopardy so that the *sacredness of the promise* could triumph."

40:30–31   *legally established ... areas on the body*] cf. Post, *Bausteine*, I: 334ff. Post gives two examples of lists assigning value to body parts. They are meant to determine the payment required of the perpetrator when the given body part is injured, however, and not the amount the injured party can cut off as compensation. In one case the list gives the number of cattle that must be paid by the one who caused the loss of the part in question, in the other the list gives the number of lashes the perpetrator is to receive for causing the loss of the body part.

40:32–33   *Twelve Tables legislation*] In 450 BC the Roman senate passed a reformed legal code which was then recorded on twelve tablets that were set up in the Forum. These laws remained the core of the Roman legal code until the end of the empire.

40:34–35   *"si plus ... ne fraude esto."*] "If they have secured more or less, let that be no crime." This is taken from paragraph 6 of table III of the Twelve Tables of Roman law. Nietzsche's quotation is not quite correct. Where he has *ne fraude* it should read *se [=sine] fraude* (... let it be honestly done). Geuss' note in the Diethe translation suggests this is a difference between older and more recent editions of the text. It seems very likely that N took the quote from Kohler, *Law as a Cultural Phenomenon*. In N's personal copy of Kohler's book, however, the text—underlined by N—reads "se fraude."

41:7   *"de faire ... plaisir de le faire,"*] to do evil for the pleasure of doing it. Prosper Mérimée, *Lettres à une inconnue*, Paris, 1874, I, 8. The letter warns the *inconnue*: "know, too, that there is nothing more common than doing evil for the pleasure of doing it."

42:9   *sympathia malevolens*] ill-willing sympathy. This phrase is a formulation of Spinoza's idea (Ethics III, P 32) that we wish a person ill if we imagine him enjoying something that only one person can possess. Nietzsche found this formulation in H. Höffding's *Psychologie in Umrissen* (*Psychology in Outline*, Leipzig, 1887), p. 319. See William S. Wurzer, *Nietzsche und Spinoza* (Meisenheim am Glan, 1975), p. 104.

42:21   *court of the Duchess*] *Don Quixote*, Book II, chapters 30–57.

42:29   *"prelude"*] The original "vorspielen" also has the nuance of "enact before an audience" in addition to the musical idea of "prelude."

43:8–9   *moralization*] The German here is a coinage of N's: *Vermoralisierung*, which implies more than just moralization. The usual German word for this would be *Moralisierung*. The prefix *ver-* can add a number of different nuances to a verb stem; the most probable here are: *thoroughly moralize* or *wrongly moralize* (and hence spoil).

43:15–17   *"impure begetting ... saliva, urine, and feces"*] The traits are summarized from sections 2 (Of the Vileness of Matter), 3 (Of the Flaw of Conception), 4 (With What Kind of Food the Fetus is Fed in the Womb), and 8 (What Fruit Man Produces) of *De Miseria Condicionis Humane* (1195) by Cardinal Lotario dei Segni (after 1198 Pope Innocent III). During the Middle Ages the work was extremely popular throughout Europe.

44:19   *Luther*] Martin Luther (1483–1546), instigator of the 16th century Reformation and of Protestantism. Luther was the son of a miner and entered the Augustinian Order of monks in his youth. Luther found the concept of a "righteous," judging God oppressive, and in his struggles to reconcile his feelings of guilt with his sense that Christianity should make one happy, he developed his doctrine that it is faith that saves us, not our works. The consequences of Luther's work for German culture were tremendous, and not only in religious and political matters. Luther's translation of the Bible (New Testament, 1522; Old Testament, 1534) had a profound influence on the development of the modern German language. N's reading of Janssen's *History of the German People* (see note 100:25) had a major impact on his view of Luther. In a letter to Heinrich Köselitz, dated October 5, 1879, he wrote: "on the subject of Luther I am now ... unable to say anything of a praising nature: the aftereffect of a powerful collection of material about him, that J. Burckhardt brought to my attention. I mean Janssen, Hist. of the German People, vol. II, which appeared this year (I own it). For once it is *not* the falsified Protestant construction of history that speaks, the construction according to which we were taught to believe. ... The dreadful, arrogant, ascerbic-envious cursing of Luther—who wasn't happy unless, driven by rage, he could spit on someone—disgusts me too much." Still N never entirely lost a certain admiration for Luther's achievements. In a note on the German people in general, written around the time of GM, N observed: "Our last event is still *Luther*, our only book still the *Bible*" (KSA 11, 25 [162]).

44:22–23   *Homer ... the fates of humans?*] cf. *Odyssey*, 8: 579–80.

46:15   *"Elend," êlend*] The New High German *Elend* (misery) derives from the Old High German adjective *elilenti* (in another land or country; banished) via the shortened Middle High German *ellende* or *êlend* (foreign, miserable). Exclusion from the protection of the tribal laws was a severe punishment and the Modern High German adjective *êlend* and noun *Elend* are still forceful expressions.

46:20   *criminal is above all a "breaker,"*] There is a play on words here in the original, since the German word for 'criminal' is *Verbrecher*, the stem of which (*brechen*) is the verb for 'to break.' Kaufmann translates this as 'lawbreaker,' which makes the play on words visible but at the same time meaningless—to a native speaker of English a 'lawbreaker' is obviously a 'breaker' and there is no need to call attention to this; with the German *Verbrecher*, the root meaning has long been assimilated into the meaning 'criminal' and is no longer consciously heard by native speakers—unless it is called to their attention.

47:1 *vae victis!*] Woe to the conquered! The phrase is from Livy, *Ab urbe condita*, Book V, 48, 9, where Livy narrates a surrender of the Romans to the Gauls where the Gauls demanded a payment of one thousand pounds of gold. As it was being paid, the Romans discovered that the Gauls were using false weights to weigh the payment and complained. The Gallic leader is said to have responded by uttering this phrase while throwing his sword into the balance as well.

47:14 *compositio*] cf. Post, *Bausteine*, I: 171, 181ff. Post describes "composition systems" as the precursor to state imposed fines. The tribe or clan avoided a blood feud by paying an agreed upon settlement or *compositio* to the family of the one murdered by a member of their family or tribe. As long as the payment is paid by the family or tribe to the injured family or tribe, it is *compositio*. When a state develops and takes over the function of punishing, a "fine" is paid to the state.

48:2 *his beyond-the-law*] N plays here with the expressions "Vorrecht" (privilege; literally, before-law) and "Jenseits des Rechts" (=beyond the law). The translation of this word play is further complicated by the fact that the German word "Recht" encompasses the meanings of both "law" and "right" in English.

48:26 *E. Dühring*] Eugen Karl Dühring (1833–1921), prolific philosopher and political economist who was blind from the age of 30. In his autobiography (1882) he claims to have been the founder of anti-Semitism, and he was a major figure in the anti-Semitic movement in Germany (see Katz, note 114:16). N's library included Dühring's autobiography as well as his *Werth des Lebens* (Value of Life, 1867) and *Cursus der Philosophie* (Course in Philosophy, 1875). See the following two notes.

48:28–29 *the homeland ... ground of reactive feeling*] Dühring, *Der Werth des Lebens*, 219: "The conception of law and along with it all special legal concepts have their final ground in the drive for retaliation, which in its higher intensification is called revenge. Legal sentiment is essentially ressentiment, a reactive sensation, i.e., it belongs with revenge in the same affective grouping." In N's copy of this book he has underlined the word "ressentiment." This passage stems from the appendix entitled *"Die transcendente Befriedigung der Rache"* ("The Transcendental Satisfaction of Revenge"). This appendix displays frequent underlining and marginal marks—with the exception of one or two earlier passages, this is the only part of this book that N has marked.

49:18–19 *"the doctrine ... red thread of justice"*] This is a shortened version of the original from Dühring's autobiography, *Sache, Leben und Feinde* (Cause, Life, and Enemies), Karlsruhe and Leipzig, 1882: 283, "The doctrine of revenge was first most pointedly sketched in an appendix to the 1st edition of *Value of Life*, and in its theoretical and practical applications runs through all my works and efforts as the red thread of justice." This book was part of N's personal library.

50:29   *"purpose in law,"*] a reference to the jurist Rudolf von Ihering's book *Der Zweck im Rechte* (The Purpose in Law, 1884).

52:19   *Herbert Spencer*] see note 11:34.

52:26   *Huxley*] T[homas] H[enry] Huxley (1825–1895), English biologist. Huxley was a largely self-taught scholar who never earned an academic degree—though he was awarded several honorary ones. He began training at Charing Cross Hospital but left after his scholarship ran out and secured a position on an exploring ship. He wrote reports of his findings during the expedition and sent them back to England for publication. When he returned four years later he was well known in biology circles. He was one of Darwin's close associates and perhaps his chief defender in the public debates concerning the theory of evolution. Huxley's views on science and religion eventually led him to advocate "agnosticism"—he coined this term himself. In his later years he was very involved in educational reform and was a member of the London School Board.

52:26   *"administrative nihilism"*] T. H. Huxley, "Administrative Nihilism," *Fortnightly Review* 16 (November 1, 1871): 525–43.

53:34   *Chinese law*] The annotations in KSA refer here to a pamphlet N had in his personal library: Josef Kohler, *Das chinesische Strafrecht. Ein Beitrag zur Universalgeschichte des Strafrechts* (Chinese Penal Law. A Contribution to the Universal History of Penal Law), Würzburg, 1886. This particular aspect of Chinese law is not actually discussed in the pamphlet. In his copy of Post's *Bausteine*, however, N has marked a passage (I: 204) that indirectly raises this issue: "The decline of capital punishments in Europe is presumably to be attributed essentially to the development of punishments of imprisonment, which make it possible to apply state-of-emergency punishments only in light measure. Since China knows no punishment of imprisonment at all, it must apply many more state-of-emergency punishments for the preservation of ethnic balance."

55:7–15   *in the consciousness … can no longer fight*] cf. Post, *Bausteine*, I: 175. Post observes that there are cultures that consider it "immaterial *whether the perpetrator intended his deed* or was simply the accidental cause of the disruptive occurrence. The punishment is an ethnic *necessity* that strikes *the individual* like a *stroke of fortune* and to which he must submit with resignation, *as to any inevitable natural occurrence.*" The emphasis is N's, as found in the copy of Post in his library.

55:18   *Kuno Fischer*] (1824–1907), professor of philosophy at Heidelberg, author of the ten-volume *Geschichte der neuern Philosophie* (History of Modern Philosophy). The sections dealing with Spinoza are found in volume I, 2: *Descartes' School. Geulinx, Malebranche, Baruch Spinoza.* 2nd Edition. Heidelberg, 1865.

55:20   *morsus conscientiae*] sting of conscience. *Ethics* III, Prop. 18, Schol. 2.

55:23–24   *sub ratione boni*] for the sake of the good. *Ethics* I, Prop. 33, Schol. 2.

55:24–25 *"that, however, ... greatest of all absurdities"*] *Ethics* I, Prop. 33, Schol. 2.

55:27–30 *"the opposite ... all expectation."*] Nietzsche has manipulated the quotation somewhat. In Curley's English translation the original reads: "Finally, Gladness is a Joy which has arisen from the image of a past thing whose outcome we doubted, while Remorse is a sadness which is opposite to Gladness."

55:33 *"something ... gone wrong here,"*] There is a play on words in the German, between the expression "to go wrong" (=schief *gehen*) and the term "crime/trespass" (=Ver*gehen*), suggesting that the word "Vergehen" might still retain traces of this earlier attitude.

57:4–5 *thin as if inserted between two skins*] Although it seems relatively clear what N means here, the image he uses is puzzling; the verb he uses can mean not only "to insert" (as a sheet of paper in a typewriter) but also "to harness" (a horse to a carriage) or "to stretch" (as a canvas into a frame). None of these clearly fit the context "thin as if ... between two skins"—which is itself far from clear. N may mean something like "between two layers of skin," as on an onion.

57:36 *Heraclitus*] Fragment 52: "Lifetime is a child playing, moving pieces in a backgammon (*pessoi*) game; kingly power (or: the kingdom) is in the hands of a child." (Translation from Heraclitus *Fragments*, Transl. by T. M. Robinson. Toronto: U of Toronto P, 1987, 37, 116–17.)

59:9–10 *"labyrinth of the breast,"*] from the final stanza of Goethe's poem "An den Mond" ("To the Moon"):

Selig, wer sich vor der Welt	Blessed whoever closes himself
Ohne Haß verschließt,	Toward the world without hate,
Einen Freund am Busen hält	Holds a friend to his bosom
Und mit dem genießt,	And with him enjoys,
Was, von Menschen nicht gewußt	That which, unknown to man
Oder nicht bedacht,	Or not considered,
Durch das Labyrinth der Brust	Through the labyrinth of the breast
wandelt in der Nacht.	walks in the night.

60:28 *redemption*] The German here is *Ablösung*, which means redemption or discharge of a debt. In both German and English this legal or economic term is related by root to—in English it is identical with—the religious term "redemption," *"Erlösung."*

61:26 *mimicry*] in English in the original.

62:9 *causa prima*] first cause. Aquinas uses this term in describing God as the creator of the world.

62:18 *the faith in our "creditor,"*] N is playing here on the words "Glaube" (faith, belief) and "Gläubiger" (creditor). Although the two ideas are connected in

English as well (through the Latin root "credo"), the word play does not translate easily.

62:34   *"Original Sin"*] the doctrine introduced into the West by Augustine (354–430) according to which all human beings are burdened with a hereditary disability of the will and a liability to punishment due to Adam's disobedience to God. All of the theologians in the Augustinian tradition, including Luther and Calvin, connect a general human disability or unfreedom of the will to Adam's sin. Augustine develops the doctrine to justify the already existing African practice of infant baptism—a nice illustration of N's point that the practice comes first and the "meaning" is then interpreted into it—in *De peccatorum meritis et remissione* (On the merits of sin and their remission, 412). See Althanase Sage, "Peche originel. Naissance d'un dogme," *Revue des etudes augustiniennes* X (1967), 211–248. (James Wetzel supplied information for this note.)

64:30–33   *"A wonder ... even counter to fate."*] *Odyssey* 1, 32–34. We have translated N's version rather than using a common English translation since the wording is important to him—at least the opening word: *Wunder!* ("wonder!" or "strange!") Lattimore's "O, for shame" loses the sense of amusement and approval that N is underscoring here. The Liddell-Scott Greek-English Lexicon gives the translation of the exclamation *o popoi* as either "O, strange" or "O, shame."

Third Treatise

67:epigram   *Thus Spoke Zarathustra*] The epigram is from "On Reading and Writing" in part 1 of Z, but is slightly reworded. The original begins with four adjectives, the first of which is "brave" (*mutig*), which N omits here, and it has the conjunction "and" rather than a comma between the last two clauses.

67:0   From an examination of the printer's manuscript, it is clear that when N began writing it out, the third treatise began with what is now section 2, and that N added section 1 later, but before he sent the treatise to his publisher. See John Wilcox, "What Aphorism Does Nietzsche Explicate in *Genealogy of Morals*, Essay III," *Journal of the History of Philosophy* XXXV/4 (October 1997) 593–610, for convincing textual evidence that the "aphorism" N refers to in the preface to GM (7:6) is section 1 of GM III, and not, as has so often been assumed, the epigram that precedes the treatise. The same journal issue contains Maudemarie Clark's "From the Nietzsche Archive: Concerning the Aphorism Explicated in GM III," which details the evidence in support of Wilcox's interpretation that can be gathered from examining the original manuscript. Also see Christopher Janaway's almost simultaneous and independent article, which makes many of the same points: *European Journal of Philosophy* 5:4 (December 1997) 251–68.

67:11   *novissima gloriae cupido*] last thing, passion for glory. Tacitus, *Histories* IV, 6: "Erant quibus adpretentior famae videretur, quando etiam sapientibus cupido gloriae novissima exuitur." ("Some thought that he was rather too eager for fame, since the passion for glory is the last thing from which even philosophers divest themselves.") N cites a longer version of this passage in *Gay Science* 330.

67:14 *horror vacui*] horror of emptiness—an Aristotelian expression for nature's horror of empty space—as demonstrated by the fact that a vacuum can only be partially achieved and temporarily maintained. As soon as the force maintaining it ceases, matter rushes in to fill the void.

67:19 *Richard Wagner*] (1813–1883), German composer and music theorist. Because of his socialist leanings and his involvement in the revolution of 1848–49, Wagner fled from Germany and spent most of the next 11 years in Zurich and Paris. During this exile Wagner wrote several theoretical pieces on social and artistic revolution—"Art and Revolution," "The Artwork of the Future," "Opera and Drama"—and began to work out the plans for his major work, *The Ring of the Nibelung*, a four-part opera based on Germanic legends, specifically the legends of Siegfried. Wagner conceived the character of Siegfried as a new type of human being freed from the corruption and oppressive influences of society. While in Zurich Wagner was introduced to Schopenhauer's works and began to move away from his socialist views toward a more pessimistic view of life. The opera *Tristan and Isolde* was the first expression of his new outlook. The last of the four operas in *The Ring of the Nibelung* also lost the revolutionary tone that marked the first three. N had followed Wagner's music for several years, and finally met him in November 1868 while Wagner was visiting his sister in Leipzig, where N was a student. Wagner invited N to visit him—he had again fled Germany, this time for personal reasons, and now lived in Triebschen, Switzerland. N was appointed professor in Basel, Switzerland soon after this and made his first visit to Wagner in May of 1869. He became a close family friend and visited the Wagners frequently over the next six years. N's first book, *The Birth of Tragedy Out of the Spirit of Music* (1872) suggested that Wagner's new kind of opera was a rebirth of the spirit of ancient Greek tragedy. By 1876, when N published his essay ("Richard Wagner in Bayreuth," the fourth of his *Unfashionable Observations*), the friendship had become strained. This essay already shows subtle signs of N's movement away from Wagner, and after the festival opening of Wagner's opera house in Bayreuth the two did not meet again. All accounts of the breakup of their relationship are controversial, but N himself believed that it was connected to the development of his own philosophy, in particular, to his movement away from the early form of his devotion to Schopenhauer (see note 4:15). By the time he wrote GM, N had come to see Wagner's final opera, *Parsifal*, with its strong Christian asceticism, as the ultimate symbol of the gulf between them. *Parsifal* was premiered in 1882 and Wagner died the following year in Venice. In N's final year of productivity (1888), he published one book—*The Case of Wagner*—and wrote another one—*Nietzsche Contra Wagner*—which attempted to explain his objections to Wagner. For a very helpful account of Wagner's music and its relationship to Schopenhauer, see Bryan Magee, *The Philosophy of Schopenhauer*

(Oxford: Oxford UP, 1997), 350–402. Magee's account of *Parsifal* at the end of this material (395–402) provides readers of GM III with excellent background for understanding N's objection to it.

68:9   *Meistersinger*] *Die Meistersinger von Nürnberg* (The Mastersingers of Nuremberg), Wagner's ninth opera. At the competition of the mastersingers a young contestant enters a new type of song and finds that the mastersingers are too set in their ways to give him a fair hearing. Only Hans Sachs takes his side and helps him get his song heard. The opera deals not only with the difficulties of musical innovators but is also a defense—some would say glorification—of German art and music.

68:10–11   *"Marriage of Luther,"*] Luther rejected the Catholic notion that priests should be celibate and in 1525 married Katharina von Bora, a Cistercian nun who had left her convent in 1523.

68:21   *"Protestant freedom"*] This expression presumably stems from the title of Luther's *On the Freedom of a Christian Man* (Von der Freiheit eines Christenmenschen, 1520) in which Luther posits: "A Christian is a free lord over all things and subject to no one." It was used in reference to more than Luther's abandonment of celibacy, however. The consequences that some of his followers drew from this book tended more in the direction of libertinism, a development that disturbed Luther and fueled the attacks of his opponents. Already during his lifetime the expression "Protestant freedom" (*"evangelische Freiheit"*) appeared in the works of his critics in ironic usage. Erasmus, for example, wrote in 1523: "Under the pretext of the Protestant freedom some seek senseless license to serve their bodily lusts; others cast a covetous eye on church possessions; still others boldly waste their own possessions through drinking, whoring, and gambling while consoling themselves with the theft of others' goods; finally there are also those whose affairs stand such that rest brings danger for them." Quoted from Johannes Janssen, *Gesichte des deutschen Volkes*, 7th edition, 1897, vol. 2, p. 447. N owned the first edition of this volume (see his letter to Heinrich Köselitz, October 5, 1879) though it is not part of his library as preserved in the Herzogin Anna Amalia Bibliothek in Weimar. The footnote on page 311 of this same volume also refers to a polemical text from 1524 with the title "A Mirror of Protestant Freedom" (*"Ein Spiegel evangelischer Freiheit"*).

69:25   *Feuerbach*] Ludwig Feuerbach (1804–1872) was in his own time the most famous of the "Young" or leftist Hegelians—only later eclipsed by Marx— and was influential not only among philosophers but also writers, especially the writers of the movement known as "Young Germany." Feuerbach's philosophy was a radical humanism. In *Das Wesen des Christentums* (The Essence of Christianity, 1841), Feuerbach analyzed religion as man's alienated knowledge of himself: in religion, we worship what we take to be the best qualities of human beings, but without recognizing them as such. This book and two of his other works, *Tod und Unsterblichkeit* (Death and Immortality, 1831) and *Grundsätze der Philosophie der Zukunft* (Principles of the Philosophy of the Future, 1843), had a strong influence on Wagner's thinking in his earlier theoretical works—Wagner dedicated his book *Das Kunstwerk der Zukunft* (The Artwork of the Future, 1850) to Feuerbach.

69:26 *"healthy sensuality"*] cf. Feuerbach, *Principles of the Philosophy of the Future*, 1843, §31ff.

69:28 *young Germans*] The Young Germans—or *Junges Deutschland* (Young Germany)—were a group of poets and writers—Karl Gutzkow, Ludwig Börne, Georg Herwegh, and others—often closely associated with the Young Hegelians and dedicated to politicizing literature. Heinrich Heine was claimed by the Young Germans as a model though he was not directly associated with them.

69:30–31 *Parsifal-trombones*] The first act of *Parsifal* opens with the trombones—unaccompanied and in unison—playing one of the central leitmotifs, the so-called *"Glaubensmotiv"* (faith motif).

69:36 *"blood of the Redeemer"*] This phrase occurs in *"Heldentum und Christentum"* (Heroism and Christianity, 1881), the second of the three expositions that were appended to Wagner's *Religion und Kunst* (Religion and Art, 1880, in *Sämtliche Schriften und Dichtungen*, X, 280f). This precise phrase does not occur in *Parsifal*, but the "blood" of the "Redeemer" nonetheless figures prominently in each of the three acts: during the unveiling of the grail in act I; in the conversation between Parsifal and Kundry in act II; and in Amfortas' and Parsifal's redemption scene at the end of act III.

70:14–15 *contiguity*] This word appears in English in the original. The British philosopher most closely associated with "contiguity" is Hume. In *A Treatise of Human Nature* (1739–40), Hume lists "contiguity in time or place" as one of the three natural relations between ideas and gives it an essential role in his famous analysis of the relation between cause and effect. Contiguity plays the same role in Hume's *Enquiry Concerning Human Understanding* (1748), but is not mentioned by that name in its analysis of causality. Although there may be, as Thatcher claims, no evidence that N knew Hume's *Treatise*, it seems highly unlikely that he was unaware of Hume's analysis of causality, considering its importance to both Kant and Schopenhauer and the fact the N's own analysis of causality in *Gay Science* 112 is so Humean in spirit. Thatcher suggests as N's immediate source for the word Afrikan Spir's discussion of J. S. Mill's *An Examination of Sir Walter Hamilton's Philosophy* in *Denken und Wirklichkeit* (Thought and Reality, 1873)—on pages 131–32 the word "contiguity" occurs three times.

70:27–28 *the valuable part of his friends*] Nietzsche himself, for example. Perhaps N has chosen this somewhat awkward phrasing ("der wertvolle Teil seiner Freunde")—rather than something more usual like "der wertvollere Teil seiner Freunde" (=the more valuable part of his friends) to draw attention to the expression—even to suggest that he was Wagner's only valuable friend.

71:10 *"the time had come"*] cf. Luke 9: 51. The wording of this passage varies considerably in the various translations. The King James version reads: "when the time was come."

71:15–16   *milk of a ... pious way of thinking*] N is paraphrasing and parodying a line from Schiller's *Wilhelm Tell*, act IV, scene 3 (line 2573), Tell's mono-
logue in which he deliberates on the justifiability of assassinating the imperial
governor, Gessner. Tell claims that Gessner's cruelty has transformed *"Die Milch
der frommen Denkart"* (the milk of the pious way of thinking) into fermenting
dragon's poison. N modifies the adjective "fromm" (pious) into "reichsfromm"
('imperially pious,' or 'devoted to the empire').

71:25   *Herwegh*] Georg Herwegh (1817–1875), one of the most prominent of
the Young German poets. Herwegh's poems dealt with concerns of the working
class. His song *"Mann der Arbeit, aufgewacht!"* (Man of work, awake!) became the
anthem of the socialist movement. Wagner met Herwegh in 1853 in Zurich where
both had sought asylum. In October of 1854 Herwegh brought Wagner a copy of
Schopenhauer's *The World as Will and Representation*. It was apparently also Herwegh who introduced Wagner to the ideas of Karl Marx.

71:27   *"Opera and Drama,"*] Excerpts of *Oper und Drama* appeared in *Deut-
sche Monatsschrift für Politik, Wissenschaft, Kunst und Leben* in 1851. The complete
work was first published in 1852. N read this shortly after meeting Wagner in
1868. The ideas on opera and drama presented by Wagner in this work were a
starting point for ideas that shaped N's *Birth of Tragedy.*

71:34–35   *in majorem musicae gloriam*] for the greater glory of music.
Nietzsche is parodying the motto of the Jesuits: *Ad maiorem Dei gloriam* (for the
greater glory of God).

72:27   *without interest*] *Critique of Judgment* (1790), Part 1, Section 2, Book
2, "General Note on Aesthetic Reflexive Judgments," (page 114 of the original
edition, page 267 in the Akademie edition). There are other passages which dis-
cuss this topic, but this comes closest to the wording of N's quote: "The beautiful
is that which pleases in mere judgment (that is, not by means of sense impression
according to a concept of the understanding). From this it automatically follows
that it must please without any interest."

72:29   *Stendhal*] pseudonym of Henri Beyle (1783–1842), French author.
Beyle wrote under a number of pseudonyms and first used the name Stendhal in
1817 for *Rome, Naples et Florence*. Stendhal is the name of the Prussian town
where the art critic J. J. Winkelmann was born. N read Stendhal (and other
French "moralists") together with Malwida von Meysenbug and her other guests
during his stay in Sorrento in the winter of 1876–1877. Over the next ten years N
read and reread numerous works by Stendhal. In *Beyond Good and Evil* 256 he
lists Stendhal among the people he thinks of as "future" Europeans and on February 23, 1887, he writes to his friend Overbeck that he has discovered Dos-
toievsky by chance——as he had Schopenhauer at 21 and Stendhal at 35—and
adds: "my joy was extraordinary: I must go back all the way to my first acquain-
tance with Stendahl's *Rouge et Noir* to remember equal joy."

72:29   *une promesse de bonheur*] a promise of happiness. The phrase is from
Stendhal's *Rome, Naples et Florence* (first published in 1817, reworked and

expanded for a new edition in 1826): "October 28, 1816, at 5 o'clock in the morning on returning from the ball. I just returned from the *Casin' di San Paolo*. In all my life I have never seen a gathering of such beautiful women; their beauty made one lower one's eyes. For a Frenchman it has a noble and somber character that makes one dream of the happiness of passions much more than of the fleeting pleasures of a lively and merry affair. Beauty, it seems to me, is but a *promise of happiness.*"

73:6   *sense of touch!*] Perhaps N alludes here to *Anthropology From a Pragmatic Point of View* (1798). In its brief chapter "On the Sense of Touch," Kant describes this sense in a way that might suggest that he has no awareness of the role it plays in human sexuality.

73:25–26   *World as Will and Representation, I: 231*] The pagination N cites is that of the edition by Julius Frauenstädt (1873). The passage in question is in vol. I, section 38, p. 196 of the translation by E. F. J. Payne (New York: Dover, 1969).

74:21   *being-here*] The German word *Dasein*—literally "being there/here" is generally translated as "existence"—as it is in the next sentence. We have translated it more literally here in order to preserve the connection to the expression *Dableiben*—"remaining here"—which follows it.

75:9–10   *"surpasses all understanding,"*] Philippians 4: 7, in German, literally: "is higher than all reason (Vernunft)." The context is important, since a biological phenomenon (instinct) has replaced a religious one: "And the peace of God, which surpasses all understanding, will guard your hearts and your minds in Christ Jesus."

75:23–24   *"Râhula ... forged for me"*] quoted from page 122 of Hermann Oldenberg, *Buddha. Sein Leben, seine Lehre, seine Gemeinde* (Buddha. His Life, His Teachings, His Following), Berlin, 1881. This book was part of N's library.

75:26–29   *"narrowly ... leaving the house."*] quoted from Oldenberg, *Buddha*, 124.

76:1–2   *pereat ...philosophus, fiam!*] let the world perish, let there be philosophy, let there be the philosopher, *let there be me!* This is a parody of "Fiat justicia et pereat mundus" (let there be justice though the world may perish), the motto of Emperor Ferdinand I of Germany (1503–1564). Thatcher points to a similar play with this motto in Schopenhauer, at the beginning of the dialogue between Demopheles and Philalethes in *Parerga und Paralipomena* ("On Religion"—Chapter 15, §174, "A Dialogue").

77:17–19   *Heraclitus ... "empire"*] Diogenes Laertius 9. 3: "He had a habit of retiring to the temple of Artemis and playing dice with the children. When the Ephesians came and stood around him, he said, 'Why are you surprised, you scoundrels? Isn't it better to do this than involve myself with you in your political affairs." Quoted from Heraclitus, *Fragments*, 166 (see note 57:36 in the second treatise).

77:19–20   *Persia, you understand me*] The circumstances N describes apply equally well to the newly founded (1871) German Empire.

78:29–30   *"to what end … the world?"*] cf. Deussen, *Das System des Vedânta* (The System of the Vedanta), Leipzig, 1883, p. 439, 448. In Deussen the passage reads: "To what end do we need progeny, we whose soul is this world!"

79:30   *"ephectic"*] The adjective "ephectic" stems from the Greek verb *epekhein*, to hold back, to reserve (judgment). An "ephectic" drive is thus a drive to hold back, to reserve judgment, to "wait and see." The Greek skeptic philosophers were also referred to as "ephectics" since their skepticism led them to reserve judgment.

79:32–33   *sine ira et studio*] *without* anger and partiality. In *Annales* I, 1, Tacitus states his intention of taking this attitude toward the work he is beginning.

80:1   *Fraw Klüglin*] This name—in Luther's Early New High German spelling—means something like "Lady Shrewd." The expression is not unique to Luther; Grimms' *Deutsches Wörterbuch* notes other instances of its use as an epithet for 'reason.' The source in Luther's writings could not be identified. Notice that N's use of this phrase to describe reason as a "shrewd whore" fits the idea of reason as a capacity for finding means to ends given from elsewhere (see note 10:37). N's claim here that philosophy violates reason therefore may be intended to suggest that philosophy itself involves a reflection on ends.

80:3   *nitimur in vetitum*] we strive for *what is forbidden*. Ovid, *Amores*, III, 4, 17. The phrase occurs in a poem questioning surveillance as an effective method for ensuring fidelity in a wife. Cf. BGE 227.

80:16   *"je combats l'universelle araignée"*] I combat the universal spider. Thatcher notes that "universal spider" was a popular nickname for Louis XI, coined by Jehan Molinet and found in *Les Faictz et Dictz* (1537).

80:27   *worthier of questioning*] The German for "more questionable" is "fragwürdiger," which translates literally as "question-worthier," hence N's interpretative paraphrase *"worthier* of questioning."

80:30–31   *penalty … a wife for oneself alone*] cf. Post, *Bausteine*, I, 67. N has marked a passage that mentions "a custom, that treats a marital union between two individuals as a violation of the rights of the members of the tribe."

80:31–32   *jus primae noctis*] right of the first night—the alleged right of the feudal lord to have sexual intercourse with his vassal's bride on the wedding night. Recent research suggests that this was a fiction invented during the Enlightenment to discredit the nobility.

81:12–24   *"Nothing … pregnant with ruin!"*] The quotation is not exact; following the colon in the second sentence N has added *überall* (everywhere) and *an sich* (the essence of).

84:23   *Crux, nux, lux*] Cross, nut, light. In Peter Pütz' edition of GM published by Goldmann Verlag, this line appears as "Crux, nox, lux" ("Cross, night, light"). This is presumably an intentional "correction" since the annotation to the text repeats and translates this version. The word "nux" is not a misprint for "nox," however—it is clearly "nux" in the manuscript and is "nux" in the first edition. In N's notebooks from 1885 there is also a brief note (34 [174]) using the same image: "Nux et crux. A Philosophy for Good Teeth." Given N's depiction of modern psychological probing into humans as "nutcracking" (GM III: 9) the term may well fit in this series.

85:3 *"intelligible character of things"*] Kant, *Critique of Pure Reason*, e.g., B 564ff.

87:1 *Dance of Death*] also known as *danse macabre*, the Dance of Death was a genre of allegorical plays, popular in Medieval Europe, in which Death led persons of all conditions into the grave—reminding the spectator of the transitory nature of life.

88:26–27 *"beautiful souls"*] The expression "beautiful soul" has its source in Plato: in the *Symposium* 209b Diotima speaks of "a soul which is at once beautiful, distinguished, and agreeable"—(*psyche kale*). The German *"schöne Seele"* and the French *"belle âme"* gained widespread currency in the 18th century, above all among the Pietists—this expression or a similar one can be found in Zinzendorf, Lessing, Wieland, Rousseau, and Hemsterhuis among others. Goethe used the expression in several places. Goethe was already familiar with the expression in his childhood through contacts with Pietism, and one of its prominent occurrences underscores this connection. The sixth book of *Wilhelm Meister's Apprenticeship*, "Confessions of a Beautiful Soul" (written 1795) contains the writings of a woman who was a Pietist. Goethe's understanding of the expression is perhaps best expressed by the words he has this character write: "That I may always go forward, never backwards, that my actions may come to resemble ever more clearly the idea I have conceived of perfection, that I may daily feel more ease in doing that which I hold to be right … ." Schiller uses the expression in a similar sense. In his essay *"Über Anmut und Würde"* ("On Grace and Dignity," 1793) the expression is used to describe the human being in whom duty and inclination coincide (in contrast to Kant's idea of the morally good person, which is defined in opposition to acting from inclination). Already in Goethe's and Schiller's time the expression had begun to be used ironically as well. Hegel criticizes both Kant's notion of moral goodness and the "beautiful soul" ideal in the section on morality in *Phenomenology of Spirit*, Hoffmeister's German edition, page 421ff.; Miller translation (Oxford UP, 1977) page 364ff.

88:35 *woman is a hyena*] Post, *Bausteine*, I: 67: "The highly characteristic legal saying of the Bogos provides an example: Ogheina woga gen—that is, woman is a hyena, whereby one expresses the fact that among them woman is outside of all legal organizations and has neither any rights or any duties."

89:21 *"inverted world"*] Hegel, *Phenomenology of Spirit* (Force and Understanding, Appearance and Supersensual World), page 121ff. in Hoffmeister's German edition; page 96 ff., in Miller's English translation. Cf. also page 374 in the

Hoffmeister edition "world of inversion" ("Welt der Verkehrung"); page 319 in Miller, translated as "world of perversion."

91:37   *nervus sympathicus*] sympathetic nerve. The sympathetic nervous system is one of the major branches of the autonomic nervous system and governs the internal organs, intestines, blood vessels, etc., by reflex action.

92:24   *one thing is needful*] Luke 10: 42.

93:14–15   *"pain of the soul" ... "soul"*] The German for "soul" is *seelisch* in the first instance and *Seele* in the second, words which can be used in both psychological and spiritual senses—these two expressions could also be translated as "psychic pain" and "psyche."

93:30   *knows and has it*] Kaufmann reads here: "the only perspective known to the priest." The German is not unambiguous here, but the point seems to be that the priest knows this perspective as no one else does, not that he knows no other. Cf. *Thus Spoke Zarathustra* IV, "The Festival of Asses": "Oh Zarathustra," the pope answered, "forgive me, but in the things of God I am more enlightened even than you. And it is only fair that it is so."

94:25   *Sir Andrew*] a character in Shakespeare's *Twelfth Night*. The passage in question is I, iii:

Sir Andrew: [...] Methinks sometimes I have no more wit than a Christian or an ordinary man has. But I am a great eater of beef, and I believe that does harm to my wit.

Toby: No question.

Sir Andrew: An I thought that, I'd forswear it.

In the German translation of Shakespeare by Schlegel and Tieck, Sir Andrew is called "Junker Christoph" and this is the name Nietzsche uses in the original.

95:1   *first*] The second option is given at the beginning of the next section.

95:7   *Pascal*] Blaise Pascal (1623–1662), French mathemetician, physicist, and religious philosopher. Pascal was educated by his father, a tax court judge, and at age 17 published a mathematical essay that attracted the attention of Descartes. In 1646 Pascal came into contact with members of the convent of Port-Royal, the major center of Jansenism, a Roman Catholic movement that denied free will and taught that man attained salvation through God's grace rather than good works. For the next eight years he devoted himself to scientific studies but his interest in religious matters continued, and in January 1655, following a religious experience he referred to as "the night of fire," he entered Port-Royal, where he remained the rest of his life. During this time he wrote only at the request of the convent and never again published under his own name. It was here that he wrote the work he is best known for, a work conceived under the title "Apology of the Christian Religion." It was unfinished at the time of his death, and the editors who prepared and published it gave it the title "Pensées."

95:7   *il faut s'abêtir*] one must make oneself stupid (literally: make oneself an animal). The phrase does not seem to be from Pascal, however. Pascal does use the word *abêtir* in the *Pensées*, but not this phrase. In the famous passage on the wager (Brunschvicg 233, Latuma 418), he observes that one can go through the motions of religious observance even if one does not believe—*"Naturellement cela vous fera croire et vous abêtira."* Krailsheimer (Penguin edition) translates this as "That will make you believe quite naturally and will make you docile." Levi (Oxford UP edition) translates the last clause as "and according to your animal reactions." The passage Nietzsche quotes comes much closer to one from Montaigne's *Apology for Raymond Sebond*, from the section "Man's Knowledge Cannot Make Him Happy": *"Il nous faut abêtir pour nous assagir, et nous éblouir pour nous guider."* In the Donald Frame translation (Stanford UP): "We must become like the animals in order to become wise, and be blinded in order to be guided." Montaigne makes this statement in a discussion of brilliant men whose brilliance drove them to insanity. Nietzsche's wording is closer to Montaigne, but his use of the quote is more in keeping with the sense of the passage from Pascal.

95:15   *sportsmen*] This word is in English in the original.

95:26   *Hesychasts of Mount Athos*] a movement dedicated to the practice of inner prayer and originating among the monks of Mount Athos in the 14th century. Their prayers and other ascetic practices were to lead them to 'quietude' (Greek: 'hesuchia'), hence their name.

95:38–96:5   *"Good and evil ... over both he passed beyond"*] N's quote is a slightly modified version of a passage in H. Oldenberg, *Buddha*, 50: "Over both he passed beyond, the immortal one, over good and evil, that which has been done and that which has been left undone cause him no pain. His realm does not suffer through any deed."

96:13–14   *the knowing one*] The German original is "den Wissenden," which Kaufmann rendered as "man of knowledge." This an acceptable translation here, but obscures the fact that this is *not* the same expression with which the preface opens: "wir Erkennenden," which Kaufmann renders as "men of knowledge." Cf. note 1:1.

96:13–17   *"Redemption ... eternally pure"*] presumably quoted from Deussen, *System des Vedânta* (see note 96:19), XXXV: 3 (p. 435).

96:18   *Shankara*] Indian philosopher and theologian (ca. 788–ca. 820). Shankara travelled all over India discussing philosophy with different schools and is said to have founded four monasteries. Shankara held that the knowledge of Brahman is the only thing that can secure release from the cycle of rebirth. According to biographical writings he was involved in a major debate with a member of the Mimamsa school—a group which stressed the performance of duty and ritual as the key to release from the cycle of rebirth.

96:19   *Paul Deussen*] (1845–1919), a friend of N's since their days at Schulpforta—Deussen arrived there in 1859, one year later than N. Deussen went on to study philosophy in Bonn, Tübingen, Berlin, and Marburg. After several years as a teacher at a *Gymnasium* and as a private tutor, Deussen was made professor in Berlin in 1880. He left there in 1889 to assume a professorship in Kiel, where he remained until his death in 1919. Among his major works were *Das System des Vedânta* (The System of the Vedanta), Leipzig, 1883, and *Die Sûtra's des Vedânta* (The Sutras of the Vedanta), Leipzig, 1887. Nietzsche owned both books.

96:23–31 *"When he has ... evil works do not."*] cf. Deussen, *Sûtras* (see previous note) III, ii, 7 (p. 375). In the source Shankara quotes from several different Upanishads. N has worked the material into a single quotation.

96:31–37 *"In deep sleep ... animal to the cart."*] cf. Deussen, *System* (see note 78:29) p. 199.

97:10 *training*] This word is in English in the original.

98:13 *cenacle*] the anglicized form of the Latin *cenaculum* (dining room), the word designating the "upper room" in the Vulgate New Testament (Mark 14: 15; Luke 22: 12). The Germanized form in N's original is *Cönakel*. According to tradition, this "cenacle" was where the early Christian community first met, and as the community grew, the term was used more generally to refer to other gathering places. In the nineteenth century the word also had more current meanings: in France the group of Romantic writers around Victor Hugo called themselves "le cénacle," and in England, according to the Oxford English Dictionary, the term "cenacle" was frequently used to refer to literary gatherings.

98:20 *Geulincx*] Arnold Geulincx (1624–1669) Flemish metaphysician, logician, moralist. Geulincx studied theology and philosophy at Louvain and was made professor of philosophy there in 1646. He was dismissed 12 years later, probably because of his sympathy with Jansenism, a movement within Roman Catholicism that emphasized man's dependence on God's grace rather than good works for salvation. He then moved to Leiden where he converted from Catholicism to Calvinism. He studied medicine at the university in Leiden and in 1665 became professor of philosophy and ethics. He is best know for the philosophical doctrine of occasionalism, a theory of causation that asserts that there is no connection between human willing and external human action, but rather human willing is only an occasion for God to cause a change which then seems to be caused by the human act of willing it. Nietzsche's source for the quotation from Geulincx was presumably Kuno Fischer's previously mentioned *History of Modern Philosophy: Descartes and His School,* Part 2, Book 1, Chapter 3. The context from which the phrase is taken is: "Humilitas est incuria sui. Partes humilitas sunt duae: inspectio sui et despectio sui." (Humility is neglect of oneself. There are two parts to humility: examination of oneself and contempt of oneself.)

98:37 *Plato ... a hundred passages*] for example: *Republic* VIII, 550c–555a; *Statesman* 301a–303b; *Laws* III, 691c–d; IV, 711d–712a, 713c, 714d, 715a–d; IX, 875b.

100:1 *Plato*] cf. *Republic* III, 414b–c ("noble" = *gennaion*); II, 382c; III, 389b; V, 459c–d; *Laws* 663d–e.

100:14   *Thomas Moore*] (1779–1852), Irish poet and musician. Thatcher points out that Moore's involvement in the burning of Byron's papers is a legend—"In fact, Moore was probably the only witness who protested against it."

100:15   *Dr. Gwinner*] Wilhelm von Gwinner (1825–1917), a jurist and civil servant in Frankfurt am Main and a personal friend of Schopenhauer's. As executor of his estate Gwinner destroyed Schopenhauer's autobiographical writings. He afterwards wrote three biographical works on Schopenhauer: *Arthur Schopenhauer aus persönlichem Umgang dargestellt. Ein Blick auf sein Leben, seinen Charakter und seine Lehre* (Leipzig, 1862; "Arthur Schopenhauer Depicted From Personal Contact. A Glance at His Life, His Character, and His Teachings"), *Schopenhauer und seine Freunde* (1863; "Schopenhauer and His Friends"), and *Schopenhauers Leben* (1878: "Schopenhauer's Life"—a later and expanded edition of Gwinner's first Schopenhauer biography).

100:18   *able American Thayer*] Alexander Wheelock Thayer (1817–1897), American diplomat and musicologist. Educated at Andover and Harvard, Thayer worked as assistant in the Harvard library after his graduation and there conceived the idea of writing a biography of Beethoven. After several extended stays in Bonn, Berlin, and Vienna, and intermittent work as an editor for the *New York Tribune*, Thayer settled permanently in Europe in 1858 in order to continue his research. In 1862 he became an assistant to the American minister in Vienna, and in 1865 was appointed American consul in Trieste where he took up permanent residence. He wrote his life of Beethoven in English and it was translated for publication by a friend, Hermann Deiters. Volume I appeared in 1866, II in 1872, and III in 1879. Volumes IV and V were completed after his death by Deiters and Hugo Riemann and published 1907–1908. His biography not only became the standard Beethoven biography, but also set standards in musicological circles for more objective biographies.

100:23–24   *autobiography of Richard Wagner*] Wagner's autobiography, *Mein Leben* (My Life), was divided into four parts, which first appeared separately in private printings issued between 1870–1881. N was familiar with the work through the private printings. In 1911 an abridged edition of all four parts was published in Munich. The passages omitted in this edition were published separately in 1929–30. A complete edition was not available until Martin Gregor-Dellin's edition of 1963.

100:25   *Janssen*] Johannes Janssen (1829–1891). Educated in Münster, Louvain, and Bonn, Janssen was a professor at a *Gymnasium* in Frankfurt. He was ordained a priest in 1860 and became a member of the Prussian Chamber of Deputies in 1875. The first six volumes of his eight-volume work, *Geschichte des deutschen Volkes seit dem Ausgang des Mittelalters* ("History of the German People Since the End of the Middle Ages") were published in Freiburg, 1876–1888. The remaining two were completed after his death by L. v. Pastor and published in 1893–1894. Although his strongly Catholic interpretation was criticized in its time by many Protestant historians, more recently there has been some interest in the broad approach of his work—as an early example of interest in social and cultural as well as political history. See also N's letter to Peter Gast, October 5, 1879.

100:31   *Taine-like*] Hippolyte Adolphe Taine (1828–1893), French philosopher, historian and critic. Taine and Renan (see note 114:16) were the leading French intellectual figures of their period. As Nietzsche made clear in letters (October 26, 1886, to Reinhart von Seydlitz and November 14, 1887, to Jacob Burckhardt), he had the greatest admiration for Taine and considered Taine and Burckhardt, the great historian and N's former colleague at Basel, his only two readers, the only contemporary readers who could understand his work. The present passage brings out Nietzsche's preference for Taine over the influential German historian Ranke (see note 100: 35). In contrast to Ranke, who emphasized the foreign affairs of powerful and rising states, Taine attempted in his history of France to understand the national weakness that led to the French defeat by the Germans in 1870–71. His work also promoted the idea of history as concerned with the whole of social life. Further, in contrast to Ranke's emphasis on "pure knowing" or objectivity, Taine made his value judgments very clear. He belongs to the anti-democratic critics of the French Revolution and his presentation of the horrors of the revolution outraged liberals, after the first volume of his history of France, the *Ancien Regime*, had already angered conservatives because of its criticism of the injustices and errors of the royal governments from Louis XIV to the Revolution. On the other hand, Taine was committed to understanding human beings scientifically. A complete naturalist from early on, he accepted human beings as simply a part of nature and therefore believed they could be understood in terms of the operation of natural forces. His underlying impulse was philosophical, following Spinoza and Hegel: to understand the underlying necessity in all things. His originality lies especially in his attempt to introduce scientific method into the study of literature and other cultural products. Every social phenomenon and intellectual creation, he argued, is determined by the interplay of three major factors: "race, milieu, and moment"—national character of the creator(s), the physical or socio-political circumstances that complete or counteract this character (among which climate receives special emphasis), and by the particular place of the creation in a cultural history. What N would have found especially important about Taine was the fact that in his attempt to introduce science into the study of works of art and the epochs they exemplify, he did not abstain from value judgements and was not out to demean individuals, but in fact was able to use his method to bring out the true greatness of writers like Shakespeare and Stendhal.

100:35   *Leopold Ranke*] (1795–1886), highly successful and influential historian, author of over fifty volumes of history. Ranke was professor of history at the University of Berlin and, like N, had attended the famous school at Schulpforta before studying at Leipzig. Contemporary historian Peter Gay calls Ranke "the most admired, most quoted, most imitated professional historian of the century" (*The Bourgeois Experience*, Vol. IX: *The Naked Heart* [New York: Norton &

Co., 1995], p. 198). Ranke's approach to history was strongly influenced by the methods he encountered in Niebuhr's history of Rome, and he won general acceptance for this "Historical Method," which emphasized archival research, the search for documents and the intensive examination and criticism of primary sources. He is perhaps best known for his *"Objektivitätsanspruch"* or "claim to objectivity": it is not the historian's task to judge history or to instruct the present, but rather he should "simply show how it actually was." According to Gay, Renan never doubted that such objectivity is best assured by emphasizing "direct testimony uncontaminated by secondary accounts" (209); Ranke "proposed to enter the past humbly, hat in hand, that he might faithfully transmit the messages he had learned to decipher. This empathy required him to strip away current interests and private preferences and to confront early modern France or England burdened with as little baggage as possible" (Gay, 199). Cf. N's idea of "objectivity" in GM III:12. N's reference to Ranke's "prudent indulgence towards strength" may be explained in terms of the overriding importance Ranke's view of history gives to the state, dealings among states, and especially to states that are in the process of increasing their power. According to Gay, "the great powers remain [for Ranke] the divine scheme for humanity... Ranke's eye for power reduced his perceptions of the shaping role of economic forces and internal social strains; his celebrated doctrine that foreign affairs have primacy over domestic affairs is typical of him. It endorsed success. In Ranke's historical creed, the first shall be first" (Gay, 202). Further, Ranke's view of history fit well with the mood of his German contemporaries, especially following the defeat of France and the founding of the second *Reich* in 1871–72. Cf. previous note 100:31.

101:7   *that diplomat*] Charles-Maurice de Talleyrand (-Périgord), Prince de Bénévent (1754–1838). French statesman and diplomat known for his lack of scruples and for his capacity for political survival—he was Bishop of Autun prior to the revolution, held high offices during the French Revolution, served as a representative of Napoleon in London in 1792, after the restoration of the Bourbon monarchy he represented France at the Vienna Congress in 1815, and under King Louis Philippe he again represented France in London from 1830–34.

101:7–8   *"Let us mistrust ... always good"*] N's translation of the statement is a bit unusual—he quotes the original in his notebooks as "méfiez-vous du premier mouvement; il est toujours généreux." KSA 12: 500 (10 [78]). A more accurate translation would be: "...they are almost always generous."

102:26   *hideous animal*] Luther's *Table Talk*, Winter 1542–1543, Nr. 5513.

103:8   *not of this world*] John 18: 36.

103:10   *tragic situations*] Goethe, *Conversations with Eckermann*, February 14, 1830.

103:35   *St. Vitus' and St. John's dancers*] In modern German "St. Vitus' Dance" refers to epilepsy. N's reference here is to an older sense of the expression. He is not concerned with an actual medical condition so much as with a medieval religious phenomenon which reached epidemic proportions in the years 1021, 1278, 1375, and 1418. Caught up in a group hysteria or "ecstasy," people gathered in groups reported to have numbered in the thousands and danced until they fell into convulsions or began foaming at the mouth. They claimed to have seen heavenly visions while in these ecstatic states. In some cases the dancing groups moved from place to place, wearing wreaths or other decoration and often engaging in wild excesses. In one of his notebooks N mentions the similarity between these outbreaks and ancient Bacchanalia (KSA 7, 1 [33, 34]). Since they were believed to be possessed of the devil the clergy and the families of the "possessed" dancers attempted to exorcise them by praying to St. Vitus or St. John. See also 7, 7 [50]; 8, 23 [11].

104:23–24 *magno sed proxima intervallo*] next, but by a great distance. Adapted from Virgil, *Aeneid* Book 5, line 320: *"longo sed proximus intervallo"* (next, but by a long distance).

105:6–7 *"Salvation Army"*] The Salvation Army did attack the theater as an evil influence in society, but Thatcher points out that there seems to be no evidence that they ever singled out Shakespeare in their attacks.

105:11–12 *"Here … no other"*] The final words of Luther's famous reputed reply on April 18, 1521 at the Diet of Worms when asked to renounce his teachings.

105:12 *courage of my bad taste*] Cf. Julien Sorel in Stendhal's *Le rouge et le noir*: *"Il n'a pas peur d'etre de mauvais goût, lui"* (He isn't afraid of having bad taste). See also KSA 11, 25 [169] and N's letter to Peter Gast written December 19, 1886.

105:25 *No cock will crow about this*] cf. Matthew 26: 69ff; Mark 14: 66ff; Luke 22: 54ff. The German here is idiomatic and means roughly "no one gives a damn" (Kaufmann). Rather than giving this English equivalent we have opted for a literal translation of the German since it preserves the slighting allusion to the New Testament story of Peter's weakness and the crowing of the cock.

105:26 *"crown of eternal life"*] cf. James 1: 12, Revelations 2: 10.

106:4 *"devil's sow, the pope"*] Luther, *The Misuse of the Mass* (*Vom mißbrauch der Messen*) 1522, part III: *"Von des Bapsts priestern, gesetzen und opffern"* (Concerning the Pope's Priests, Laws, and Sacrifices). In *Dr. Martin Luthers Werke* ('Weimar' edition), Weimar: Böhlau, 1889, section 1, vol. 8, p. 540. *The American Edition of Luther's Works*, vol. 36, p. 201, translates the phrase as "the devil's swine, the pope." N's source for this quote may have been Johannes Janssen, *Geschichte des deutschen Volkes* (*History of the German People*). In the edition of 1896 this quote appears in volume 2, p. 211. In a letter to H. Köselitz from October 5, 1879, N comments on reading this volume at the suggestion of Jacob Burckhardt. In the English translation of Janssen, this passage is found in vol. 3, p. 233 (book vi, chapter II).

108:26 *"makes blessed"*] cf. Mark 16: 16; Luke 1: 45; John 20: 29.

108:33   *anti-Christians*] The German is ambiguous here and could also be rendered as "anti-Christs."

108:33   *immoralists*] See note 2:28.

109:10   *Assassins*] A secret Islamic order, founded in the 11th century by Hasan ibn Sabbah. They terrorized Islamic princes and statesmen as well as Christian crusaders. The name of the sect—Assassins—stems from their reputed use of hashish (Arabic *hasisi:* hashish-eater) and made its way via returned crusaders into both French and English as a term for a murderer or, particularly in English, a murderer with political motives.

109:13   *tally-word*] The German here is *Kerbholz-Wort,* a coinage of N's. A *Kerbholz* or "tally" was a stick or long, thin piece of wood into which one cut notches (*"kerben"* means "to notch, to score"—cf. English "score" as a "tally" of points) in order to keep track of some kind of debt—such as drinks consumed. The German word *Kerbholz* now survives only in the idiom: *etwas auf dem Kerbholz haben* (literally: "to have something on one's tally"), which now has a moral rather than legal meaning—to have a sin or crime on one's conscience. The *Kerbholz* or "tally" was generally split lengthwise across the notches or "scores" and each party involved in the transaction was given one half. The correspondence between the two halves could then be used to confirm the size of the debt and the identity of the creditor. The latter point is presumably what N has in mind here—in a notebook used between fall 1885 and fall 1887 he wrote: "'Paradise is under the shadow of swords'—also a symbolon and tally-word by which souls of noble and warlike descent betray themselves and recognize each other—" (KSA 12, 2 [19]). N's use of "symbolon" here likewise supports this reading—"symbolon" is the Greek word for "mark, token, watchword, symbol." In GM the word appears simply as "symbol." Kaufmann is thus not wrong to translate this expression as "watchword," but in doing so he eliminates an overtone that is significant in GM: the "Kerbholz" is another example of a moral phenomenon evolving from an economic one. The expression must have had some significance for N, since "Kerbholz-Wort" is as obscure to German speakers as "tally-word" is to English speakers—there are much easier ways to convey the idea of "watchword" in German.

111:10   *outworks*] German *Außenwerk,* a detached outer part of a fortification. N's figurative use of this word has an English parallel in John Donne's lines: "All our moralities are but our outworks, our Christianity is our citadel" (Quoted from the *New Shorter OED*).

111:26   *Plato contra Homer*] This antagonism is illustrated in Plato's *Republic,* Book III, where Socrates criticizes Homer's portrayal of gods and heros (388c–392c) and again in Book X where Socrates faults Homer for depicting things he does not know firsthand (esp. 595a–607a).

112:10   *"poor of the spirit"*] cf. Matthew 5: 3. Although N is clearly referring to the passage in Matthew, he does not use the familiar Biblical wording—as he does elsewhere in his writings. This may be meant to underscore the connection between this phrase and other variations in GM: "physiologists and vivisectors of the spirit," "actor of the spirit," "stage heroes of the spirit," "skeptics, ephectics, *hectics* of the spirit," and "*rich* of the spirit."

112:25   *Copernicus*] Nicolaus Copernicus (1473–1543), Polish scholar and astronomer, founder of modern astronomy. A canon in the Catholic church, Copernicus was asked by the church to revise the calendar to correct the inaccuracies that were becoming increasingly problematic. In the course of this project he developed his theory of the motions of heavenly bodies—demonstrating that it is we who are moving, not the heavens. In other words the earth is not the center of things but rather a detached sphere rotating around its own axis and around the Sun. This shattered the medieval conviction that Earth and man were at the center of God's creation.

112:31   "*penetrating ... nothingness?*"] source not identified.

112:34   *it annihilates my importance*] Kant, *Critique of Practical Reason*, 289: "The first of these sights, that of a countless multitude of worlds, annihilates, as it were, my importance—as an animal creation that must return the material from which it was made to the planet (a mere point in the universe) after having been outfitted with the force of life for a short time (one knows not how)." Thatcher's suggestion that N has misunderstood Kant or misused the quotation—since Kant is speaking here of the vastness of space and not of astronomy—is unfounded. N may be speaking a bit eliptically, but it was the science of astronomy that gave birth to this sense of space through its discovery that Earth was not the center of the universe and was not contained in a finite spherical heaven, but rather was only one among a multitude of worlds in boundless space.

112:38   *ataraxy*] imperturbability, tranquility of the soul (from Greek *ataraxia:* impassiveness). This was an important concept for Epicurus and his school—together with bodily health it was the basic goal of life, as a form of lasting pleasure. It was also a central concept for the skeptics, tied to the ephectic attitude (see note 79:30) "like a shadow"—according to the skeptic Timon (as reported by Diogenes Laertes).

113:1–2   *holds in contempt ... how to respect*] hold in contempt =*verachten*; respect =*achten*.

113:14   *Xaver Doudan*] actually Ximenès Doudan (1800–1872), French politician and author. Doudan was a political advisor to Victor de Broglie, minister for public instruction, then for foreign affairs, and finally president of the council of ministers. The duke retained Doudan as a personal secretary and he lived more or less continuously with the family Broglie. He published only a few articles during his lifetime. After his death his friends collected his letters, which appeared in four volumes under the title *Mélanges et Lettres de Doudan* (1876). In the ensuing years the publication found a resonance that established a reputation for Doudan. In his letters he revealed himself to be a sensitive and subtle writer, a perceptive observer, and a sceptic. Politically he held to the "*juste milieu*" and in questions of art and aesthetics Doudan likewise preferred measure and rationality, and was put off by what he saw as the excesses of romanticism and realism. N owned a copy of *Mélanges*, and as early as 1879 asked his sister to translate passages from Doudan for him. His notebook for fall 1885 through fall 1887 contains several excerpts from *Mélanges et Lettres*.

113:14–16   *l'habitude ... dans l'inconnu*] "the habit *of admiring* the unintelligible instead of staying quite simply in the unknown." From Doudan's *Lettres*, 4 vols., Paris:, 1879; Doudan to Piscatory, March 3, 1855 (vol. 3, p. 23f.). Cf. also KSA 11, 26 [441], KGW VII 4/2: 188.

114:16   *Renan*] Ernest Renan (1823–1892), French historian of religion and critic, best known for his *La vie de Jésus* (Life of Jesus, 1863), the first volume in his multivolume work, *Origins of Christianity*. Renan was elected to the chair of Hebrew at the Collège de France in 1862, but when his reference to Jesus as "an incomparable man" in his inaugural lecture caused an uproar, he was suspended and not reinstated until 1870. He and Taine (see note 100:31) were the most influential French intellectuals of their time. Renan had studied for the priesthood, but left both the seminary and the Roman Catholic church in 1845 after a lengthy struggle with doubts engendered by philological analyses of the Bible. He rejected Christianity's supernatural doctrines due to the findings of historical criticism, which he thought showed the Bible to be a merely human document, but he did not abandon a Christian outlook. Influenced by German idealism, especially Hegel's, he believed that the goal of the universe is "the development of mind," and that religion, and especially Christianity, plays a major role in this development. His interpretation of Christianity as a development of spirituality, and of Jesus as the herald of an "unritualistic, inwardly directed religion," made it possible to retain a Christian identity while rejecting the authority of the church (Katz, p. 134). Renan's interpretation of Christianity is also part of the intellectual background of the anti-Semitic movement that developed in Europe during the 1880's. For an account, see Jacob Katz, *From Prejudice to Destruction: Anti-Semitism, 1700–1933* (Cambridge: Harvard UP, 1980). According to Katz (p. 133ff), in his *Life of Jesus*, Renan contrasts the "allegedly more lenient Judaism" of the North, i.e., of Galilee, Jesus' homeland, with that of Jerusalem, and concludes: "The North alone created Christianity, Jerusalem on the contrary was the true homeland of obstinate Judaism founded by the Pharisees, fixed by the Talmud, and transmitted during the middle ages until our day." Renan also introduced the idea of race into the discussion of Judaism. In a later essay, he contrasts the contributions of Aryans and Semites to human culture, and finds an "absence of philosophical and scientific culture" among the latter, which he claims is due to "the lack of extension, of variety and consequently of analytical spirit which distinguishes them" (quoted in Katz, p. 137). Compare N's very different view: "Whenever Jews have won influence they have taught human beings to make finer distinctions, more rigorous inferences, and to write in a more luminous and cleanly fashion; their task was ever to bring a people to listen to *raison*" (GS 348). In his later works, Renan turned to a new kind of writing; he wrote philosophical dialogues and dramas as well as an autobiography (1883). Gay (see note 100:35) describes the latter as "a cunningly arranged feast of reminiscences, stories, maxims, and opinions," which served Renan's search for a "faith purged of legends and superstitions" and involved a reenactment of romanticism's earlier attempt at an aesthetic re-enchantment of the world (Gay, 129–31). In the notebook from Summer-Fall 1884, N quotes Doudan's description of Renan's later style: "That dreamy, sweet, ingratiating style, circling around the questions without drawing very close to them, like little snakes. It is because of the sounds of this music that one resigns oneself to ridiculing everything so much, that one supports despotism while dreaming of liberty" (KSA 11: 269). See BGE 48 for N's more extended discussion of Renan, including a quote from him and the charge that his soul is "in the more refined sense, voluptuous and inclined to stretch out comfortably." N describes his own soul, in contrast, as "less beautiful and harder."

114:18   *the Fate*] The Greek fates were three sisters; one spun the thread of life, one measured it, and the last one—the one N has in mind here—cut it.

114:24   *chasm' odonton*] "chasm of teeth." N is citing the first lines of Poem 24 from *Anacreontea*, a collection of poems in the manner of Anacreon (Greek lyric poet ca. 570–485 BC), composed by various poets over the centuries following Anacreon's death.

Nature gave bulls
horns, hooves to horses
speed to hares
to lions a chasm of teeth

114:31–32   *smelling out the infinite ... infinite smells of bugs*] In the notebook entry quoted in note 114:16, N noted that Doudan had said of Renan: "he gives the people of his generation that which they want in all things, bonbons that smell of infinity" (KSA 11, 269).

114:32–33   *whited sepulchers*] Matthew 23: 27.

114:35   *magic concealing-cap*] German *Tarnkappe*. The *Tarnkappe* is a familiar element of German mythology. This "cap" had the power both to make its wearer invisible and to allow him to take on whatever appearance he chose. Siegfried uses it in several of his exploits.

115:10–11   *"Deutschland, Deutschland über alles"*] Germany, Germany above all else. The opening line of the first stanza of August Heinrich Hoffmann von Fallersleben's song *Das Lied der Deutschen*, 1841. The song was meant to encourage Germans from the various German states—Prussia, Saxony, Bavaria, etc.—to forget regional differences and work to form a unified German nation. In 1922 this song was made the national anthem of Germany. Since 1952 only the last of the three stanzas is used as national anthem.

115:18   *la religion de la souffrance*] the religion of suffering. These are the final words of Paul Bourget's novel *Un crime d'amour* (1886): "He felt that something had sprung up within him through which he might always find reasons for living and acting—the religion of human suffering." For Nietzsche's reaction to this book see his letter to Overbeck, April 10, 1886.

116:4–5   *The Will to Power*] N never completed this work. N collected material for it in his notebooks but did not compile any of it into a more organized form. The work by this title that appeared in 1901 was a selection and compilation of his notes, prepared by his sister, Elisabeth Förster-Nietzsche, and Peter Gast (Heinrich Köselitz). In 1906 they published an expanded second edition. Both versions contained many editorial "errors" that have since been shown to be intentional manipulations by the original editors. The ideas attributed to N on the basis of *The Will to Power* nonetheless have had a serious impact on interpretations of his philosophy—because it has so often been read and interpreted as one of his works.

116:7–8   *the comedians of this ideal*] This passage is often taken as evidence that N's own strategy for overcoming the ascetic ideal is to be a comedian of it; after all, he claims that these "comedians" are the only real enemies the ideal has, "for they arouse mistrust" of it. However, although N's description of these comedians in GM III:26 is certainly funny, it is not designed to arouse mistrust of the ascetic ideal "*as long as it is honest*" (114:29). Instead, his biting humor seems directed against those who, like Renan, combine ascetic idealism with an aesthetic and easy-going style (see note 114:16). Finally, it seems clear that these comedians of the ascetic ideal are the same ones N refers to at 115:20, the ones who would have to be exported out of Europe for its air "to smell cleaner again."

116:25   *Samkhya philosophy*] The Samkhya or Sankhya (=enumeration) tradition, whose roots date back to 800–400 BC, is devoted to "enumerating" the categories it uses to delineate the structure of the world. Samkhya holds that reality consists of a unitary substance, and this reality or cosmos is conceived of as alternating between periods of dissolution and periods of organization. It is this alternation that gives rise to the world and to souls. Only through interaction with the world do souls gain the consciousness necessary for escape from the cycle of rebirth. This theory of creation through alternating periods made it unnecessary to posit a god in accounting for the creation of the world.

117:11   *my unknown friends*] Thatcher calls attention to Emerson's journal for April 19, 1848: "Happy is he who looks only into his work to know if it will succeed, never into the times or the public opinion; and who writes from the love of imparting certain thoughts and not from the necessity of sale—who writes always to the unknown friend." As Thatcher notes, however, the journals were not published until 1909 and this expression does not occur in any of the essays Nietzsche is known to have read.

Index

End Notes, marked "en," are found in End Notes for the page listed. "Int" refers to the Introduction, and is followed by the number of the section of the Introduction in which the entry is found. Footnotes, marked "fn," are found on the page or section listed. "B" refers to the Selected Bibliography.